MILTON, TOLERATIO
NATIONHOOI

CW01486341

John Milton lived at a time when English nationalism became entangled with principles and policies of cultural, religious, and ethnic tolerance. Combining religious and political thought with close readings of key texts, this book examines how Milton's polemical and imaginative writings intersect with representations of English Protestant nationhood. Through detailed case studies of Milton's works, Elizabeth Sauer charts the fluctuating narrative of Milton's literary engagements in relation to social, political, and philosophical themes such as ecclesiology, exclusionism, Irish alterity, natural law, disestablishment, geography, and intermarriage. In so doing, Sauer shows how literary and historicist inquiry enriches the study of toleration and nationhood. Her book makes a salient contribution to Milton studies and to scholarship on Early Modern literature and the imagining of the early nation-state.

ELIZABETH SAUER is a professor of English at Brock University, Canada, and winner of a Killam Research Fellowship from the Canada Council for the Arts. She has published widely on Milton and Early Modern culture, including co-edited collections such as *The New Milton Criticism* (2012) and *Reading the Nation in English Literature* (2010).

MILTON, TOLERATION,
AND NATIONHOOD

ELIZABETH SAUER

Brock University

CAMBRIDGE
UNIVERSITY PRESS

32 Avenue of the Americas, New York NY 10013-2473, USA

Cambridge University Press is part of the University of Cambridge.

It furthers the University's mission by disseminating knowledge in the pursuit of education, learning and research at the highest international levels of excellence.

www.cambridge.org
Information on this title: www.cambridge.org/9781107615199

© Elizabeth Sauer 2014

First published 2014
First paperback edition 2015

A catalogue record for this publication is available from the British Library

Library of Congress Cataloguing in Publication data
Sauer, Elizabeth, 1964–
Milton, toleration, and nationhood / Elizabeth Sauer, Brock University.
pages cm
Includes bibliographical references and index.
ISBN 978-1-107-04194-3 (hardback)
1. Milton, John, 1608–1674 – Political and social views. 2. Milton, John, 1608–1674 –
Criticism and interpretation. 3. Politics and literature – Great Britain – History – 17th
century. 4. Nationalism – England – History – 17th century. 5. Nationalism in
literature. 6. Nationalism and literature. 7. Great Britain – Politics and
government – 1603–1714. I. Title.
PR3592.P64S28 2013
821'.4–dc23 2013023410

ISBN 978-1-107-04194-3 Hardback
ISBN 978-1-107-61519-9 Paperback

Contents

Acknowledgments

The debts accumulated over the past decade and a half in the composition of this book are many. The book owes its existence to Dr. Ray Ryan's encouragement, counsel, and confidence in the project. I also benefited greatly from the acute and constructive reports of the Cambridge University Press readers, which guided, redirected, and sharpened my argument. Validation and invaluable support received from the Canada Council and Killam Trusts in the form of a Killam Research Fellowship ensured the book's completion. Generous research funding from the Social Sciences Humanities Research Council of Canada made five research trips to the archives in London, England, and Washington, DC, possible. A Folger Institute seminar on "Religious Conflict and Toleration in the Early Modern World," led by Benjamin Kaplan, developed into lasting conversations and a virtual archive.

The genesis of this book was a conversation with the late Balachandra Rajan that resulted in an essay on "Religious Toleration and Imperial Intolerance" (1999). Among the projects that followed were *Imperialisms: Historical and Literary Investigations* (2004), *Milton and Toleration* (2007), and *Reading the Nation in English Literature* (2010), which I was privileged to edit with Balachandra Rajan, Sharon Achinstein, and Julia M. Wright, respectively, scholars whom I could not admire more. The volumes' contributors played a major role in my education, as did the panelists who accepted invitations to participate in special sessions organized at the Modern Language Association Convention on "Comparing Imperialisms," "Imperialisms: East and West," "Toleration and Nationalism in Early Modern England," and "Milton and Toleration: Then and Now." Additionally, this book was enriched by the award-winning criticism on early nationalism and tolerationism by Paul Stevens, Achsah Guibbory, David Loewenstein, Richard Helgerson, Andrew Escobedo, Alexandra Walsham, Rachel Trubowitz, Jason P. Rosenblatt, Joan S. Bennett, Blair Worden, Victoria Kahn, Andrew Hadfield, and John Kerrigan. Students

I was honoured to teach in a graduate seminar at Queen's University, Canada, and in senior courses at Brock University, were, along with my colleagues Barbara Seeber, Jane McLeod, and John Sainsbury, held hostage over the years to impromptu disquisitions on Milton and toleration. I thank them all for their indulgence and tolerance. Sean Morton and Christopher Stampone served as diligent, rigorous, and conscientious research and editorial assistants.

Finally, I am indebted to members of the Northeast Milton Seminar, the Brock University intellectual community, and, among others, Peter C. Herman, Laura Knoppers, Stephen Fallon, and the late Douglas Brooks, whose expertise, kindnesses, and *very different perspectives* inspired and challenged my thinking about this project. Permission to use material from "Disestablishment, Toleration, and the New Testament Nation: Milton's Late Religious Tracts," in Nigel Smith and Nicholas McDowell (eds.), *The Oxford Handbook of Milton* (2009), pp. 325–41, and from "Milton's *Defences* and the Principle of '*sanior pars*'," in Laura Lunger Knoppers (ed.), *The Oxford Handbook of Literature and the English Revolution* (2012), pp. 146–61, was generously granted by Oxford University Press.

Note on Editions

Unless otherwise stated, all references to Milton's *Paradise Lost* are from Alastair Fowler (ed.), *Milton, "Paradise Lost,"* 2nd edn. (London: Longman, 2007), cited as PL. References to the 1671 volume are from Laura Lunger Knoppers (ed.), *The 1671 Poems: "Paradise Regain'd" and "Samson Agonistes,"* vol. 2, Thomas N. Corns and Gordon Campbell (gen. eds.), *The Complete Works of John Milton* (Oxford: Oxford University Press, 2008), cited as PR or SA. References to Milton's other shorter poems are from John Carey (ed.), *Milton, The Complete Shorter Poems,* 2nd ed. rev. (London: Longman, 2007), cited individually by title. References to Milton's prose works are from Don M. Wolfe (gen. ed.), *Complete Prose Works of John Milton*, 8 vols. in 10 (New Haven, CT: Yale University Press, 1953–82), cited as CPW. Biblical quotations are from *The Holy Bible, Conteyning the Old Testament, and the New: Newly Translated out of the Originall tongues* (London, 1611).

Introduction

While decrying the "bloody *Tenent* of *Persecution* for cause of *Conscience*," Roger Williams, arguably having ignited the debate in the 1640s, delineated the outer limits of toleration in protesting, "I have desired to labour in *Europe*, in *America*, with *English*, with *Barbarians*, yea, and also I have longed after some trading with the *Jewes* themselves ... yet ... I cannot see but that the first and present great *Designe* of the *Lord Jesus* is to destroy the *Papacy*." In Williams's prophecy of the unfolding of the "great *Designe*," culminating in the apocalyptic destruction of the antichrist, the "*wild, yet wise Americans*," the European Jews, and even Catholics (as distinct from Roman Catholics or Papists) are designated as marginally tolerable.[1] When the "great *Designe*" mutated thereafter into the failed Western Design – an assertion of English sovereignty in Spanish-occupied America – Oliver Cromwell interjected his declaration of war against Spain with comparisons between English colonialists and Spanish conquistadores and with several protestations on the persecuted Amerindians' right to liberty. The terms of toleration and accommodation served a vital function in the public discourse on international relations and on England's "moral exceptionalism" and national sovereignty.[2]

The conjunctions of nationhood and toleration in an era when liberty became an animating feature of English identity formation present a compelling subject for critical inquiry. This book demonstrates how evidence from the polemical and imaginative literature intersects with imaginative and extraliterary representations of Protestant nationhood and cultural, religious, and ethnic difference. Building on the influential concepts of the imagined community (Benedict Anderson) and the Janus-faced nation (Tom Nairn), Homi Bhabha, Richard Helgerson, Claire McEachern, Adrian Hastings, David J. Baker, Jean E. Howard and Phyllis Rackin, Andrew Hadfield, Willy Maley, Andrew Escobedo, Patrick Schwyzer, Paul Stevens, David Loewenstein, Raymond Tumbleson, and Rachel Trubowitz studied the forms of the discursively constructed nation and demonstrated the significance of imaginative writings for interpreting the early nation.[3] Given the metaphorical, discursive, and polemical nature of nationhood, literary analysis in fact emerges as a key methodology for examining the imagined community of the nation. While interrogating developmental narratives of nationhood, this book focuses on John Milton's mimetically produced nation, the religious character of which lent it a dimension extending beyond its state identity and enabled its transformation into an abstract entity independent of an institutional affiliation. For Elie Kedourie and, decades later, for Krishan Kumar, Ernest Gellner, E. J. Hobsbawm, Colin Kidd, and Anthony Giddens, the England of Milton's time is not yet nationalist because it lacks horizontal ties that "ris[e] above the ties of class, region and religion."[4] Indeed, Benedict Anderson, in his seminal *Imagined Communities*, had described the nation as the product of a "deep horizontal comradeship."[5] Milton, however, imagines the nation in terms of its embrace of such values as Christian liberty and tolerance, which transcend state power. At a time when state policy and secularized discourses of reason increasingly came to the fore, Milton's interventions in controversies over nationhood, civil and ecclesiastical politics, and the terms of toleration remained couched in the language of religion and liberty of conscience. While not presuming to offer a full treatment of Milton's articulations of Protestant nationhood and toleration in all their manifestations, *Milton, Toleration, and Nationhood* seeks to illustrate how a study of these conjoined subjects enriches appreciation of Milton's works, broadens understanding of the role of literature in the conceptualizing of early nationhood, and opens up possibilities for further scholarship in this field.

Milton's powerful engagements with key debates on nationhood and toleration have a considerable literary, cultural, and philosophical significance. His poetry and prose are central to this investigation because they were produced in a period when English nationalist consciousness – with its relationship to questions of rights, accommodation, integration, and certainly exclusivism – was heightened. Theologian and cultural historian of nationalism, Adrian Hastings, who extends nationhood as far back as ancient Israel, situates England's "greatest intensity" of nationalist experience in the early modern era and notably in Milton's lifetime.[6] Literary critics and historians continue to feature Milton's writings in the most influential studies on seventeenth-century Britain's literary, political, and religious history and identity.[7] Examinations of the Miltonic oeuvre in terms of Protestant nationhood and toleration provide an important complement to and extension of scholarship on Puritan radicalism, liberalism, a largely secularized republicanism, and imperialism, through which Milton's identity as a nationalist has generally been interpreted.[8] Because Milton was fully immersed in the historical moment in which nationalism became entangled with ideas and policies on toleration, a book highlighting this involvement should be a salient contribution to Milton studies and to literature on the early modern nation and pre-Lockean toleration.

This project seeks to advance knowledge about these concepts as categories of analysis in literature, cultural history, and nationalism studies. Although they locate nationhood in later centuries, historians and cultural theorists of the nation, beginning with Benedict Anderson, usefully underscore the invention of the nation and its ascribed significance rather than its natural or organic identity. Because the members of a national community are unknown to each other, nations are best understood as intellectual and cultural creations, forged or invented largely in and through language. According to this theory, nations are sustained in the minds of their citizens and of the international community. Anderson underscored the role of print culture, in such forms as literature, maps, and surveys, in inciting individuals to imagine themselves as part of a nation, the composition, coordinates, and identity of which remained provisional. In conjunction with Anderson's hypothesis, cultural historians and theorists, including Linda Colley, Anthony Smith, Ernest Gellner, and E. J. Hobsbawm, described the nation as the product of various kinds of communication, relations, and social and cultural exchanges that enabled the conception of "a national community where previously there had been only unrelated groups or individuals."[9] The constructivist nature of nationhood and its status as artefact are central to an understanding of early modern writings on the nation at large.

In the acclaimed *Forms of Nationhood*, Richard Helgerson explained that his work involved various kinds of boundary (and border) crossing, and that only one-third of his book engages with texts "that normally belong to [his] home discipline of literary history."[10] The other chapters take into their purview writings traditionally associated with the province of history – legal and cartographic tracts, for example. The present study demonstrates that the subjects of "nation" and "toleration" summon, preoccupy, and test the abilities of Milton the polemicist, the social critic, and the apologist as much as they inspire the poet. Thanks largely to the New Historicism and cultural poetics, of which Helgerson was among the pioneers, the category of literature has been expanded to accommodate poetry and prose in the widest range of canonical and popular forms. Accordingly, one can more readily argue for the literary value of

Milton's entire oeuvre and also of the writings with which he was in conversation. Indeed, the number of his interlocutors that set the stage for, and shared the stage with, Milton in his contributions to debates on toleration and nationhood was enormous. In this book alone, the cast of national and international figures ranges from the philosophers and statesmen of antiquity through to the church fathers and such key figures of the early modern era as Edmund Spenser, David Paraeus, Samuel Purchas, Hugo Grotius, Thomas Edwards, Robert Baillie, Katherine Chidley, John Goodwin, Hubert Languet, John Temple, Roger Williams, Thomas May, William Prynne, Andrew Marvell, Samuel Morland, John Lilburne, Thomas Fuller, James Harrington, Oliver Cromwell, Marchamont Nedham, Henry Spelman, Henry Vane the Younger, Peter Heylyn, Sir Robert Filmer, Gilbert Burnet, and John Locke.

Throughout the centuries, Milton's own prose and polemics in particular have fallen in and out of favour with critics, largely depending on their own literary tastes and politics. Long after the Whigs revived the revolutionary Milton and the Romantics reawakened him following the Neoclassicists' efforts to suppress the political identity of the classical poet,[11] mid-twentieth-century critics elevated the status of Milton's prose in reaction to the New Critics' concentration on the aesthetical value of the verse. Don M. Wolfe produced the first annotated edition of Milton's prose in the collaborative *Complete Prose Works of John Milton*, published in 1953–82.[12] A. S. P. Woodhouse's *Puritanism and Liberty* helped prepare the way for that project by locating Milton as a *revolutionary* prose writer within a seventeenth-century political, intellectual, and religious climate of liberal Puritanism.[13] His colleague and former student, Arthur Barker, thereafter raised the prose to the status of the poetry to give the former its rightful due.[14] "Historicist Critics," including especially Woodhouse, Barker, William Haller, Merritt Y. Hughes, and Arnold Williams, determined that Milton's writings at large needed to be put alongside Milton's extra-aesthetic experiences and alongside research on his life, thought, and intentions.[15]

A little more than two decades later, Keith Stavely commended Northrop Frye for giving Milton's prose the "high aesthetic praise" that the achievements of the left hand justly deserved, and he proceeded in his study on *The Politics of Milton's Prose Style* to demonstrate that the polemicist's writings are "a medium of imaginative expression," the scrutiny of which will generously reward the literary critic.[16] The contributors to Michael Lieb and John T. Shawcross's volume, *Achievements of the Left Hand: Essays on the Prose of John Milton*, which Stavely acknowledges, made that case equally persuasively in the previous year.[17] A decade and a half later, David Loewenstein and James Grantham Turner's *Politics, Poetics, and Hermeneutics in Milton's Prose* would reiterate and develop the thesis of the literary merits of Milton's prose and of the interrelationships of verse and prose, literature and politics. In his chapter on "The Poetics of Engagement," Turner even discovered a surprising number of examples of Milton dismantling and reversing the conceptual hierarchy of poetry and prose.[18]

Most recently, in a direct challenge to the approaches of Barbara Lewalski and David Loewenstein – who, like most Miltonists of the current generation, align the poetry and prose – Annabel Patterson showed that Milton made a concerted effort to separate the two modes of expression.[19] It is true that Milton characterizes the job of the polemicist as inferior to the work of the poet in the autobiographical digression of *The Reason of Church-Government* (CPW 1:808). This prose tract proceeds to describe the poet and his art as a divinely ordained medium of civil and spiritual regeneration that "inbreed[s] and cherish[es] in a great people the seeds of virtue and public civility" (CPW 1:816). Despite such assertions, however, Milton behaves in the *Reason of Church-Government* as though he would rather be writing in the "cool element" of prose, Gordon Campbell and Thomas N. Corns perceive.[20] His subjects in the treatise, including the nature of ecclesiastical polity, the tyranny of bishops, and the accommodation of sectaries, are central to his writing of the English nation and his championing of toleration, which calls forth the polemicist. Yet Milton's anti-prelatical tracts generally and his mid-career prose at large exhibit aesthetic and literary value in their heavy reliance on classical oratorical and rhetorical forms, figures, and tropes.[21] In *Defensio Secunda* (1654), Milton congratulates himself, in the ancient Roman tradition, for the erection of an immortal "monument that will not soon pass away, to those deeds that were illustrious, that were glorious, that were almost beyond any praise" (CPW 4:685). The poet-polemicist lays the philosophical epic foundation for the ideal nation he imagines into being and for the heroic representatives thereof he celebrates and immortalizes in the art of prose. The point of this meditation on mediums is to justify the relatively equal attention given to Milton's verse and prose in a book intended for the literary reader first and foremost and the historian and political theorist secondarily.

To demonstrate the interaction between verse and prose expression within and outside of Milton's oeuvre, I have incorporated some poetic analyses in all the chapters despite the concentration on Milton's prose treatises in the first four. In Chapter 1, for example, which studies Milton's literary ecclesiology, observations on *Lycidas* (comp. 1637) are interpolated. As announced in the addition to its prose headnote in the poem's second printing, *Lycidas*'s new occasional or topical relevance complements and completes the work undertaken by the polemicist in the 1641–42 anti-prelatical treatises. Chapter 2, which deals with discourses on reductionism and civilizing conquests in Ireland, concludes with remarks on Milton's "On the late Massacre in Piedmont," a sonnet that reproduces the shared imagery of testimonies of the massacre of Waldensians on the French-Italian border in 1655. Popular accounts of the atrocity, with which the sonnet is in dialogue, are largely derived from a collection of depositions assembled by Jean Baptiste Stouppe, the Swiss minister and acquaintance of Milton. In the later chapters of *Milton, Toleration, and Nationhood*, which examine at length all the major poems, the mutually enriching nature of verse and prose is more apparent. Chapter 5, for example, shows that Samuel Purchas's *Hakluytus Posthumus or Purchas His Pilgrimes* (1625) proved authoritative for Milton and informed his prose and poetry, as evidenced in his work of travel literature, *A Brief History of Moscovia*, and in the epics, which in turn also derive various geographical place names from the *Moscovia*. The final chapter in *Milton, Toleration, and Nationhood* develops a conversation between Milton's divorce tracts and his most controversial poem in terms of the question of mixed marriages, whereby the representations of international relations and of cultural, gender, and religious difference take on new historical and literary significance.

Nation and Toleration as Categories of Analysis

What is early modern nationhood? The term "nation" itself was a multilingual construct. Derived from the Middle English "nacioun," "nation" enters the English language by way of the Middle French term "nation," originating from the Latin *natio* meaning birth, race, and nation (from *natus*, the past participle of *nasci*, meaning to be born). In the early modern era, Thomas Thomas's Latin-English dictionary defines *natio* as "A nation, a countrie, a people having their beginning in the countrie where they dwell: also a sort of companie, a people."[22] The terms "realm," "kingdom," "country," and "commonwealth" still appeared with greater frequency than "nation," the significance of which nevertheless continued to develop throughout the sixteenth and seventeenth centuries. At the same time, the concept and the term belied any single definition in early modern discourse. The nation assumed a corporate identity based on crown, church, or land; it was conceptualized as a public space and a geographical and historical entity whose boundaries were constantly redrawn; its connotations included empire, public sphere, kingdom, commonwealth, republic, and nation-state. It remained a discursive construct that also generated new discourses.[23] A cognate of nation, "nationhood" is the condition of "being a nation; national independence or autonomy; national, ethnic, or cultural identity."[24] The first example in the Oxford English Dictionary used to illustrate the definition is taken from a mid-nineteenth-century Irish ballad in which "freedom" and "nationhood" are juxtaposed.[25] As this book shows, however, the concept of nationhood predates the coining of the term; literature and cultural history regularly embarrass the Oxford English Dictionary.

Historical and literary evidence in this book reveals that from the early seventeenth century on, "nation" came to refer to a politically autonomous community and notably to a people with a claim to liberty. The institution of political and legal systems, the emergence of cultures of dissent, the expansion of a mercantile class, the formation and documentation of a collective historical memory reliant on symbols and myths, and the enlargement of a public sphere through the spread of various literacies and print technologies are among the numerous factors that informed the discourse, lineaments, and category of the nation. While acknowledging the impact of these developments, *Milton, Toleration, and Nationhood* foregrounds the resonant and contested issue of early modern toleration as represented especially in literary and imaginative writings.

The complex and expansive history of toleration in Europe, notably in England, has traditionally been charted in historical, religious, intellectual, and political terms. Resisting models of religious opposition and complicating both anachronistic Whig readings of a liberal English nation and the revisionist history of English intolerance, social and cultural historians have studied the politics and practices of tolerance in European religious rituals, architectural spaces, church structures, and the coexistence of diverse ethnic, religious, and cultural communities.[26] To such investigations of social, cultural, and religious mediation, *Milton, Toleration, and Nationhood* adds literary evidence, which likewise redefines the conditions and conjunctions of nationhood and toleration.[27]

What is early modern toleration? Conventionally understood as the temporary forbearance of difference or the accommodation (often reluctantly) of "beliefs … deemed to be conscionably held," toleration became a pivotal and decisive development in Europe.[28] Certainly toleration was

a contentious and divisive issue in the early modern era, one not synonymous with contemporary notions of liberalism, even though it assumed,
often controversially and to varying degrees, some of the forms associated with the concept today, including principled resistance to religious
persecution, divergence of belief and a plurality of churches, humanitar-
ian sensibility, and respect for conscience. The exercise of conscience itself
was understood in terms of the freedom to adhere to God's laws above
all other laws; on that basis, "liberty and authority [were not] antithetical," liberty of conscience having little to do with individualism or self-
sufficiency – a marked difference from Western concepts thereof today.[29]
Appeals to conscience could fragment societies, as anti-tolerationists, who
constituted the majority, regularly complained. In Milton's day, the term
was often used derisively and the practice of toleration was judged as an
inducement to libertinism and atheism. "There hath been much these
dayes bygone concerning a general *Toleration*, and liberty of Conscience,"
James Hay announces in a 1655 appeal for the enforcement of religious conformity in the name of national order and political stability.
"[B]y granting too large a *Toleration*, you dishonour God, and disorder
the State."[30]

An advocate of liberty of conscience, Oliver Cromwell in 1648 urged
religious unity as a means of consolidating a pluralistic society: "I profess to thee [Colonel Robert "Robin" Hammond] I desire from my heart,
I have prayed for it, I have waited for the day to see union and right
understanding between the godly people (Scots, English, Jews, Gentiles,
Presbyterians, Independents, Anabaptists, and all)."[31] Cromwell's promotion of the Protestant League in 1654–55 anticipated his plea for "brotherly
consent and harmony"[32] among warring Protestant parties. The realization
of such a vision also required the management of any threats to liberty of
conscience or religious union, not infrequently achieved through subjugation, reduction, or conquest. Marked by the entanglement of notions
of toleration and intolerance, the Interregnum government's mission to
advance English nationhood and its interests gave rise to a culture of
nonconformity, anti-popery in the European theatre, the proposed readmission of the Jews in 1655, relative press freedom, hostility to English
Levellers and Quakers, ruthless military campaigns against the Irish, and
the considerably less popular war against the Spanish. The early conception of tolerationism within the context of Protestant unity, supremacy,
and the advancement of the Reformation helps explain how the tolerationist Milton could in good conscience reconcile anti-Catholic hostility
with the doctrine and discipline of the true religion.

While querying reports on the coexistence and the mutual toleration of European Protestants and Catholics, Richard Perrinchief distinguished between forbearance and toleration in observing that "whence it is evident, that the one beareth indeed with the other, but neither gives Toleration to other."[33] The difference Perrinchief discerned is one akin to that between negative toleration – resistance to constraints or persecution and reluctant accommodation – and positive toleration, or an embrace of alterity or heterodoxy. Jurist Hugo Grotius had earlier described the difference between complete and incomplete toleration in his work of international law, *De Juri Belli ac Pacis*: "[P]ermission which is accorded by a law ... is either complete, which authorizes the doing of something with the fullest possible liberty, or incomplete, which only grants freedom from punishment among men, with the right of non-interference by another."[34] Milton's own oeuvre reveals how his thinking about and his treatment of toleration were subject to historical contingencies of various kinds and shifted from positive to negative, on which both then frequently settled. The literary evidence in this book thus regularly dismantles the Whiggish history and theory of toleration, and within that, the theory that Milton was the voice of liberty.[35] Certainly in his optimism about the liberty-loving nation, Milton sees toleration empathetically as an embrace of Christian principles of liberty. In confronting the backsliding, persecutory tendencies of a nation that betrayed its exceptionalism, Milton, however, condemns policies on and instances of intolerance without consistently raising toleration to a positive value. His later works oppose a religious settlement and are founded largely on a negatively formulated toleration. The narrative presented here, one that resists a teleological construction, is designed to illuminate the ways that Milton's varying positions on the practices, violations, and poetics of toleration subtend his writing of a nation, whose elect status is correspondingly also interrogated.

Elect Nationhood?

In the history of early nationhood, peculiar status was originally less a nation-specific designation than a distinction reserved for a people bound by a common religion. England's elect status developed before the early modern era, in a rivalry with France, whose identity was established through its papal legitimization of monarchical authority. The effort to emulate France's dominant status involved the cultivation of a royal mystique and a "political theology" prominently featuring a providential narrative.[36] Interpreted in relation to an international Reformation movement, an evolving English nationhood was distinguished by a resistance to the universal acclaims of Roman Catholicism.[37] In an expression of political autonomy, Henry VIII in the Tudor revolution renounced the foreign jurisdiction of the Holy Roman Empire and was declared "Supreme Head of the Church of England" by the first Act of Supremacy in 1534.[38] After Henry's death, Humanist and diplomat, Sir Thomas Smith announced the transference of elect status through the succession of divinely ordained British monarchs. At a time when the kingdom was assailed by foreign foes as well as shaken sorely within, Smith judged that England was "a chosen Realme," blessed by the transmission of divine favour to "the late King of most famous memorie, Henrie the Eight, *and* now more amply ... [to] his most swete sonne, the Kings *Majestie*, that now reigneth."[39] The consolidation of England's national identity occurred in conjunction with the Reformation and then with Protestantism, and by 1565, unifying compulsions led to the formation of a national church, liturgy, and theology.[40] Still, even by Shakespeare's time, only a minority subscribed to Protestant nationalism.[41] Among the most influential English writers of the day, John Foxe, whom Milton would claim for England as the "Author of our Church History," remained more an internationalist than a nationalist.[42] Not until the 1580s is it appropriate to speak of a *Protestant* Reformation, represented by new religious beliefs and conversions to the faith, although, even so, the number of "informed godly Protestants" remained relatively small. Christopher Haigh, who offers a revisionist history of the Reformation, including a critique of the early modern advancement of religious radicalism, thus distinguishes between a Protestant nation and a nation of Protestants.[43]

In her seminal work on the subject, Linda Gregerson sees the assertion of theological independence in the Henrician era as decisive in England's coming of age as a nation.[44] The event, however, is double-edged, because the construction of a national identity involved pitting unifying measures against separatist origins that would also eventually splinter. First aligned with monarchical authority, as Sir Thomas Smith protests, the concept of English nationhood would come to reflect a reformed relationship. Connecting the nation with the idea of an elect people of God offered leverage to critics and opponents of the monarchy. Even so, contemporary scholarship on the nation tends to chart an evolutionary march toward nationalism through John Foxe to John Aylmer, to the Golden Speech of Elizabeth I, and eventually to Milton's "chauvinist rhetoric."[45] Protestant internationalism and English nationalism in conjunction with the universal and exclusive designations of election readily ran together. Indeed, nationhood was relational, mercurial, internally fractured, and compatible with broadly defined sympathies embracing other communities and nations.

In the early modern era, the English nation would be torn by the terms of its origination as opposition to the royal mystique that launched a nationalist movement seeded a new form of nationalism whose "democratic and libertarian connotations" came increasingly to the fore.[46] Nationhood came to be distinguished by a host of related competing interests, notably civil, religious, and political liberties, as well as shifting relations between church and state government, ranging from disestablishment to comprehension – an ecclesiastical settlement accommodating divergent opinions on nonessential issues.[47] The gradual alignment of Englishness with the liberty of the subject ultimately led to the reconstitution and reformulation of the nation's institutional and state identity and to the displacement of monarchical authority by a sovereign people.[48] Still, the persistent suspicion of and outright hostility to toleration in the early modern era certainly unsettle any contemporary theory of a progressive nationhood or of a people readily severing allegiances to kingship or state power.

The configuration of the nation remained a subject of debate among conservatives and nonconformist sympathizers in the early modern era and was directly tied to questions of toleration of cultural, political, and religious difference. England is hailed by early modern historians as superior, a status ascribed to the nation in Edward Chamberlayne's royalist *Angliae Notitia, or The Present State of England* (1669): "In a word, the *English* were then ['before the late Troubles'] according to their *Native Tempers*, the Best *Neighbours*, best *Friends*, best *Subjects*, and the best *Christians* in the World."[49] Added to subsequent editions of the treatise are Chamberlayne's reactions to the spread of nonconformity, the by-product of the rebellion:

> As for those other Perswasions whose Professors are commonly called *Presbyterians, Independents, Anabaptists, Quakers, Fifth-Monarchy-Men, Ranters, Adamites, Behemists, Family of Love*, and the rest of those Mushromes of *Christianity*; as most of them sprang up suddenly in the late unhappy Night of Confusion … the State of *England* doth account them no other Members then the *Pudenda* of the Nation.[50]

For royalists and social conservatives, England's peculiar status was rooted in the stability of the restored monarchy, supported by policies designed to secure allegiance to the national church. Interestingly, by the twenty-first edition of Chamberlayne's treatise, changes in government and state legislation in the era following the Glorious Revolution ushered in new policies on toleration and accommodation for nonconformists: "a free

Toleration is granted to all the dissenting Protestants, and none is to be molested upon any account of his Religion, that takes the Oath of Allegiance to Her present Majesty."[51]

The historical and literary evidence in this book suggests that early modern writers conceived of England as both "an" and "the" elect nation, that is, continuous with other peoples and nations professing the Reformed religion, and as specially chosen. In contrast to Christopher Hill, who describes England as "the" elect nation, Patrick Collinson judges that English Protestants "eschewed grossly ethnocentric exclusivism" and that even Milton designates "England's peculiarly elect role" as "a blessing intended for all Christian nations."[52] Joad Raymond likewise observes that England was deemed by the intellectuals of the day to be "a" (not "the") peculiar nation whose providential destiny was attributable to its insularity.[53] Claire McEachern noted the tension in the English church between "international filiation" and "national figuration," and later she reasserted that England's status as "the" elect nation was not unqualified in the second half of the sixteenth century.[54] Still, contemporary scholarship on the parallel between Israel's and New Israel's peculiar status tends to exaggerate what was, according to David Armitage, a "quite restricted, particular and contested" argument among English Protestants. Armitage also disputes the connections among religion, nationhood, and imperialism by maintaining that biblical precedents do not establish "a foundation for exclusive *dominium*, or the grounds for secular *imperium*."[55]

Anthony Smith approaches the question of early modern elect nationalism from a different direction and to different ends. Having in the 1970s judged that nationalism was the philosophical product of the interweaving of Enlightenment and Romantic precepts, Smith in later decades makes a case for the antiquity of nations.[56] In "Nation and Covenant," he concedes that, despite the seductive thesis of a secular nationalism, some nations did predate the Industrial Revolution. Smith discerns a covenantal nationalism in England, Scotland, and the United Provinces. In galvanizing society against the corrupt Roman church, the writers of these nations availed themselves of a discourse of election through recourse to the Old Testament, which was translated into the political and national mythology of the nationalists. The concept of election to which covenantal nationalists subscribed, however, was conditional insofar as it depended on performance or "the continuing conduct of the community in executing God's laws."[57] Witnessing becomes a sign of the covenant, as does adherence to the laws, statutes, and rituals of the covenanted nation, whose exclusiveness is thereby preserved. Another key mandate for and sign of special intimacy with God is the emergence of the covenanted people as a model for all nations.[58]

Early modern defences of England's elect status often rested on the premise that the English led Christian nations in the advancement of the Reformation, the most important aspect of which was the realization of a polity that guaranteed liberty of conscience. Liah Greenfeld articulates this position while arguing for the diminished authority of religion in the history of the nation. Correspondingly, she singles Milton out as "a leader of 'the new religion of patriotism'" for his embrace of an "increasingly secular nationalism and the accentuation of its libertarian implications."[59] Modern theorists of the nation like Greenfeld have traditionally underplayed the role of religion in narratives of nation formation.[60] The revived interest in religious history and in early modern theological contexts and positions can be explained in terms of the increased discontent with Marxist and Whig readings of history driven by proletarian or liberal movements.[61] Published in the same year as Greenfeld's *Nationalism*, Helgerson's study of the *Forms of Nationhood* – albeit a Whiggish historical narrative of nationmaking – shows that the "language of politics was most often the language of religion" and not vice versa.[62] Milton himself subscribed to a political theology rather than political theory, as his meditations on nationhood and toleration amply demonstrate.

The Literary Narrative

Each chapter in this book highlights a feature of nationhood, signaled by the titles "'Temple-worke,'" "Reduction," "Natural Law," "Disestablishment," "Geography," and "Exogamy." All of these themes also represent expressions, extensions, and complications of English and, notably, Milton's positions on and figures of toleration. From the early stages of his literary career, Milton's championing of an English Protestant national identity and his embrace of liberty are inflected with anti-prelatical and anti-Catholic overtones. The Latin epyllion "In Quintum Novembris," on the failure in 1605 of the Gunpowder Plot and Catholic conspiracy, commemorates England as the paradisal chosen nation that spurns a popish Satan. Milton proceeds to assault the prelates in such tracts as *Of Reformation, Of Prelatical Episcopacy, Animadversions upon the Remonstrants Defence*, and *The Reason of Church-Government*. In these and other works, he censures the Episcopal Church for its vestiges of Laudianism, regularly elided with Catholicism. Milton's Puritan revulsion against ritual and idolatry fed his contempt for the trappings of Catholicism: "easy Confession, easy

Absolution, Pardons, Indulgences, Masses ..., *Agnus Dei's*, Reliques, and the like" (CPW 8:439). Further, just as Milton implicates English bishops in a treacherous plot to dethrone monarchs, so does he accuse papists of indenturing themselves to a foreign authority. In all cases, Milton judges Catholicism as irreligious, menacing, un-English, and intolerant – and thus intolerable.

Milton's oeuvre is balanced by numerous positive tolerationist statements, beginning with his early religious tracts. In *Of Reformation*, for example, Milton argues for a Presbyterian church discipline in lieu of an episcopacy. Implicit in his ecclesiology and theory of religious toleration is a sense of social, civic, and religious obligation and of mediation between the desire for individual liberties and systemic change. Other early writings proposing toleration include *The Doctrine and Discipline of Divorce* (1643, 2nd ed. 1644) and *Areopagitica* (1644), founded upon theological arguments and biblical examples, such as the wheat and tares – a touchstone for tolerationists. His biblically and theologically inflected meditations on England as a community of the elect serve as an impetus for imagining a Protestant nation. In *Areopagitica*, Milton recalls England's history of liberation enabled through the early reformers: "the favour and the love of heav'n we have great argument to think in a peculiar manner propitious and propending towards us. Why else was this Nation chos'n before any other, that out of her as out of *Sion* should be proclam'd and sounded forth the first tidings and trumpet of Reformation?" (CPW 2:552). The treatise featuring the poetic vision of a holy nation is replete with rhetorical and imaginative flourishes that serve as speech acts, calling the nation into creation as a "mansion house of liberty," "a Nation of Prophets, of Sages, and of Worthies," and "a noble and puissant Nation" (CPW 2:554, 554, 558). The concepts of liberty and tolerance in fact engender and depend on the mythos of a nation.

Chapter 1 develops this connection by locating the seventeenth-century designation of national election in the context of debates on ecclesiology and the controversy over toleration. In an assault on Independency and the threat it posed to the national Church, the anti-tolerationist orthodox Presbyterian Thomas Edwards identified "the Disciplinary Controversie" as "the chiefe question ... in our dayes in this Kingdome."[63] Milton sows the seeds of his radical position on church discipline in his early anti-episcopal tracts with their advocacy of freedom of conscience. Elect nationhood and the Christian commonwealth take the form of a reformed ecclesiology, in which "temple-worke" emerges as a key metaphor. Milton's ecclesiology, however, gets transmuted into a belief in an invisible church, one without a counterpart in a specific organization or temporal structure. In contrast to secularized conceptions thereof, Milton's notions of toleration issue from the vision of the church as a spiritual community and initially out of his identification of nation and church as coterminous.[64] As he responds to the crises over toleration in his day, Milton redirects his assaults on episcopacy at the Presbyterians themselves, while, in *Areopagitica*, appropriating the Presbyterians' architectural metaphors and tropes for the nation in the cause of liberty of the press and liberty of conscience.

The relationship between Milton's competing desires for toleration on the one hand and for the punishment of anti-tolerationists on the other is the subject of the second chapter, which concentrates on English literature dealing with the Irish crisis. Michael Neill insists that "nationality can only be imagined as a dimension of difference,"[65] but England's dealings with its "Daughter Iland[]" (CPW 1:614) also turns the exercise of nation formation into a (self-)encounter. Sixteenth-century writers had asserted what Andrew Hadfield called "an English hegemony within Britain, colonising the imagined space as English," and the colonial relationship to Ireland therein is perhaps the most troubling and vexing.[66] Neither Ireland nor Wales represented itself as a nation at this time, although "they did indeed have identities with an imperial British state thrust upon them," and Chapter 2 offers one particularly disturbing piece of literary evidence thereof.[67] The contentious relationship with Ireland, however, was also an expression of England's own unstable identity. For Attorney General for Ireland Sir John Davies and many of his contemporaries, the failure to execute a perfect conquest of or to reduce Ireland undermined England's entitlement to the country, exposed its shaky commitment to the Reformation, and threatened its own liberty and national security. In *Observations upon the Articles of Peace* (1649), Milton powerfully asserts strong nationalist concerns to reinforce proprietary rights over Ireland and to offer historical and rhetorical support for a reconquest.[68]

Milton's fluid conception of national character and rights is reliant on a scale of civility and virtue, which can redefine national identity and the conceptual boundaries of Englishness itself. Thus Milton attests in the *Tenure of Kings and Magistrates* that "whoever keeps peace with me, neer or remote, of whatsoever Nation, is to mee as farr as all civil and human offices an Englishman and a neighbour." An Englishman, however, renounces his national ties and privileges by "forgetting all Laws, human, civil and religious" and by violating the terms of liberty, thus degenerating into something "no better then a Turk, a Sarasin, a Heathen" (CPW 3:215). The statement is a fascinating expression of international nationalism but also of the dangers of lapsing into the condition of otherness that the true nation seeks to repel. Milton's mid- and late-career writings bring this danger to the fore and exhibit his departure from an incipient liberal nationalism while displaying his concerted effort to reconceive a nation, the ascription of whose upright moral and civic character would be reserved for the "sounder part of a nation" (CPW 4:681). The relationship between the worse part and the minority that represented the better or sounder part, which was in fact a central defining feature of Protestantism,[69] was integral to Milton's conception of the free Christian commonwealth.

Even though Charles I was charged with treacherously seeking to "subvert the ancient and fundamental laws and liberties of this nation," the execution of the king in 1649 was endorsed only by a minority.[70] In addition to accepting an assignment to answer the martyred monarch's *Eikon Basilike* (1649), Milton was commissioned by the Council of State to respond to *Defensio regia* (1649) by Claude de Saumaise or Salmasius, an internationally renowned French scholar. Composed in Latin and directed to a continental readership, Milton's post-revolutionary 1651 *Pro Populo Anglicano* refutes *Defensio regia*, using the weight of scripture and the language and principles of natural law, whereby all enjoy freedom from tyranny in a true commonwealth, to invalidate Salmasius's claim that Christ promoted subjection to secular authority. *Pro Populo Anglicano* is significant for its definition of the nation as a safeguard for Christian liberty, used here as part of the argument justifying opposition to kingship. Chapter 3 locates Milton's two *Defence*s of the English people in philosophical contexts in relation to Milton's own privileging of the moral disposition of the Protestant nation over its political identity. Like its 1654 successor, the 1651 *Pro Populo Anglicano Defensio* is a declaration of civil, political, and religious rights and liberties upheld by a virtuous few that now represent the true nation. In delimiting the concept of nationhood, Milton confronts the various positions on the law of nature and, correspondingly, on constitutional laws that inform national identity.

A number of Milton's shorter poems, including "On the New Forcers of Conscience under the Long Parliament" (1646) and Sonnet XV "On the late Massacre in Piedmont" (1655), express outrage at the violation and persecution of nonconformity. The Preface to his posthumously published theological treatise, the *Christian Doctrine* is, like *Areopagitica* and *Of True Religion*, a plea for toleration of unorthodox Christian sects, with which he consorted at least ideologically. Milton is linked to the culture of dissent by way of his millenarianism; the apocalyptic and liberal premises of his concept of toleration; his criticism of the abuses of civil power; his anti-Catholicism; associations with Quakers Thomas Ellwood and Isaac Pennington; his interest in Hebraism; resistance to censorship; criticism of prelacy and kingship; and belief in an inner light and heart-circumcision (CPW 6:543). Yet Milton's theory of toleration, for which Christian liberty and the exercise of human reason as a divine faculty were the basis, remained less secular than that of the radicals, from whom he maintained a "polemical and authorial independence."[71] He also consistently subordinated his civil and political discourses to his theological premises whose authority trumped that of the state.[72]

In conjunction with the intellectual climate of his day, Milton variously subscribed to a philo-Hebraic cultural and literary program,[73] while simultaneously and repeatedly exhibiting his religious and political intolerance, not to mention his anti-Jewish biases. In his post-regicide works, Milton prepares the way for Cromwell's campaign against the Catholic Irish, fuels English-Spanish antipathy, and lapses into silence over the proposed readmission of the Jews at a time when Amsterdam Rabbi Menasseh ben Israel presented his vision of England as a religiously and culturally inclusive society. During this period, Milton also produced his *History of Britain, That Part especially now call'd England*, designed to "instruct and benefit them that read" it and thereby contribute to "the good of the *British Nation*" (CPW 5.1:4). Here his theories of fundamental rights and liberties focus on the people's ability to exercise them properly. His *History of Britain*, however, conveys doubts about national election that would resonate especially throughout Milton's final and most significant writings. Despite its providential designation as *peculiar*, England has a profoundly mixed history of cultural, political, and religious fitness, as Milton demonstrates in his anatomy of national character. His exasperation over the moral degeneracy of the nation accounts to varying degrees for his reformulations of toleration and republicanism.

In the tracts of his earlier years, most notably *Areopagitica*, Milton expressed what Feisal Mohamed has called a "liberal" vision of "a tolerationist state guiding the nation's progress towards enlightenment."[74] But even at this stage, Milton displays an obvious skepticism about the role of the state in civil society. Certainly Milton's later polemics, especially those on disestablishment, as Mohamed has pointed out in an observation critical to my project, do not entertain the possibility of the state leading the nation and of advancing policies consistent with the preservation of Christian liberty. Chapter 1 reviews the various configurations of the relationship of the church, the state, and the imagined nation while noting that the interrelationships among them were tenuous and fragile in the early seventeenth century. The radicals of Milton's day who lobbied for church reform conceived of the counter-cultural, anti-establishment New Testament community as distinct from a national church and from the nation at large,[75] and it is this position that Milton eventually supports, spurred on in part by his case for disestablishment, the subject of Chapter 4. The pre-Restoration pamphlets *A Treatise of Civil Power in Ecclesiastical Causes* (1659) and *Considerations Touching the Likeliest Means to Remove Hirelings Out of the Church* (1659) urge church disestablishment as a means for achieving a more inclusive political culture and for fostering a republican ethos.

In *A Treatise of Civil Power*, in which he maintains that "no man or body of men in these times can be the infallible judges or determiners in matters of religion to any other mens consciences but thir own," Milton nevertheless refuses to promote toleration of or defend liberty of conscience for Catholics on political grounds, that is, "for just reason of state more then of religion" (CPW 7:242–3, 7:254). The treatise thus reinforces the political associations of Catholicism and offers Milton's first extensive argument for disestablishment, which undergirds his theory of toleration. What are the limits of toleration? "[S]hall divers Religions be allowed in the Gospel?" asks anti-tolerationist Nathaniel Hardy in a fast-day sermon. "I have read indeed of a *Turk*, who resembled the diversity of Religions in his Empire, to the variety of flowers in a garden; but Christian Magistrates must account them as weeds, which if not pluckt up, will soon overtop the flowers of Orthodox doctrine ... sure I am, a free toleration of divulging errors in matters necessary, will prove pernicious." National security or the commonwealth's safety, maintains Hardy in citing Solon, the ancient Athenian statesman and lawgiver, depends on the people's regulation by magistrates, and the magistrates' observance of the law.[76] Milton's late pro-tolerationist tracts contest obstructions to the freedom of the church, whose independence from the state is essential, and which is for Milton the foundation for an "undisturbd" Christian commonwealth (CPW 7:276). Politico-historical conditions would demand concessions on Milton's part in his pre-Restoration religious pamphlets, and thus he would, for example, eventually grant magistrates a civil function, although specifically as exorcists of a politicized popery.

What evidence is there of any ongoing investment in issues of nationhood and toleration in the post-1660 era? One answer to the question lies in the study of Milton's conceptualization of space and his use of geography as a figure in the discourse of nationhood, to which chorographies of his day contributed.[77] Chapter 5 of this book thus examines the cataloguing and spatial arrangement of Milton's geopolitical knowledge in the formulation of nationhood, foreign relations, and the terms of toleration. *Paradise Lost* in particular advances the chorographical projects of Ortelius, Richard Hakluyt, Samuel Purchas, and Peter Heylyn, among others, in applauding an expansionary English nation. The encyclopaedic scope of Milton's epic and the genre in general permitted the anatomising and management of space "under the commanding eye of English standards," as Bruce McLeod observes.[78] At the same time, the geographic evidence highlights the nation's fraught relationship to foreign lands. Robert Ralson Cawley assures us that Milton's immersion in geographies and travel literatures – the "vast body of peripheral literature" – did not really compromise "Milton's essential nationalism."[79] Implied here is a distinction between Milton's esteem for his native land and his admiration for foreign nations.[80] A survey of Milton's epics reveals the poet's mobilization of a formidable repertoire of geographic place names, epic catalogues, and spatial arrangements of geopolitical knowledge that convey a national consciousness in conjunction with a pronounced internationalism. A review of Milton's descriptive geography and poeticised cartography exposes his indebtedness to biblical and classical geographical allusions and to early modern cosmographies, geographic compendiums, and travel narratives. The textual evidence displays Milton's uses of poetic space to reconstitute geographic place. The transformation of places into charged spaces is a common practice among historical geographers, but more evocatively, the feat of the epic poet, whether through the compilation and positioning of place names specifically or the design of the stanza form more generally.

Milton's late writings – his great poems in particular – are less national and more universal, and yet they still possess contemporary preoccupations specific to England. Like ancient Israel, England had reverted to a state of subservience, which is reflected in what Victoria Kahn characterized as the "disappointed nationalism" of Milton's late poems.[81] As a victim of renewed censorship in a repressive climate that saw the restoration of monarchy, Milton again modulates the concept of national election and transfers his lingering hopes for reviving liberty to a remnant nation. Changing his notes to tragic (PL 9.6), the poet asserts divine providence in the native tongue, lamenting and memorializing the fallen New Israel. National salvation now depended on the excision or colonization of Judaism, the transference of elect status, and the internalization of the Hebraic in the heart-circumcised Christian, the "Jew inward."[82] At the same time, "lived history" and all its revolutions and particularities, as Jeffrey Shoulson observed, unsettled the poem's and the nation's typological narratives.[83] In the wake of dashed political aspirations and expiring liberty, the writing of the *New* Israelites' providential history takes the form of tragedy.

Milton's Greek tragedy of the Restoration era features a Hebrew narrative that rescripts the Judges story of Samson and Delilah as a drama of nationhood, whose forms are at once biblical, mimetic, legal, civic, and philosophical. In *Samson Agonistes*, Milton reaches back to a period of Israel's history before the time of kingship, thus invalidating the dynastic origins of nationhood.[84] Configured as an ethnic body, the nation is marked by a common bloodline or genealogy, but as a civic construction, the nation is bound by laws, duties, and rights ideally designed to preserve the liberty of its citizens, and thus it is deemed less exclusionary than an ethnicity. In his final poetic illustration of the conjunctions of toleration and nationhood, Milton, as discussed in Chapter 6, resets the scale of toleration by confounding ethnic formulations of the nation, by broadening the parameters of the law – biblical, civic, natural, national, and international – and by destabilizing the rigidly oppositional relationship between Israelite chosenness and Philistine reprobation. In *Samson Agonistes*, Milton pushes hard against the boundaries and registers of nationhood as he imagines Israel out of dislocation and in relation to contraries and dissimilitudes that are marked as "foreign." Milton's "most indeterminate poem," one that "offers debate, not certainty," as Stephen Fallon and David Norbrook contend, tests the tolerance for ethnic, religious, and national difference in a drama on intermarriage and holy war.[85] Connections between the divorce tracts and *Samson Agonistes* are used to show that more than ethnicity, self-integrity, a consensual relationship to a righteous law, and a liberty-affirming nature establish the character of the true nation.

In defiance of the anti-sectarian climate of the Restoration era, Milton continued to explore and defend liberty of conscience in the works he produced in his final years. In 1673, the authorities legislated against the practice of Catholicism by issuing "An Act for preventing Dangers which may happen from Popish Recusants" (Test Act), which denied civil or military office under the Crown to those who refused allegiance to the Church of England. The rights of nonconformists themselves were compromised by the delay of the "Bill for Ease of his Majesty's Protestant Subjects, Dissenters in Matters of Religion." In that same year, Milton made a final public plea for freedom of speech and religious toleration by composing *Of True Religion, Hæresie, Schism, Toleration* (1673), the product both of a particular moment marking a conjunction between fierce anti-Catholic aggression and indulgence for nonconformist sects and schisms. As "the greatest Heresie," popery remained intolerable, the "dialectically and symbiotically linked" relationship of tolerance and intolerance fully on display again in Milton's last major intervention in the history of Protestant nationhood.[86]

In *Of True Religion*, we find more examples of what is ultimately most compelling and conspicuous about Milton's writing of the nation from the start – the renegotiation of rigidly defined contraries and the confounding of the terms of toleration by which nationhood is circumscribed: "it is a general complaint that this Nation of late years, is grown more numerously and excessively vitious then heretofore ... no wonder if Popery also grow a pace" (CPW 8:438–9). The nation takes a dangerous course as it collapses into what it had always defined itself against: idolatry, licentiousness, popery, and the "inward vitious rule" of "blind affections" (CPW 3:190). "Let us," Milton urges, "amend our lives with all speed; least through impenitency we run into that stupidly ... the worst of superstitions, and the heaviest of all Gods Judgements, Popery" (CPW 8:440). In producing *Of True Religion* in a period of anti-popish sentiment that marks the Restoration era, Milton seizes the opportunity to consolidate all the adherents of what he and his contemporaries singled out as the true reformed religion. He champions comprehension for Protestants, thus esteeming toleration as a key feature of and basis for the advancement of the Reformation. "What Protestant," Milton asks rhetorically, "would persecute, and not rather charitably tolerate such men as these [sectarians], unless he mean to abjure the Principles of his own Religion?" (CPW 8:426). Yet, as Milton's oeuvre intermittently reveals with regret, frustration, and irony, in the "long and hot Contest" (CPW 8:429) over the terms of toleration, popery – whose destruction Milton, Williams, and others had prophesied –resurfaces as a feature of English nationhood itself.

CHAPTER I

"Temple-worke": Milton's Literary Ecclesiology

For Puritans like Milton, the elect status of England – often used inter-changeably with "Britain" – was associated with the progress of the Reformation and with the restoration of the church to its original form, one predating medieval Catholicism. Milton's increasingly unorthodox ecclesiology moves him closer to his ideal nation and sharpens his theories of toleration. Ecclesiology concerns the structure and terms of church polity, the relationship of ecclesiastical and civil power, and the nature of church discipline, defined by Milton as "the *execution* and *applying* of *Doctrine* home" (CPW 1:526). This chapter focuses on the consolidation and galvanizing of national sentiment through the formulation of a literary ecclesiology in early works by Milton, in which the labour of reformation is expressed biblically, polemically, and metaphorically as "temple-work." The moderate Episcopalian and member of the Westminster Assembly Thomas Hill celebrates a "constellation of providences" first in Scotland and then England, as evidenced by the willingness of "the remnant of our people … to bee ingaged in *Temple-worke*," a figure for the "*blessed worke of Reformation*" assigned to the chosen, the sons of Sion.[1] In his anti-episcopal tracts, Milton participates in and also enacts the advancement of temple-work, that is, building the Reformed English church.

Embracing a broad Puritanism, Milton's early religious writings exhibit positions on church polity that resemble Presbyterianism but increasingly gesture toward Independency. As outlined by Joan S. Bennett, Milton's religious allegiances shifted from "an unexamined Calvinism … inspired by the courage of the reforming Presbyterians, to an Independency based initially on a reaction against Presbyterian intolerance."[2] When he responds to what his contemporary Thomas Edwards calls "the Disciplinary Controversie"[3] over toleration in his day, Milton redirects his assaults on episcopacy at the Presbyterians themselves while appropriating and reworking the Presbyterians' tropes for the national church in the development of his ecclesiology. Milton emerges as an "independent

Independent,"[4] and, correspondingly, congregationalist notions of an invisible church would enable his envisioning of the nation as a diversified but unified spiritual community independent of institutional form.

Of Reformation

Although it certainly has universal applications, the scriptural paradigm of a chosen people as applied by Milton is specifically designed to reflect the conditions of English nationhood. Monitoring the character of the English, Milton constantly adjusted the concept of elect nationalism, which gave way to a history of moral vicissitudes and intolerance that called for the reworking of the paradigm. England-Israel identifications as correlative and antithetical correspond most directly with England's fluctuating commitment to Christian liberty. Of the two forms that the biblical Covenant between God and people initially assumed, the second – the conferring of elect status on the Israelites through the creation of a "kingdome of Priests, and an holy nation" (Exod. 19:6) – is dependent on the obedience of the people, as Moses reminds Israel in Deuteronomy 7:9–12, 8:1–2. Possibly indebted to *De Republica Anglorum* by Sir Thomas Smith are Milton's remarks in the Commonplace Book on the failed fitness of historical nations for liberty. In ancient Rome, Brutus and Cassius misjudged the nation they sought to liberate; although they "felt themselves of spirit to free an nation," they failed to realize that "the nation was not fit to be free."[5] The Son in Milton's Restoration work, *Paradise Regained*, would also be tempted to liberate the Jews but would resist, given that "inward slaves" must save themselves (PR 4.145), a lesson that Samson would also need to learn (Chapter 6, "Exogamy"). In the *Christian Doctrine*, Milton would outline the conditional nature of election, which he divorces from predestination early in his treatise, and the obligations of the people in fulfilling the Covenant.[6] Milton thus also converted the Calvinist doctrine of predestination into an Arminian position by asserting the need for the cooperation of believers in confirming their election. "All the Jews were not elect," he judges,[7] thereby substituting worthiness for chosenness as the criterion for election.

The conditional concept of peculiar status informed Milton's reading of Reformation England. *Animadversions upon the Remonstrants Defence Against Smectymnuus* claimed God as "*Brittains* God" who designated the English as his elect, "pittying us the first of all other Nations, after he had decreed to purifie and renew his Church that lay wallowing in Idolatrous pollutions" (CPW 1:704). Among the aims of the more radical reformers and architects of the chosen Reformation nation were the reconstitution of church government and the advancement of toleration for variances in doctrine and disciplinary practices. These objectives developed alongside and in conjunction with an anti-episcopal campaign. Milton himself prepared five pamphlets denouncing prelacy as a legitimate form of church polity. The tracts defend five Presbyterian divines, Smectymnuus, who opposed episcopacy and collectively authored a book (published in 1641) upholding Presbyterianism and refuting Bishop Joseph Hall's treatise on the bishopric.[8] Hall had insisted in his *Humble Remonstrance* on the immutability of the established religion on the basis that "if Antiquity may be the rule, the civill Politie hath sometimes varied, the sacred, never."[9] Further, he rehearsed the hotly contested position that "Bishops, Presbyters, and Deacons … [represent] three distinct subordinate Callings, in Gods Church" and that Timothy and Titus, to whom he assigned the title of bishop, established the model for apostolic succession.[10] Presbyterian church government, by contrast, would splinter the church into "Atomes," Hall warned, and would destabilize both the church and commonwealth.[11] Presbyterianism had contentious beginnings despite the reputation it would acquire and earn as an instrument for imposing rigid conformity in church and state affairs.

Adopting the method of polemical warfare characteristic of the controversialist literature of the period (animadversion and response, counter-response, response) the aforementioned Smectymnuan pamphlet, *An Answer to a Booke*, anatomized Hall's contentions about the Episcopal Church while using the example of the primitive church and its informal practices of discipline and prayer to ground anti-prelatical arguments.[12] Debates on the degree of diversity that the church could accommodate inevitably raised the question of schism. *An Answer to a Booke* announces that the threat schismatics pose pales in comparison with the injuries and injustices inflicted by episcopacy, the office of which, moreover, cannot be justified under the pretence of removing schisms. The incidence of dissent among bishops and archbishops is at least as high as among presbyters, the pamphleteers explain.[13] As the papists charge Protestants with generating "schisme," so do the prelates falsely accuse the presbytery of sedition. But "the Prelats are more Schismaticks then we," retort the Smectymnuans.[14] According to *An Answer to a Booke*, the prelacy's appropriation of the right to establish the national church undermines monarchical authority and treacherously subjects civil power to autocratic ecclesiastical power.

Hall's rejoinder to Smectymnuus, *A Short Answer to the Tedious Vindication of Smectymnuus* (1641), which offers a defence of the antiquity of liturgy and the divine right of episcopacy,[15] prompted Milton to intervene in the debate over church government and take up the antiepiscopal position of Presbyterianism. Later he would categorize his 1641–42 pro-Smectymnuus pamphlets as defences of ecclesiastical liberty (to be followed by domestic or personal liberty and then civil liberty [CPW 4:624]). The program of national reform Milton urged in the pamphlets involved a reconstitution of the English ecclesiastical and political bodies through the exclusion of bishops and the promotion of the Presbyterian system of church organization as the "one right *discipline*" (CPW 1:605). The opposition to the episcopacy, whose power had been upheld by the monarchy, led to debates over church government and escalated in the civil wars. As reformers, Presbyterians and their supporters sought to check the authority that the bishops lorded over the ecclesiastical realm. The Bible offers no model for the office of the bishop as separate from that of the presbyter ("elder," *presbuteros* Gk.), Milton insists, repeating the refrain of the Smectymnuan pamphlet throughout his anti-prelatical tracts, including *Of Prelatical Episcopacy*: "a Bishop and *Presbyter* is all one both in name, and office."[16]

Even at this early period in his life, before his development of more radical positions on religion and church government, Milton does not fully embrace Presbyterianism. Nevertheless, his anti-prelatical tracts betray a strong attraction to the movement and do not anticipate the intolerance of the Presbyterians, which would materialize as "new fetters and captivity after all our hopes and labours lost" (CPW 2:479), Milton announces in lobbying for the reform of divorce legislation several years later. In the *Compassionate Samaritane*, William Walwyn would attribute the repression experienced by separatists in supporting liberty of conscience to the usurpation by Presbyterian ministers of the bishops' authority: "some say the tyrannie over conscience that was exercised by the Bishops, is like [sic] to bee continued by the Presbyter: that the oppressors are only changed."[17] When his own attacks on the Presbyterians became more aggressive, Milton declared, "New *Presbyter* is but old *Priest* writ large": etymologically and for Milton now semantically, "Presbyter" is an expansion of the much earlier term and the office of the "priest."[18] In the Restoration era, Milton's national epic would rehearse the same battle against intolerance: the forcers of "spiritual laws by carnal power" are charged with persecuting God himself by binding the "Spirit of grace" and of "liberty" and thereby "unbuild[ing] / His living temples, built by faith to stand /

Their own faith not another's."[19] Milton adopts the trope of the living Temple from Corinthians and Ephesians, written when the primitive church was heavily persecuted, as Milton's angelic historian informs his postlapsarian audience in the epic.

At an early stage of his career as a polemicist, Milton produced *Of Reformation Touching Church-Government in England* (1641), an exercise in formulating a position on ecclesiastical polity in relation to theories of nationhood and toleration. Set forth anonymously by the printer Thomas Underhill, and appearing in only one edition in Milton's time, this treatise on church government boldly announces England's peculiar status, thus particularizing the ideal of national exceptionalism that emerged after John Foxe. England is destined to be "the new Lampe of *saving light* to all Christendome" and enjoys the God-given "*Precedencie* ... to be the first *Restorer of buried Truth*" (CPW 1:525, 526). Abuses in church discipline and, more generally, the corruption of the episcopacy – the form of church government inherited from the early Roman Catholic Church – have, however, choked the Reformation. How does it happen, Milton laments, that England, God's standard-bearer for all Christian nations, should now be "most unsettl'd in the enjoyment of that *Peace*, whereof she taught the way to others"? (CPW 1:525). In *Of Reformation*, Milton rehearses the narrative recounted in the Smectymnuan Postscript, one that charts the dynastic history of England and details the succession of corrupt prelates ("a sad and dolefull succession of illiterate and blind guides" [CPW 1:603]) at every turn.[20] Possibly having authored the Postscript himself[21] – and certainly indebted to the historical sources on which the Postscript author and Milton in his Commonplace Book also relied (Holinshed, Speed, Stow) – Milton echoes the premise of the Smectymnuan pamphlet that the Reformation is a process in need of precipitation (CPW 1:536). In "*Edward* the 6. Dayes ... a compleate *Reform* was not effected," Milton declares, underscoring his objection to those who stall the Reformation by "endeavour[ing] to reduce our Religion to the first times of King *Edward*, which wee conceive were comparatively very imperfect."[22]

In one of the many analogies in *Of Reformation's* Second Book, which, according to Nigel Smith, "might readily be titled 'Of a Christian Commonwealth,'"[23] Milton compares the commonwealth to a perfectly proportioned body, "one huge Christian personage, one mighty growth, and stature of an honest man, as big, and compact in vertue as in body; for looke what the grounds, and causes are of single happines to one man, the same yee shall find them to a whole state" (CPW 1:572). While lending a Christian application to the ancient (Aristotelian) principle that the state is manifested in its ethical citizenry, Milton relies on the figurative to transport his design for the commonwealth above political philosophy. At the same time, he determines that the character, progress, and writing of the godly nation depend upon a single person, "the inspired poet himself."[24] Among the many representations of England cited by the prophet-poet is that of a mother in mourning, possibly indebted to the figure of the widowed Judah after the fall of the sinful Jerusalem in the Lamentations (of Jeremiah): "if we could but see the shape of our deare Mother *England,* as Poets are wont to give a personal form to what they please," judges Milton, she would appear "in a mourning weed, with ashes upon her head, and teares abundantly flowing from her eyes, to behold so many of her children expos'd at once, and thrust from things of dearest necessity, because their conscience could not assent to things which the Bishops thought *indifferent*" (CPW 1:585). Here Milton attributes the degeneration of England to its intolerant, repressive episcopacy, which constrains a nurturing, liberty-loving nation. The bishops' designation of church discipline and ceremonies as indifferent is, for example, a direct violation of liberty of conscience and the principle of indifferency, which allows subjects to choose rather than be coerced in the name of ecclesiastical doctrine.

Milton builds into his own model of the (Pauline) Christian community and of the ideal commonwealth a position on toleration for diversity in a body whose features are, in accordance with the law of nature, not wholly uniform or unvaried: "because things simply pure are inconsistent in the masse of nature, nor are the elements or humors in Mans Body exactly *homogeneall.*" Rooted in the classical political theory of Aristotle is Milton's recommendation for a commonwealth that boasts a mixed and balanced government by aiming at "a certaine mixture and temperament, partaking the severall vertues of each other State, that each part drawing to it selfe may keep up a steddy, and eev'n uprightnesse in common" (CPW 1:599). In *The Reason of Church-Government Urg'd Against Prelaty*, the body is the trope for God's temple, the church, whose architectural dimensions are figured as the "immortall stature of Christs body which is his Church, in all her glorious lineaments and proportions" (CPW 1:758). In *Areopagitica*, the assembly of the body of truth constitutes an ongoing act of church-building: truth's "body is *homogeneal,* and proportionall," Milton explains, and "this is the golden rule in *Theology* as well as in Arithmetick, and makes up the best harmony in a Church" (CPW 2:551).

The pattern for the Reformation church and national government is supplied by the example of the primitive church, which feeds its flock and exercises "coequall and compresbyteriall" authority in the ordination of ministers (CPW 1:537). The conversion of the bishop into a primitive cleric thus involves a divesting and a displacement of the prelate by the "undiocest, unrevenu'd, unlorded" elected minister.[25] While promoting the complementarity of state and church governments, Milton already anticipates at this point his disestablishment position, or at least his position on the exemption of ecclesiastical affairs from state jurisdiction: the "Piety, and Conscience of *Englishmen* as members of the Church [must] be trusted in the Election of Pastors to Functions that nothing concerne a *Monarch*" (CPW 1:600). Election by merit, the condition for leadership in the church, was recommended by Smectymnuus[26] and is a practice and principle for church discipline that Milton adopts as he gradually transfers authority to the laity: "the *godliest,* the *wisest,* the *learnedest* Ministers in their severall charges have the instructing and disciplining of *Gods people* by whose full and free Election they are consecrated to that holy and equall *Aristocracy*" (CPW 1:600).

At a time when the church and nation were for him still coterminous, Milton appeals for national unity in arguing for the congruity of the ecclesiastical and political bodies. Later he will insist on the differences of the true church from any national grouping, such as a nation state, as discussed in Chapter 4, "Disestablishment." But at least up until the mid 1640s, the commonwealth remained for Milton a well-balanced, *limited* monarchy. Political authority was to be disciplined by the law and checked by worthy citizens represented in government by elected officials in the House of Commons:

> There is no Civill *Goverment* that hath beene known ... more divinely and harmoniously tun'd, more equally ballanc'd as it were by the hand and scale of Justice, then is the Common-wealth of *England:* where under a free, and untutor'd *Monarch,* the noblest, worthiest, and most prudent men, with full approbation, and suffrage of the People have in their power the supreame, and finall determination of highest Affaires. (CPW 1:599)

The argument put forth by supporters of episcopacy that Presbyterianism undermines kingship (CPW 1:605) is turned on its head as Milton charges the prelates themselves with insolence, schism, and high treason: "have not some of their devoted Schollers begun ... openly to argue against the Kings *Supremacie?*" (CPW 1:594). The program for national reform then takes on an international dimension as Milton directs attention to the Reformation movement on the Continent. Decoupling support of a prelacy from fealty to the nation, Milton invokes the examples of the anti-episcopal Swiss, the Dutch, and the French Huguenots, who all retained their loyalty to the state (CPW 1:609).

The refutation in *Of Reformation* reviews arguments against Presbyterianism, including the imprudence of adopting extremist positions, the sanctity of an episcopacy founded on antiquity, and the charge that any other discipline would infect and contaminate the church more than episcopacy. In each case, Milton responds forcefully by aligning prelacy with papacy, by urging the advancement of the Reformation, and by judging prelacy as dangerous to monarchical authority. Sir Thomas Aston, who surveys pro-Presbyterian positions for the purpose of dismantling them, accuses the anti-episcopal movement of sabotaging temple-work and subverting "*Gods house*, the Church" through innovation rather than reformation.[27] His arguments are largely summarized in the refrain, Presbyterians "assume to themselves (to the little Bishop, absolute Pope of every parish) that their office is *jure Divino*."[28] Their proposal for annual elections, according to Aston, will destabilize church government entirely: "what must this produce but a little Civil war in every parish?"[29] George Digby likewise complained that a new discipline under presbyters would "set up a Pope in every Parish,"[30] a threat that Milton dismisses by lashing at those who fear the presbyters' "zealous, and meek censure of the *Church*" (CPW 1:605). "[W]hat if I prove Prelacie and Popery to be the same *in re* [res (thing)], and onely to differ in name?" asks Robert Greville, Lord Brooke, a Parliamentary leader in the House of Lords, who would make a case for the toleration of Independency years before Milton.[31] Arguing against the bishops' jurisdiction in the civil realm and for the prerogative to elect ecclesiastical authorities, Brooke invokes the peculiar status of the people whose potential, he maintains, cannot be realized under the conditions of a corrupt church government and ecclesiastical discipline: "Is not the flock of Christ stiled by the Spirit of Christ, *An Holy Priesthood, a Royall People?* Shall it then bee fit, or lawfull; For any man to transmit this Trust to any whomsoever? especially to such a crue of faithlesse Hirelings? God forbid."[32] For Milton as for Brooke, elect nationhood is bound up with an ecclesiology that accommodates an anti-episcopal church government, one that supports "the most needfull constitution of one right *discipline*" (CPW 1:605).

As he envisions a nation awaiting the imminent Second Coming, Milton, like his millenarian contemporaries, combined the language of apocalypse with the idea of chosenness. His apostrophe to the Godhead in the fiery epilogue of *Of Reformation* prophesies that out of a history

of warfare marked by "the impetuous rage of five bloody Inundations" –
the assaults of the Romans, Picts and Scots, Anglo-Saxons, Danes, and
Normans, followed by internal revolution – Britain will rise "to a glorious and enviable heighth with all her Daughter Islands about her" (CPW
1:614). Here Milton returns to the image of the corporate body of indivis-
ible nations (CPW 1:597) while particularizing peculiar status, which he
ascribes to the warrior nation. The English, Milton declares optimistically,
may yet fulfil the promise of the Reformation through their translation
into "the *soberest, wisest,* and *most Christian People* at that day when thou
the Eternall and shortly-expected King shalt open the Clouds" [Matt.
24:30, John 1:51] (CPW 1:616). The vatic strains of the apocalyptic perora-
tion reinforce the connection between the poet-polemicist and the godly
nation he imagines into being.

Poetry and its textual afterlife helped render Milton's prophecy of
church reform self-fulfilling. The bishops would in fact be ousted in 1642,
whereby Milton's poetic vision in 1637 of the apocalyptic demise of the
corrupt ministers of the Caroline Church, governed by the Archbishop
of Canterbury, was realized. Milton's monody *Lycidas* predates the anti-
prelatical tracts discussed in this chapter, but it anticipates them in its censure of the bishops and then reflects back on their ruination in its second
printing. The poem was published in 1638 in a collection of elegies and
other memorial works for Edward King, who had, like Milton, attended
Christ's College. In a significant revision of the elegiac form, which is
made to accommodate political commentary, Milton incorporates in
Lycidas a passage ascribed to the "dread" warning voice of St. Peter, the
last in the procession of mourners.[33] Milton can justify the inclusion of a
digression on church politics because King himself was destined for the
ministry. In his speech, St. Peter denounces the "Blind mouths!" because
they abandon the "hungry sheep" and fail to imitate the Good Shepherd.[34]
The etymology of "bishop" is *episkopos* (Gk) or overseer. Through St. Peter,
Milton not only strikes the bishops blind but figures them as "mouths," as
predators rather than spiritual nourishers.

The poem uses and appears to need prose to assert its topical relevance
in 1645. Seven years after its original appearance (eight after its composition), *Lycidas* supplements the headnote that was originally recorded
in the Trinity College Manuscript version of the ode. Milton seizes the
moment at the outset of this occasional poem to speak of another, more
timely event. "And by occasion foretells the ruin of our corrupted clergy
then in their height" signals the political significance of the elegy and
implies that the work undertaken in the anti-episcopal tracts came to

fruition in the clergy's ruin, which the poet had foretold and the polemicist lobbied for in 1641–2. Between its two printings in 1638 and 1645, episcopacy was temporarily overthrown and William Laud executed. St. Peter's dread voice silences Charles's dread Archbishop of Canterbury, and Milton's voice in the extended headnote claims the speech of St. Peter as a prophecy on church polity.

The Reason of Church-Government

In pursuing his objective for ecclesiastical and thus national reform, Milton produced *The Reason of Church-Government Urg'd Against Prelaty,* on which his name appears and which would become the most important of the five pamphlets he wrote between 1641–2. Relying on the genre of animadversion and direct-encounter tactics,[35] Milton builds his argument on the scaffolding of the classical oration. The opening calls into being a nation modeled on the primitive Christian community, as Milton envisioned it: "England shortly is to belong … to the faithfull feeding and disciplining of that ministeriall order, which the blessed Apostles constituted throughout the Churches" (CPW 1:749). Milton's larger challenge here is to prove that the ministerial orders of the Presbyters and deaconate are distinct from what he characterizes as the virtually indistinguishable patriarchal sees of the papacy and prelates, Lucifer himself having been "the first prelat Angel," one who presumed to aspire above his designated order (CPW 1:762). The proof text for Milton's argument about church government and the role of the Presbyters therein will be scriptures, which he scours in invalidating his opponents' biblical precedents, including the reign of Aaron and his sons, commonly cited as an example of and justification for episcopal authority.

The dominant trope that emerges in Milton's framing of church discipline and government in *Of Reformation* and *The Reason of Church-Government* is the body of Christ, the ultimate expression of temple-work in the bible. In the Old Testament, the temple Ezekiel envisions and whose coordinates he details while prophesying the re-establishment of the nation in Palestine (ch. 40–8) prefigures what Milton calls "a new and more perfect reformation under Christ," manifested in "the stately fabrick & constitution of his Church, with al the ecclesiasticall functions appertaining." Ezekiel's vision is to be read typologically, that is, "in such manner as never yet came to passe, nor never must literally, unlesse we mean to annihilat the Gospel" (CPW 1:757). The "Church militant," animated by the warfaring Christian (CPW 1:757, 2:515), establishes the new covenant or the alliance between God and his people, and thus completes the transference of the chosen Jewish heritage to the Christian community. The temple's vessels, altars, and sacrifices were but a type and shadow for the constitution of the mystical body of the Church of Christ "in all her glorious lineaments and proportions" (CPW 1:758). Because the Gospel with its message of liberty of conscience fulfils and thus supersedes the Law, the prelates' efforts to erect church government on the shifting foundation of the Old Testament are foolhardy, Milton declares in the partition of his oration (CPW 1:763).

The mainstay of Milton's argument is in the confutation or refutation in which he dissects the arguments of Bishop Lancelot Andrewes and James Ussher (Archbishop of Armagh), who focus on biblical precedents for episcopacy stretching back to ancient Israel (CPW 1:761–8). *Church-Government* was written in response to a 1641 pamphlet titled *Certain Briefe Treatises ... Concerning the Ancient and Moderne Government of the Church* (1641), which contains, among various other tracts, the late Bishop Andrewes's *A Summarie View of the Government both of the Old and New Testament ... Whereunto is prefixed ...* [Richard Hooker's] *a Discovery of the causes of the continuance of these Contentions concerning Church-government* and *The Originall of Bishops and Metropolitans* by Martin Bucer, John Rainolds (Rainoldes), and Archbishop Ussher.[36] The elaborate hierarchical edifice designed by Andrewes (the Episcopalian predecessor of William Laud), who categorizes the estates, tribes, and cities of the "*Commonwealth* of Israel," is built on genealogies, beginning with the forms of church government under the key Israelite governors and then proceeding to a series of correspondences between the Old and New Testament forms of church government.[37] In the table, the "Princes of Priests" in the Old are the types for bishops in the New, and the Old Testament priests correspond to presbyters in the New.[38] Milton would break down the edifice – just as decades later he would stage the destruction of the theatre that displaced the temple – and erect in its place the spiritual architecture of "living temples."

Biblical and classical models of governance offer precedents for the voluntary and necessary removal of the governing body or administrative structure to enable the successful formation of the national community, the church, or the state. In the New Testament accounts of John and Peter, explains Milton, the apostles, like the Roman patricians, sought to relinquish their offices, knowing that they served "but as the scaffolding of the Church yet unbuilt, and would be but a troublesome disfigurement, so soone as the building was finisht" (CPW 1:791). Invoking the regular turnover of the Roman dictatorships that began in 501 BCE, Milton returns to his figure of temple-work in characterizing alternatives to the conformist and Laudian establishment that had served as the model for national unity and obedience. The construction thereof will involve confrontations with error. Natural law dictates that the conversion of one substance or formation into another generates, like the act of creation itself, a "struggl of contrarieties" (CPW 1:795), which occasions opportunities for reformation: temple-work "is never brought to effect without the fierce encounter of truth and falshood together ... there fall from between the shock many fond errors and fanatick opinions, which when truth has the upper hand, and the reformation shall be perfeted, will easily be rid out of the way" (CPW 1:796). Toleration is urged for the interval, that is, during the process of church or temple building, when truth and error contend and dissent abounds.

The rise of the sectaries was allegedly the occasion for the appointment of bishops by the apostles, explained Lancelot Andrewes in *A Summarie View of the Government.*[39] In *The Originall of Bishops and Metropolitans*, Bucer, Rainolds, and Ussher concur that church authorities more ancient than Jerome confirm the institution of the episcopate in response to the rise of sects and heresies in the Church.[40] Milton refutes the contention, arguing that the prelates not only failed to prevent dissension, they actually generated discord by undermining the work of the councils or presbyteries, the mechanism for maintaining Christian unity. In developing his discussion of schism and sectarianism in chapters 6 and 7 of *Church-Government*, Milton thus counters the claim that prelacy was instituted to discourage dissent that would fracture the church and nation: "As for the rending of the Church, we have many reasons to thinke," Milton accuses, "it is not that which ye labour to prevent, so much as the rending of your pontificall sleeves: that schisme would be the sorest schisme to you, that would be Brownisme and Anabaptisme indeed" (CPW 1:786). That the emergence of sects was perceived as a threat to the prelates' absolutism (or what Milton describes as a "hatefull thirst of Lording in the Church" [CPW 1:783]) was most evident, as Milton testifies, in the prelates' response to Brownists and Anabaptists, who subscribed to disestablishment and to the governance of congregations by elected officials. Even the primitive Christians themselves were reviled as "Familists and Adamites, or worse" by their detractors (CPW 1:788). "The Christian faith ... was once a schism," he later reiterates in *Areopagitica* (CPW 2:529). Such a defence of dissent would have not satisfied Presbyterians any more than the prelacy, however. Still, *Church-Government* is ultimately no unqualified disquisition on tolerance for dissenters. Gordon Campbell and Thomas N. Corns interpret Milton's support of sectaries in *Church-Government* as confirmation of his desire to produce a tolerationist tract instead of an anti-prelatical one.[41] Yet the treatise constructs a defence of nonconformists through negation by seeking to quell fears about dissent in order to further the greater cause of temple-work: "I leave it as a declared truth, that neither the feare of sects no nor rebellion can be a fit plea to stay reformation, but rather to push it forward with all possible diligence and speed" (CPW 1:800), the precipitation of the Reformation being urged even more forcefully than in *Of Reformation*.

Book 1 accommodates a sober appeal to assist the persecuted brethren who had fallen prey to the rebellious Irish (CPW 1:799). Milton then invokes an account of the rebuilding of the Temple from Jewish biblical history and applies it to the contemporary situation in urging that reformation continue at all costs. In Nehemiah 4:10–7, the Israelites, as Milton recalls, rely not only on building implements but also on material weapons to fend off the assault of their foes so that the mission of church building and, by extension, nation formation would be advanced and protected against violence (CPW 1:799). This argument would eventually be put to the service of justifying the regicide. Milton's Interregnum *Defensio Secunda* (1654), discussed at length in Chapter 3, "Natural Law," numbers among the anti-monarchical tracts that cite *Vindiciae contra Tyrannos*, the English translation of which appeared in 1648 (long after its publication in 1579). The treatise makes a case for armed defence against tyrannical kings who transgress God's law and hinder the reconstruction of what *Vindiciae* identifies as the "Temple of the Land."[42]

In the Preface to Book 2 of *Church-Government*, Milton as prophet, poet, and polemicist undergoes a commissioning, consecrating himself for a life of national service. In so doing, he models the kind of ministry, the role of the "spiritual deputy," that he recommends as an alternative to prelacy, one dedicated to the cultivation of the discipline and the health of "the innerman, which may be term'd the spirit of the soul" (CPW 1:837). Those charged with carrying out this priestly duty constitute, in the biblical language of election, "a rightfull Clergy of Christ, a chosen generation, a royal Priesthood" (CPW 1:838). The title of "clergy," Milton continues, was assigned by Peter to all God's people until its appropriation by the pope (Pope Hyginus, 154–58 CE), who bestowed it on and reserved it for the episcopate and members of the church hierarchy. The constitution of the invisible church or spiritual church government that Milton delineates would, by contrast, accommodate all the virtuous and meritorious.

The church members would thus assume their rightful place as a peculiar people, "a holy generation, a royall Priesthood, a Saintly communion, the household and City of God" (CPW 1:844). The account of the Israelites' peculiar status is transferred here from the First Epistle of Peter to the congregation of the reformed church that Milton envisions as the embodiment of the elect nation. In this nation, the prelates, by whom Milton claimed to have been "Church-outed," are cast as outliers themselves for allegedly undermining true Christianity and the English government itself (CPW 1:823, 858). In his divorce tracts, Milton would direct the same accusation at the canon doctors (Chapter 6, "Exogamy").

Milton seizes the opportunity in *Church-Government* to indict the twelve bishops impeached on 30 December 1641 for treason, that is, for "indeavouring to subvert the fundamentall Lawes of the Realme"[43] by petitioning the king to declare the invalidity of legislation enacted in the House of Lords since their expulsion from the assembly. Establishing a metonymic relationship between Parliament and the corporate body of the nation, a relationship he would refine and defend in *Defensio Prima* (discussed in Chapter 3), Milton charges the bishops with "perpetually mutin[ing] against their own body" (CPW 1:860). The body refers to Parliament, but, as indicated by the final judgement issued in the tract, that body takes on larger proportions in being comprised of members that include civil government, monarchy, the people, religion, law, liberty, and learning (CPW 1:861) – the sutures and lineaments of the commonwealth nation. If the bishops are indeed guilty of endangering the nation, as Milton has decided they are, then may divine vengeance destroy them, cries the prophet, so that the Reformation nation, "the elect people of God," are no longer afflicted (CPW 1:861).

Arguing for "the impossibility of this [Independent] Government to any Christian Common-wealth or Nation," the aforementioned harrier of sects, Thomas Edwards, called on Parliament to suppress the nonconformists, whom he blamed for divisions in the kingdom.[44] Rendering Independency and toleration synonymous, Edwards uses the terms as watchwords for social disorder and national collapse. Negatively formulated arguments about moral degeneracy undergird his promotion of a cohesive national church, one now "much troubled": "There ought to be no Toleration … Is it fitting that well meaning Christians should be suffered to goe and make Churches, and then proceed to chuse whom they will for Ministers, as some Taylor, Felt-maker, Button-maker, men ignorant, and low in parts, by whom they shall be led into sinne and errors."[45] Or, as the aforementioned Lord Brooke reported, "Now they [the supporters of the prelacy] say, Not onely Every *matter* will be preached, what every Minister pleaseth, but also Every *Person* will turne *Preacher*: Even Shoomakers, Coblers, Feltmakers, and any other."[46] If anything, Edwards's tract makes Milton look less Presbyterian and more inclined to accept the tenets of Independency. Yet Milton too remained committed to a national church, one that nevertheless accommodated a flexible structure, more specifically, a congregational discipline and church government.[47] Among the respondents to Edwards was the supporter of separatist churches, Katherine Chidley. Her *Justification of the Independant Churches of Christ* urges independence from the Established Church, whose authorities charge the Lord's people with sowing sedition. Separation is lawful and necessary for achieving toleration and protecting liberty of conscience. Refuting Edwards's allegations, Chidley determines that Christians should be at liberty to establish their own church government, whether it includes "Taylors, Felt-makers, Button-makers, Tent-makers, Shepherds, or Ploughmen, or what honest Trade soever." Contrary to the claims of ecclesiastical officials, "ill-meaning Priests are very unfit men to make Churches."[48] The doctrine and discipline practised by the Independent churches is that of the primitive Christians, a point Chidley illustrates with a figure of the spiritual architecture and composition of a New Testament community of disparate churches: whereas God commands in the Hebrew Bible that his elect obey "all the Ordinances of the house, and to doe them, *Ezek*. 43. 11," the Gospel dictates "Doctrine, Fellowship, breaking of Bread, and Prayer" across "every particular Church or Congregation." The multiplicity of churches causes no "disturbance to the Nation … Separation is not a Schisme, but obedience to Gods Commandement."[49] Chidley articulates a position on toleration by justifying religious plurality in a Reformation nation that upholds liberty of conscience and the right to elect meritorious church officials. Her recommendation for overruling the authority of magistrates – "would you [Edwards] have them be Lords over [people's] consciences?"[50] – would inadvertently set the stage for the growth of a culture of dissent that heresy hunters like Edwards judged as the greatest danger to national stability.

In her preface "To the Christian Reader," Chidley asserted that canon law, on which the English church government is founded, undermines the legitimacy of the ecclesiastical institution. She herself proposes a reformation: *The Justification of the Independant Churches* includes on the title page a quotation from Judges, ch. 4, that suggests Chidley's identification with Jael, who undertakes an iconoclastic act of temple-work: "*Hebers* wife tooke a naile of the tent, and tooke an hammer in her hand, and went softly unto him, and smote the naile into his temples and fastened it into the ground, (for he was fast asleepe and weary) and so he died." Taking up Chidley's weapon and cause against Edwards, John Lanseter declares that "when the woman came and strook the naile of *Independency* into the head of their *Sisera*, with the Hammer of Gods holy word; then their sport was spoyled and quasht."[51] His own lance was forged, Lanseter explains, to pierce the *Gangraena*, so that the reader might view the contagion that afflicts the national body through "the bitter effects of persecution (or want of publick toleration of the true Religion)."[52] Dismissing Chidley as a "brasen-faced audacious old woman resembled unto *Jael*," Edwards in *The Third Part of Gangraena* ascribes *Lanseters Lance* to Chidley and her son because the tract commends her work. In the duel with *Lanseters Lance*, Edwards promises to neutralize its effectiveness, the lance having been "made not of iron or steele, in no sort able or usefull to lance or enter the *Gangraena*, but … of brown painted paper, fit for children to play with."[53]

As the toleration controversy of the early 1640s developed, fueling a print war that accompanied the civil wars, Presbyterians defended the role of Christian magistrates in settling a national Presbyterian Church (a visible church) and enforced conformity to it while suppressing nonconformity.[54] The aforementioned Thomas Hill hints in a sermon at the prospect of "a faire *accommodation* betwixt … *congregationall* and *classicall* Divines, (who are called *Independents,* and *Presbyterians*) in point of Church government."[55] Both groups identified as the primary threat to social order the separatists who favoured gathered congregations and fought for universal toleration, and who would challenge monarchical jurisdiction, demand disestablishment, and sow the seeds of revolution. Laying claim to temple-work as a figure for Reformation but also for the institution of conformity, Hill warns that those who profess a generous toleration, "*a toleration of all wayes of Religion in this Church*," would destabilize "the building of Gods house amongst us … [and] make *London* an *Amsterdam*."[56] The dismantling of church government and the national church more broadly is the consequence of tolerating "severall opinions," by which, John Taylor claims, England was rendered alien and ungodly or "Amsterdamnified."[57]

Despite its moderate Independent position, the 1644 *Apologeticall Narration* by Thomas Goodwin, Philip Nye, and several other ministers proved instrumental in fueling the toleration controversy. The authors, members of the Westminster Assembly, defended allowances for variations in doctrine and select disciplinary practices. The *Narration* distanced "Independencie" – a name to which the ministers take exception – from

"Brownisme" (Brownists being entirely separatist oriented) and opted for a middle way between orthodox Presbyterianism and dissent.[58] The pamphlet's promotion of an ongoing reformation is cautiously justified on the basis that the Reformed churches, those that emerged "out of Popery," are themselves "in need of a further reformation." Further, it is conceivable that the English Church's reformation was delayed longer than its neighbours' because God's renewal of his elect nation was also designed to bring about the perfection of the other churches.[59] *An Anatomy of Independency* (1644) mocks the Independents while describing *An Apologeticall Narration* as inciting "faction, singularity and schisme."[60] Troubled by the spread of sectarianism, the Presbyterians distanced themselves from even the conservative Independents' proposed reforms to church government. The most extreme position against the Independents was once more taken up by Edwards, whose *Antapologia: Or, A Full Answer to the Apologeticall Narration* anatomizes in excruciating detail every premise in the *Apologeticall Narration* in order to align Independency with sectarianism and to demonstrate that the dissenting brethrens' plea for toleration is unlawful in light of the prerogative of magistrates. In accordance with the 1643 *Solemn League and Covenant, for Reformation*, magistrates – the custodians of ecclesiastical order and discipline – are called upon to institute an Erastian Presbyterian church government and religious uniformity in the three kingdoms.[61]

Presbyterians and Independents alike were attracted to the temple trope, but, in conjunction with their competing positions on toleration, they envisioned the nature, the structure, and the work required to build the church in radically different ways. Presbyterian divine Herbert Palmer in 1643 extracted a lesson from Jewish history to exhort the English to accept a church government on the basis that "all *humane authority* on earth is for the Churches good." In support of the national church, Palmer cites the decree of Cyrus, King of Persia, to build the temple (2 Chron. 36, Ezra 1).[62] The rebellious Jews' cessation of the temple-work brings down the nation itself.[63] By contrast, the radical Puritan cleric Henry Burton declared in *A Vindication of Churches, commonly called Independent* (1644) that, as a work in progress, the Reformation cannot be modeled on the construction of the Jewish temple. In response to William Prynne's call for a national Presbyterian Church, Burton maintained that the identification in ancient Israel of the nation with the church lacked a contemporary counterpart: "your Nationall Churches are a mixed multitude, consisting for the greatest part of prophane persons," whereas "that of the Jewes … was all holy, *an holy Nation, a Royall Priesthood, a peculiar People*, all the congregation holy, every one."[64] Questioning both the precedents for and the conformity Prynne ascribed to the present-day national church, Burton insists on the incompatibility of church and nation, which also points to the disestablishment argument that Milton would develop. The Presbyterians' complaint that Independency is, as Prynne accuses, the *"Seminary of schisms, and dangerous divisions in Church, State"* was also the basis for the charge of sedition against Paul, Burton points out, citing Acts 24:5.[65] Independency, Burton concedes, spawned such by-products as Roger Williams's *Bloudy Tenent*, a plea for comprehensive toleration, and bred corresponding heresies, atheism, and "Divorce at pleasure." But, he continues, using one of the most popular images of toleration, "Shall we therefore blame the wheat, because the tares come up with them [sic]."[66] From this question and the biblical exemplum of the wheat and tares would emerge Milton's theories of toleration and education and his epistemology, adumbrated in *Of Education* and in *Areopagitica*, which encourages consideration of "all kinde of knowledge whether of good or evill," given the impossibility and injustice of separating the wheat from the tares (CPW 2:512, 564).

"Brotherly dissimilitudes"

Milton's divorce from Presbyterianism would come earlier than that of the moderate Independents after he increasingly distanced himself from the Presbyterian positions on church government, marriage law, and non-conformity. *The Doctrine and Discipline of Divorce*, Milton's contribution to church reforms and to the cause of toleration in the domestic sphere – a microcosm of the state – appeared anonymously in 1643, and the second edition, printed in 1644, was dedicated to Parliament. Milton cites Hebrew laws and customs, particularly the Mosaic concept of divorce (Deut. 24), in querying the applicability of canon law to the rite of marriage no longer considered sacramental. The aforementioned Herbert Palmer was the first to express and then publish his outrage over Milton's defence of divorce. In a fast-day sermon preached before both Houses of Parliament on 13 August 1644, one week after the appearance of Milton's *Judgement of Martin Bucer, Concerning Divorce*, Palmer outlined the dire consequences of condoning toleration, now unleashed in books that promoted licentiousness under the pretence of advancing liberty. Toleration legalizes divorce for extra-biblical reasons, Palmer accuses, while noting in particular the appearance of an *"uncensored"* *"wicked booke ... deserving to be burnt*, whose *Author* hath been so *impudent* as to *set his*

Name to it and *dedicate it to your selves*," as was the case with the second edition of *The Doctrine and Discipline of Divorce* and with *The Judgement of Martin Bucer*.[67] John Ward, in his sermon *God Judging Among the Gods*, announces that the conditions for the enjoyment of true liberty have indeed been established by the expulsion of the "tyrannie of Prelacy," but with the result that another contagion, that of the sectarian opinion and licentiousness, now spreads through society "as frogs, and flies, and vermine in the Spring," images that populate anti-tolerationist diatribes.[68]

The Westminster Assembly of Divines, which had been convened to resolve disciplinary controversies, took exception to *The Doctrine and Discipline of Divorce* and, in late August 1644, a Stationers' Company petition also named Milton and Richard Overton as violators of printing regulations. Published later in the fall of that year, the unregistered and unlicensed oration, *Areopagitica: A Speech of Mr. John Milton For the Liberty of Unlicenc'd Printing* exposes and inveighs against intolerances that, despite the ousting of the prelates, choke education and infect the nation.[69] Vestiges of oppressive prelatical practices remain evident in censorship. Although the Reformation was in progress or "[w]hile things are yet not constituted in Religion" – that is, while the Westminster Assembly had yet to instruct Parliament on the new forms of church government – the restriction of the liberty of the press based on a prelatical discipline (CPW 2:541) was all the more injurious to a newly awakening nation.

More than any of his other tracts, in fact, *Areopagitica* takes considerable pains to "*imagine* the nation,"[70] notably through the use of architectural metaphors and discourses of toleration. Milton assumes the rhetorical and oratorical posture of a defender of the nation, taking up in the exordium the noble cause of promoting national liberty through the practice of civic duty. He thus diverts attention from personal motives for preparing his oration, like that of responding to attacks on his divorce tracts: "this is not therefore the disburdning of a particular fancie, but the common grievance of all those who had prepar'd their minds and studies above the vulgar pitch to advance truth in others" (CPW 2:539). The mediatory position he assumes involves the development of a correspondence between the imagined nation and the invisible church and a careful negotiation of his relationship to the state apparatus of prelacy and of parliament, which, along with the Westminster Assembly, was Presbyterian dominated ("this project of licencing ... hath caught some of our Presbyters") (CPW 2:493). Milton resists orthodox Puritanism, but his proposal for a congregational Independency was not opposed to a Presbyterian state church. Applying the nation-state relationship to the visible/invisible church dichotomy in an examination of the relations between Milton's ecclesiology and that of church separatists, Andrew Escobedo identifies a couple, concessions that Milton makes to the state but largely interprets the relationship between the nation and "inauthentic state" as incongruous. The nation depends on the state in order to secure civil rights and liberties, but, as Escobedo ascertains, "as much as possible Milton defines the nation as an intimate, spiritual community in opposition to the coercive visibility of the state."[71] Milton's declaration "The State shall be my governours, but not my criticks" (CPW 2:534) anticipates his position on disestablishment, which arguably gains momentum even at this early stage. Still, Milton's calls for the reformation of the state and its legislation demand cooperation with the Assembly to which he appeals for the restoration of the liberty of the press.[72] A true nation or "well instituted State" resorts to licensing at the expense of the Reformation movement (CPW 2:521–22, 2:507).

Although integral to *Areopagitica* (e.g., CPW 2:539–43), the campaign against the papistical episcopacy in the tract is inflected with recommendations for church reform and, by extension, national reform: "It is not the unfrocking of a Priest, the unmitring of a Bishop, and the removing him from off the *Presbyterian* shoulders that will make us a happy Nation, no, if other things as great in the Church, and in the rule of life both economicall and politicall be not lookt into and reform'd" (CPW 2:550). Nation building requires civil and political advancements, including the toleration of sectarianism, the assaults on which spark disunity, impede the assembly of the body of Truth, violate liberty of conscience, and unwittingly and inevitably backfire: "their own late arguments and defences against the Prelats might remember them that this obstructing violence meets for the most part with an event utterly opposite to the end which it drives at: instead of suppressing sects and schisms, it raises them and invests them with a reputation" (CPW 2:542). Lord Brooke had directed precisely this same charge against the episcopacy in the aforementioned 1641 *Discourse Opening the Nature of that Episcopacie*, which was indebted to Milton's *Of Prelatical Episcopacie*: "All the Livings under most of our Bishops have been committed to the Cure and Care of superstitious Formalists, Arminians, Socinians, Papists, or Atheists ... And is not This the most compendious way possible to beget and encrease *Heresies?* They cry out of Schisme, Schisme; Sects and Schismes; and well they may: They make them."[73] The textual exchange between Brooke and Milton culminates in a statement on toleration for nonconformists in *Areopagitica* (published after Brooke's

death), despite both authors' unease with – and, in Brooke's case, revulsion
for – the dissenters. Brooke exhorts us to forbearance, Milton states, that
is "to hear with patience and humility those, however they be miscall'd
[i.e., "sects and schisms"], that desire to live purely, in such a use of Gods
Ordinances, as the best guidance of their conscience gives them, and to
tolerat them, though in some disconformity to ourselves" (CPW 2:561).
One of the significant differences between Brooke's and Milton's arguments is the target of their censure: while Brooke reproaches the bishops
in 1641, Milton denounces the intolerance of the Presbyterians who now
suppress dissent in the name of national unity. Although Milton tolerated some of the ideals of radical Puritanism, *Areopagitica* remains less a
defence of sectarianism than of the liberties that the privileged few (elite/
elect) are entitled to enjoy.[74] Representing "lerned men at home" who
were echoing "lerned men of other parts" (CPW 2:539), the public orator
imagines a readership studied in civil virtue and an audience at the Court
of the Areopagus, reinvested with authority.[75] As for Milton's position on
and support of nonconformists, it is more moderate and considerably less
robust than implied by David Loewenstein and John Morrill, who insist
that *Areopagitica* "vigorously defends the freedom of sects and gathered
churches."[76]

In Milton's day, Scottish Presbyterian cleric Robert Baillie promoted
a vision of the nation that, like Milton's own, was bound up with his
ecclesiology. Developing an analogy between the biblical temple and the
Reformation church government, Baillie, in a sermon preached on 28
February 1644, maintained that national stability was directly dependent
on resisting the enemies of the church or state who "oppose the building of
the Temple."[77] Baillie connects the temple-work of the post-exilic chosen
people of Israel to the necessary but regularly disrupted work of hewing
the stones required for the "Foundation of our Building" – that is, for the
Reformation in England.[78] The constant obstruction of the "Government
of God in his House" impeded the settling of the Church, which ought
to be the first priority of the state.[79] Upon abandoning his efforts to bring
Independents in line with Presbyterianism, Baillie lamented that dissenters troubled and endangered both church and state, and he also vilified
Milton as a divorcer.[80]

Presbyterian minister and former Smectymnuan member Stephen
Marshall uses the trope of temple-work in appealing for national unity,
synonymous with religious conformity: "let confusion and division
belong to them that build *Babel;* let there be no noise heard at the rear-
ing of the Lords Temple."[81] In an elaborate and detailed explication of

Solomon's Temple, Thomas Fuller likewise referred to the "tongue-tied tools" used at the building site, where the absence of "laborious sound" allowed for "the happy conjunction, and compacting of parts ... easily matched."[82] The aforementioned Henry Burton interprets the biblical account describing the temple-work in terms of the messy and noisy removal of "old rubbish" from existing church structures. The hewing and squaring of the building materials thereafter prepare the ground-work for the spiritual architecture or construction of the invisible church: "*shall a Nation be borne at once?* ... you know, that the mate-rialls of that typicall *Temple*, the timber, the stone, were all *hewed* first, and *squared*" and ministers were sought out to "fit the crooked tim-ber, and rugged stones, for the Spirituall Temple."[83] In a fast-day ser-mon to the city officials in London, Thomas Hill characterizes the work of the Reformation and settlement of the church as "Temple-worke."[84] Preaching on the "*Harmony* of spirits" among the members of the early church, Hill uses 1 Kings 6:7 as a gloss and justification for enforcing conformity in the English church: "while the Temple was in building, there *was neither hammer, nor axe, nor any toole of iron heard in the house;* that thence wee should learn, in *Church affaires,* in matters of *Religion,* to manage all with sweet *peace* and *unanimity;* That no noise *of conten-tions and schismes ... might be heard.*"[85] Yet Hill allows for differences in religious matters, thus modulating the rigidity of the Presbyterian position. When the preacher breaks into dialogue, the subject of his exchange becomes the latitude for dissent in the church and nation: "Though unity joyned with purity bee very desirable, yet what if there should bee a toleration of divers ways in a Church, in a Kingdom?" The respondent, who promotes indulgence for dissenting Brethren, admits "as divers *Truths* admit a *latitude,* so likewise some *practises,* into which those Truths lead, in both which some *differences* may bee borne." The early Christian community tolerated divergent opinions: "*Paul* and *Barnabas* jarred, yet both Preached the *Gospel*; *Cyprian* and *Cornelius* dif-fered in judgement, yet both *pillars* of the *Christian Faith; Chrysostome* and *Epiphanius* disagreed, yet both *Enemies* to the *Arians.*"[86] Here Hill gestures to the accommodation of differences in discipline that are, as Milton would state that year, "not vastly disproportionall" (CPW 2:555). How does one distinguish between peoples who can be included in the Temple of God and those who would disturb the peace therein and, by extension, the nation? Hill turns again to the example of the primitive Christians: differences are tolerable when they do not "undermine the *power of godlinesse, or peace of the Church.*"[87]

Milton proposed a more ambitious and elaborate model of unity amenable to divergent opinions when he described God's house as accommodating congruities and "many moderat varieties and brotherly dissimilitudes" (CPW 2:555). By extension, he advocates a wide toleration of Protestant denominations while chiding those who seek to suppress dissent at the expense of truth: "There be who perpetually complain of schisms and sects, and make it such a calamity that any man dissents from their maxims ... they are the dividers of unity, who neglect and permit not others to unite those dissever'd peeces which are yet wanting to the body of Truth" (CPW 2:550–51). Repairing the ruins of England's "spirituall architecture" involved a continual process of constructing the Temple of the Lord, analogous to the assembly of the body of Truth, here associated with the true church as a community of believers. The labour of church building is a philosophical and spiritual exercise, an act of liberty enabled by the builders' engagement with Scripture.[88] The biblical narrative of Solomon's temple in the Book of Kings supplies Milton with an exemplum that he modulates into a statement on toleration. He castigates the "irrationall men" who fail to recognize that "there must be many schisms and many dissections made in the quarry and in the timber, ere the house of God can be built" (CPW 2:555). Whereas in the biblical account of temple building, the stones were hewn at the quarry to ensure that no noise would be made by the implements during the construction of the temple – the sign of a covenant between God and his chosen (1 Kings 6:7) – the ongoing process of cutting the stones is, in Milton's adaptation of the account, fundamental to the construction project. "Schism" refers to a cut or cleft (*skhisma*). The phrase "schisms and ... dissections" in Milton's abovementioned description of the Temple of the Lord resonates with "schismaticks and sectaries" (CPW 2:555), all being integral to the fabric of the nation, Milton argues, thus forging a link between a heterodox church and nation.

Proponents and critics of the state and national church had long used the metaphor of the Lord's temple in illustrating the constitution of the church and nation and the terms for membership therein. Thomas Cartwright, founder and defender of Presbyterianism against the Established Church, expounded in 1573 on the question of church polity and the sanctity of English church assemblies by declaring that the congregations do "groweth unto the Lordes building." Despite imperfections in the makeup of the churches, including failings in discipline or ministry, the English assemblies retain their status as God's elect or as "the Lordes confederates."[89] Two decades later, Puritan Calvinist preacher George Gifford adopts the trope of the temple for the Christian community in describing a building project inevitably marked by disruptions and defects:

> there bee imperfections both in doctrine and maners, all the best hewen stones have some rugged ones remaining, and men must beare one with an other in much: for charity must cover the multitude of sinnes. I.Pet.4. while the Temple of God is in the world, the stones are not perfectly set together, but the work is still in hand, this temple is still in building, we must beware of the down fall on that side also.[90]

Perfect unity is not of this world, Cartwright and Gifford point out, and because flaws, disproportions, and disagreements over church doctrine and discipline are inevitable, the exercise of toleration (as forbearance) and charity is critical. Cartwright's and Gifford's explication and application of I Peter to the English nation would not ultimately compare with Milton's celebration thereof in his scriptural exegesis of the ongoing process of temple-work and of the diversity and irregularity that constitutes the body of believers.

Milton's ecclesiology accommodates the indifferency and dissimilitudes to which the invisible church is amenable, indifferency referring to those "things [that] might be tolerated in peace, and left to conscience, had we but charity" (CPW 2:563). In *Of Reformation*, Milton had asked, "What more binding then Conscience? what more free then *indifferency?*" (CPW 1:585). This concept of "things indifferent" or *adiaphora* is a principle of the "theology of reduction," for which Christ's parable of the wheat and the tares supplies a biblical precedent.[91] The parable teaches that deviant elements should be left undisturbed until the final judgement. The meantime called for toleration. It is "more Christian," Milton professes, "that many be tolerated, rather then all compell'd ... those neighboring differences, or rather indifferences, are what I speak of, whether in some point of doctrine or of discipline, which though they may be many, yet need not interrupt *the unity of Spirit*, if we could but find among us *the bond of peace*" (CPW 2:565). The nature of that unity in the spirit was more than ever a subject of contention, and, in his vision of the temple, Milton offers what David Loewenstein characterizes as "a striking revision" of how harmony might be achieved amid religious and national divisions.[92] Milton's appeal for a "*bond of peace*" that supports neighbouring differences develops out of his radical ethical position on the inviolability of liberty of conscience, fostered by a climate of toleration: "[a] little generous prudence, a little forbearance of one another, and som grain of charity" in order that we "might unite into one generall and brotherly search after Truth; could we but forgoe this Prelaticall tradition of crowding free consciences and Christian liberties into canons and precepts of men."[93] The Pauline exhortation in Colossians to act charitably, the founding principle of the Christian community, is prefaced with an address to "God's chosen ones, holy and beloved," who are called to confirm their peculiar status through the exercise of toleration.[94]

On a scale of toleration, Milton's concept of the elect Reformation nation is decidedly less charitable than that of Baptist and New England Seeker Roger Williams, mentioned at the start of this book. An apocalyptic "warning voice" of Revelation (PL 4.1), who asserts that his anti-persecution arguments are written "in *bloud,*" Williams declares that Christ mandated the complete separation of church and state and decreed toleration for all religions, even Catholics, Jews, and Muslims.[95] In the context of a broadly conceived, generous toleration, the premise of the peculiar nation is intolerable, and thus Williams transfers chosen status to the spiritual kingdom. Ancient Israel "is proved *figurative* and *ceremoniall,* and no *patterne* nor *president* for any *Kingdom* or *Civill state* in the *world* to follow," he insists at the outset of his tract. Later he reiterates and develops the point as he states that elect nationalism is reserved exclusively for the universal nation under God: "What Land, what Country now is *Israels Parallel* and *Antitype,* but that holy *mysticall* Nation the *Church* of *God,* peculiar and called out to him out of every Nation and Country, I *Pet.* 2.9."[96] The temple of God cannot be built, not because a material construction thereof would recall Old Testament observances and institutions but because no worldly counterpart could ever exist. Williams anticipates the position of Milton, who would later urge disestablishment, challenge the applicability of the parallel of ancient Israel's national church to the present-day church, and defend the model of an invisible church.

In asserting the innate superiority of the nation, Milton characterizes Englishness in terms of the people's natural disposition to embrace Christianity: "the Englishman of many other nations is least atheisticall, and bears a naturall disposition of much reverence and awe towards the Deity" (CPW 1:796). Still, instruction in discipline and the cultivation of civility are lacking among certain classes ("the meaner sort"), thus necessitating ecclesiastical reform, which will contribute to the restoration of England's universally recognized peculiar status: if the English cultivate "a wise and well rectifi'd nurture ... [by virtue of] the goodly vigilance of the Church," England will assume a leading role as "a right pious, right honest, and right hardy nation."[97] The development of that righteous national character is enabled, according to *Of Reformation*, through the process of temple-work, that is, through the practices of "searching, trying, examining all things, and by the Spirit discerning that which is good" (CPW 1:566) and, correspondingly, in *Areopagitica* through the "musing, searching, revolving new notions … reading, trying all things, assenting to the force of reason" (CPW 2:554). In the following years, the temple-work of the Reformation nation would be advanced but also interrupted by the troubled relationship between the English and the Irish, who were cast as the Canaanite other or the infidel, that is, the "cursed off-spring" of the degenerate episcopacy itself (CPW 1:798).

CHAPTER 2

Reduction: Civilizing Conquests in Ireland

"Little England will ever be better then *great Brittain*." *A Necessary Examination of a Dangerous Design and Practice Against the Interest and Soveraignty of the Nation and Common-wealth of England, by the Presbytery at Belfast* (1649)

Chronicler of Ireland, Sir James Perrott, celebrated English prowess as inscribed in ink and blood, the nation having "bredd as worthy spirits for literature and militarie profession as any other kingdom hath possessed." England, reports Perrott, secured the "recovery of Palestine from the Turkes; conquered Ireland; subjugated Wales; supported the Netherlands; subdued Fraunce; both assisted and affronted Spayne."[1] The inventory of triumphs demonstrates that English national (and imperial) identity was not self-made but forged through ideological, materialist, and military confrontations with the Continent and, more immediately, with the other nations of the British Isles, on which the present chapter concentrates.

The four realms of England, Scotland, Ireland, and Wales were never smoothly consolidated despite various efforts to that effect, as proponents of the New British History – and their detractors – have pointed out. In light of the pioneering work of J. G. A. Pocock on the problem of Britain,[2] and in conjunction with the debates it generated, the status of England as nation, and specifically as Protestant nation, has once again come to be understood alongside the nations of the British Isles (what Pocock called the Atlantic archipelago) and with regard to the writing of the nation as relational. Nationalism studies – those that locate nationhood in the early modern era and the majority that view nations as modern constructions – address the question of the nation's dialectical engendering in terms of the resistance to an external threat on the one hand and willful adherence and identification on the other. But the case of England's relationship to Ireland in particular – a constellation of different social, ethnic, and religious identities – complicates

that model, being based on opposition as well as assimilation and identification. Milton's own writing on Ireland takes its place among other
English representations of the Irish, including early modern appropria-
tions of the pre-Medieval writings of Giraldus Cambrensis and Welsh
chronicler Geoffrey of Monmouth, which contributed to what David
Cairns and Shaun Richards aptly characterize as a "'narrower definition
of Englishness' and new practices of colonization."[3]

Ireland maintained a liminal status in the Union of Crowns, not having
been mentioned in 1603, 1660, or 1689 when the settlement of the throne
was decided in London.[4] The country's history is one of conquest, subjugation, and occupation first by the Old English (who settled in Ireland
immediately following the Norman Invasion) and then by the New
English and Scots in the early modern era. Ireland served as a crucible
for English identity by supplying an "anvil" for the forging of Englishness
in the British Isles.[5] Among the primary and most widely adaptable ideologies justifying aggression against the Irish was anti-popery, which was
intensified by the promulgation of news and myths of Irish cruelty.[6] In a
period when the antithetical relationship of tolerance and intolerance was
regularly elided, as Alexandra Walsham cogently argued, the rise of radical
tolerationism was paradoxically indebted to anti-popery.[7] The interconnections between these movements are highlighted in the mid-seventeenth-
century literature preempting and justifying Cromwell's 1649–50 anti-Irish
campaign and in the pamphlet debates over the settlement of Ireland following the conquest. Appearing three months before Cromwell's invasion,
Milton's 1649 *Observations upon the Articles of Peace* supports the reduction of an uncivilized people by a godly Protestant nation, whose election and moral character, however, were also being tested. The missions of
conquest, civilization, and Christianization can be traced to the Protestant
belief in English election, which, as mentioned in Chapter 1, was a principal source of intolerance in Milton's time. This chapter reviews the discourses of civility, reductionism, and exclusionism that were deployed to
control representations of Ireland's alterity by a new republic that emerged
as "a bulwark of English national interest," as Thomas Corns aptly noted.[8]
At the same time, what is demonstrated here is how the animus expressed
against the Irish became a comment on the troubled status of English toleration and nationhood. The latter sections of this chapter examine the
great case for transplanting Anglo-Protestant interests in Irish soils and,
more generally, in Catholic territories, as represented in Milton's sonnet
"On the late Massacre in Piedmont."

Reduction

"Reduction" refers to subjugation, conquest, and reformation, a practice of "bringing someone or something back *to* (also *from*) a particular state, condition, belief." In *The Statues of Ireland*, "An Act for the English order, habite and language" outlines "the conveyance and trayning of his people [in the English pale] … to an honest Christian civilitie and obedience."[9] Justifications for taming Ireland relied on the rhetoric of civil order, good citizenship, and national stability. The colonialists' civilizing mandate has Roman precedents, as Sir Thomas Smith insisted in writing to Sir William Fitzwilliam (Lord Deputy Fitzwilliam): "this contrey of England, ones as uncivill as Ireland now is, was by colonies of the Romaynes brought to understand the lawes and orders of thanncient orders." The new Rome is now charged with planting colonies, designed to civilize the Irish and "to leave robbyng and stealyng and killyng one of another."[10] Defences of this act of reduction served as a pretext for repressing a people vilified as degenerate and dangerous.

For Edmund Spenser, secretary to Lord Deputy Arthur Grey of Wilton, and his fellow reformers in the late sixteenth century, Ireland was held by right of conquest, or in the words of Irenaeus, "yt is in the powre of the Conqueror to take vpon him self what tytle he will over his dominions conquered."[11] In the period following the 1641 Rising, *A vewe of the present state of Ireland* (1596), which served as an anatomy of Ireland, was used to enforce conformity to English laws and customs. After decades of suppression, *A vewe* appeared in print in 1633 as *A View of the State of Ireland*, edited by Sir James Ware, who had sought to mitigate some of Spenser's harshness and rashness. Marginalia in the Huntington Library copy of the 1633 *Historie of Ireland, Collected by Three Learned Authors*, in which Spenser's *View* was first printed (with modifications), reads: "M^r. Spencer censured by S^r. Jame[s] Wares mistake of immoderation / for the Rebellion of Oct. 23. 1641. [j]ustified Spencers wisedome and deep insight into that barbarous nation."[12] But the militarism of Spenser's original *Vewe of the present state* would conceptually (but not textually) be restored in the post–1641 era. Political history and a corresponding textual history of editing, publication, reading, annotation, and appropriation transform the practice of writing the nation. The most famous reader of the published tract at the time finds new uses for Spenser's accounts of the wild Irish: Milton read Spenser's *A View* in the year prior to publishing *A Masque Presented at Ludlow Castle*, in which Comus (revelry), who roams "the Celtic, and Iberian fields," resembles Spenser's wild, loose, deviant, nomadic Irish.[13] In his Commonplace Book, Milton invests Spenser's *A View* with a contemporary relevance and applicability as he records, presumably in the period between 1642 and 1644, the following entry: "The wicked policies of divers deputies & governours in Ireland see Spenser dialogue of Ireland," thus reinforcing Irenaeus's view of the delinquent and corrupt governors of Ireland.[14]

The 1633 edition of *A View* opens with Eudoxus inquiring about the possibilities of "reducing that nation to better government and civility."[15] Irenaeus interprets reduction as reformation, and explains that many efforts have been made to that effect but to no avail, the reform of Ireland having been thwarted, possibly by God himself:

> they say, it is the fatall destiny of that Land, that no purposes whatsoever which are meant for her good, wil prosper or take good effect, which whether it proceed from the very *Genius* of the soyle, or influence of the starres, or that almighty God hath not yet appointed the time of her reformation, or that hee reserveth her in this unquiet state still, for some secret scourge, which shall by her come unto *England*, it is hard to be knowne, but yet much to be feared.[16]

England's destiny is potentially bound with that of Ireland, Irenaeus worries, in one of the rare but tellingly self-conscious moments in *A View* in which the oppositional relationship between the self and the colonized other is renegotiated. Still, the treatise proceeds by justifying the imposition of English laws on Ireland on the basis of what Eudoxus hails as the successful reduction of England to civility and on the basis of English superiority: "the English were at first, as stoute and warlike a people as ever the Irish, and yet you see are now brought unto that civility, that no nation in the world excelleth them in all goodly conversation."[17] The native Irish, however, are figuratively displaced or put outside "the pale of 'civill conversation'" by what is paradoxically the monologism of the Renaissance genre of the dialogue itself, which here in *A View* undercuts debate, effectively silencing the voice of the other.[18]

A Treatice of Ireland (ca. 1599) likewise complains about the incivility of the Irish, which the author John Dymmok interprets as disobedience to the English monarch: "the cheefe thinge wantinge in that cuntrye [of Ireland] is cyvillitye, and dutyfull obedience of the people to their soveraigne." But the English too are to blame for the barbarousness of the Irish, having failed to exert colonial mastery and fulfil their duty to implement measures and systems, including legislation, needed for "the preservation of the Englishrye." The protection and the social and moral integrity of the English in Ireland were also undermined by miscegenation, that is, by "marrying, fosteringe, and allyinge with the Irish, and takinge of coynye and lyvery, which hath beene, and yet is, the only cause of weakninge the English pale, and of so many degenerate English at this present."[19] Spenser's *View of the State of Ireland* ascribed this state of depravity to the Old English in particular: "some of them are degenerated and growne almost meere *Irish*," reports Irenaeus, to which Eudoxus responds, "is it possible that an *Englishman* ... should forget his owne nature, and forgoe his owne nation!"[20] In a statement that appears to recall Spenser's remarks on ethnic cross-contamination, Fynes Moryson in 1617 denounced the "English Irish [who,] forgetting their owne Countrey, are somewhat infected with the Irish rudenesse."[21]

The reduction of Ireland was partly about the demonstration and reassertion of England's status as a civilizing nation, although the form that the acts of reduction should take remained an issue of contention in the decades that followed. Force was largely judged as requisite to the civilizing endeavour, which included the imposition of the colonizer's religion and conversion. This course of action was followed by all the English who participated in civilizing missions during this period, explains Nicholas Canny.[22] In an early work presented to Queen Elizabeth, Francis Bacon distinguished between annihilation and reduction, declaring that "the Queen seeketh not an extirpation of that people, but a reduction; and that, now she hath chastised them by her royal power and arms, according to the necessity of the occasion, her majesty taketh no pleasure in the effusion of blood, or displanting of ancient generations."[23] Bacon thus proposed a "liberal proclamation of grace and pardon" and the extension of religious toleration while granting the Irish charters and freedoms. His plans for the institution of just laws and for the education of the citizens developed from his theories of the proper uses of knowledge. Bacon envisioned the nation in terms of the assimilation of Irish into a body, one nation composed of English and Irish, a recommendation he made for the health of the state.[24] Presented to James I in 1606, *Certain Considerations Touching the Plantation in Ireland* outlined schemes for planting Ireland with English settlers while reducing the Irish through the implementation of English programs of education, government, and legislation.[25]

In 1610, Sir John Davies, who administrated the Ulster Plantation, proposed the reduction of Ireland through the seizure of territories and the acculturation of the natives. As the "Romans transplanted whole nations out of Germany into France [and] the Spaniards lately removed all the Moors out of Grenada [Spain] into Barbary," so must the English transplant the Irish to make a civil plantation.[26] Heavily influenced by

Spenser, Davies outlined the measures for a perfect conquest of Ireland in *A Discoverie of the True Causes why Ireland was Never Entirely Subdued*. In the Ulster Plantation, James I, as the rightful King of Ireland, proposed a model for the state of coexistence that Davies recommended and for which Bacon had commended Elizabeth I. Rather than rooting out the natives, as the first colonial adventurers did, James created "a mixt plantation of *Brittish & Irish*," enabling the two peoples to "grow up togither in one Nation" wherein civility, conversation, and commerce could prosper.²⁷ Comparing the Irish to wild fruit trees, Davies determined that the trans-plantation of the Irish from the forests and mountains to the plains and open countries might cause them to "beare better & sweeter fruit," the results of which Davies characterized as James's "Maisterpiece, and most excellent part of the worke of Reformation."²⁸ In the Aristotelian tradition, to possess land was to capture and cultivate the potential in nature, or "to turn trees into chairs," as Anthony Pagden explained, in showing how the English gained sovereignty over Irish lands.²⁹ Although Davies maintained that subjugation validated a nation's possession of and title to a foreign territory, the terms for achieving dominion remained a subject of debate among seventeenth-century philosophers and political theorists and tolera-tionists, including not only Davies but also Bacon, Thomas Hobbes, Hugo Grotius, John Locke, and, at the end of the century, William Molyneux.³⁰

In the early stages of his career, as he lobbied for the conquest of Ireland, Milton chastised the government and Church for failing to con-trol, convert, or reform Irish rebels. As mentioned in Chapter 1, "Temple-worke," Milton in his anti-prelacy period directed the initial blame for the Irish Rising on the English bishops who had starved the Irish spiritually: "What can the Irish subject do lesse in Gods just displeasure against us, then revenge upon English bodies the little care that our Prelats have had of their souls. Nor hath their negligence been new in that Iland" (CPW 1:798). Lord Brooke had in the previous year denounced the bishops for their conflict of interest in Ireland, that is, for having "more parts to act then One."³¹ The prelates in Ireland failed to repress heresy and idolatry adequately, Milton judges, aligning idolatry with popery before seizing the opportunity to make a bigger point about toleration at home: He dis-tinguishes the laudable practice of tolerating "all good Christians under the name of schismaticks" from the English Church's policy of defending "all Papists and Idolaters as tolerable Christians."³² The rebellion, Milton maintains, is the consequence of the misgovernment of the Protestant church (CPW 1:798) and its misdirected efforts to extirpate radicals while indulging idolaters.

Milton thereupon alludes to the original conquest by the "Kernish Prince" (Dermot MacMurrough, King of Leinster), who assisted the single earl (Richard FitzGilbert de Clare, Earl of Pembroke) in preparing for the subjugation of Ireland by Henry II in 1171.[33] The reform of Ireland remains a priority, but the reduction of the barbarous Irish can continue without "staining of any Noble sword"[34] through the reformation of the church, Milton determines:

> And we for our parts a populous and mighty nation must needs be faln into a strange plight either of effeminacy, or confusion, if *Ireland* that was once the conquest of one single Earle with his privat forces, and the small assistance of a petty Kernish Prince, should now take up all the wisdome and prowesse of this potent Monarchy to quell a barbarous crew of rebels, whom if we take but the right course to subdue, that is beginning at the reformation of our Church, their own horrid murders and rapes will so fight against them, that the very sutlers [who sold provisions to soldiers] and horse boyes of the Campe will be able to rout and chase them without the staining of any Noble sword.... [n]either the feare of sects no nor of rebellion can be a fit plea to stay reformation, but rather to push it forward with all possible diligence and speed. (CPW 1:799–800)

In a tract on church government, remarks on the barbarity of the Irish are channeled into an argument for recommitting to the Reformation's agenda. The ecclesiastical reforms and acts of spiritual warfare recommended here will not ultimately avert bloodshed and compulsion in Ireland but will contain the conflict to a fight between the "barbarous crew of rebels" and the "sutlers and horse boyes of the Campe" while waging the main battle at home.

Others were less prepared to leave the job of combating Irish rebels to sutlers and horse boys. Adopting a literal reading of the Old Testament model of defensible slaughter, while remarking that England had yet to live up to its calling as the New Israel, Daniel Harcourt, a Protestant minister in Ireland, declared that the 1641 Rising revealed to the English the true cost of the Israelites' "cruell mercy in not extirpating the Idolatrous Canaanites."[35] The failure to eradicate the Irish would draw God's ire against the chosen. The paradoxical concept of "holy violence," which Harcourt urges is, as mentioned, the subject of Walsham's perspicacious investigation of the conjunctions of toleration and persecution, in which she historicizes the biblical mandate to enact justice against religious and moral deviance. Divine judgements would be visited on nations that disobeyed or disregarded the divine ordinance to exterminate the wicked.[36] Harcourt thus calls upon the Protestants to "joyne with Israel, to punish this damnable, and other facts of unpattern'd cruelty like them in the 20. of Judges 48. then ye men of Israel returned unto the children of *Benjamin*, and smote them with the edge of the sword."[37] During the 1649 Irish Conquest, Milton in *Eikonoklastes* (1649) justifies England's "just Warr and execution" against the Irish by invoking the same biblical precedent and proof text: "Did not all *Israel* doe as much against the *Benjamits* ... and did they not the same to *Jabesh Gilead* for not assisting them in that revenge?" (CPW 3:482). Having failed to support the Israelites' war against the Benjamites, the inhabitants of Jabesh-Gilead were massacred. Milton then issues a disclaimer: "I speak not this that such measure should be meted rigorously to all the Irish, or as remembering that the Parlament ever so Decreed."[38] As Michael Lieb discerns, however, the qualification does not temper his vituperation: Milton wholeheartedly endorsed "holy war in a just cause."[39] Indeed, in the face of any violation of "sound Doctrin or the power of godliness" (CPW 3:325), the nation could override the mandate to exercise toleration. In the anti-prelatical *Reason of Church-Government*, Milton blamed the episcopacy, but in his commissioned work on *Eikonoklastes*, Milton accused Charles of instigating the Irish Rising and retaliating against the English themselves while sympathizing with the rebels (CPW 3:483). In Milton's crusade against the prelates and monarchy, Ireland becomes a testing ground for contentious English domestic politics and civilizing policies, which the conflict with the Irish brings to the fore.

Milton explored the possibilities of defensible acts of reduction involving the civilizing of a people who had spurned "the ingenuity of all other Nations to improve and waxe more civill by a civilizing Conquest" (CPW 3:304). Indeed, the Irish proved themselves "averse from all Civility and amendment," having upheld their own "absurd and savage Customes before the most convincing evidence of reason and demonstration." Their resistance merely reinforces their primitive and barbaric behavior, Milton judges (CPW 3:304). By extension, he identifies civility with Englishness as Cromwell himself also repeatedly did. "My coming hither is to endeavor, if God so please to bless me, the reduction of the city of Kilkenny to their obedience to the State of England," Cromwell announced on 22 March 1650 in corresponding with the governor of Kilkenny.[40] As Milton and Cromwell both recognized, the Irish could only be tamed by a rigorous conquest, whereby the English might also reassert their difference from and dominance over an ignoble, sordid, and cursed race.

Likely composed just prior to *Observations upon the Articles of Peace*, Milton's *Character of the Long Parliament* – arguably a segment in book 3 of the *History of Britain, That Part especially now call'd England* – features comparisons between the fifth-century Britons at the time of the Roman withdrawal and the English of Milton's day, both peoples having failed to embrace liberty, the measure of a true nation.[41] "[S]o neare a parallel," Milton states, God drew between the state of the Britons upon the removal of the Romans and that of the English "in the late commotions" (CPW 5.1:441). The example of Roman acts of civilizing mentioned earlier in this chapter reappears here. In the case of the ancient Britons, foreign invasion was warranted and necessary: After the Romans won Camalodunum, a military force was stationed there, as Milton put it, "to teach the Natives *Roman* Law and Civilitie" (CPW 5.1:70). With the fall of the Roman Empire, the chief forms of cultural expression – "Learning, Valour, Eloquence, History, Civility, and eev'n Language it self, all these together" – all decayed.[42] The ancient history of Britain that Milton charts does not, then, celebrate either Britain or England. Further, as Corns recognizes, the peoples of the British Isles at large are represented contemptuously, whether the Scots, the Welch in their "Mountanous and Barren Corner," or the Irish in their "Bogs" (CPW 5.1:183, 59). "This not the prehistory of a chosen people; or at least, whatever the subsequent history of England, it owes nothing to that past," Gordon Campbell and Corns observe.[43] Yet even here, Milton introduces a scale of barbarism: The Scots and Picts tip the scale while the Britons distinguish themselves as latently civilizable.[44] Although Milton does betray a certain admiration for the Romans, he also acknowledges the potential invested in the Britons, who were "beate[n] … into some civilitie; likely else to have continu'd longer in a barbarous and savage manner of life" (CPW 5.1:61). William Camden's own history of Britain, *Britannia*, included a lengthy section on the Roman occupation of Britain in which he described the civilizing conquest of the Romans, who "chased away all savage barbarisme from the Britans minds …. [and who] reduced the naturall inhabitants of the Iland unto the society of civill life, by training them up in the liberall Arts, and … the lawes of the Romanes."[45] England's prolonged antagonistic response to Ireland, a nation deemed corrupt and rebellious, becomes a seventeenth-century expression of the Romans' reduction of the ancient Britons, as well as a statement on England's self-designated role as a civilizing power and on the rifts in the fabric of Britishness.

Observations upon the Articles of Peace

On 17 January 1649, two weeks before Charles I's execution, the Marquis of Ormond, an Anglo-Irishman and Charles's lord lieutenant and royalist

Irish governor in Ireland, signed the Articles of Peace with the Kilkenny Confederates, who were promised Irish independence. Royalists wanted to use Ireland, along with Scotland, for the exiled Charles II's military efforts. In November 1648, Charles proposed to disavow the treaty with the Confederacy, but it was ratified and Ormond proclaimed Charles II in Ireland.[46] The treaty posed a direct threat to the new Cromwellian government, which readily dismissed the prospect of peace with the Irish rebels. By mid-February 1649, officers and MPs began preparing the allocation of troops for a new expedition under Cromwell, who sought to thwart any plans to use Ireland for an assault on England's new regime.

The Council of State ordered its Latin Secretary, who had been appointed a month beforehand, to prepare the treaty and three other documents for publication in a composite pamphlet to be titled "Articles of Peace, made and concluded with the Irish Rebels… Upon all which are added Observations. Published by Autority." For Milton and his contemporaries, Ireland obstructed the establishment of a Protestant, Anglocentric Britain. Further, the 1641 Rising itself had ignited an intense anti-Irish fervour that could only be satisfied by a reconquest of the rebellious kingdom. In early 1649, Milton reminded the readers of *The Tenure of Kings and Magistrates* that "whole massachers have been committed on [the king's] faithfull Subjects" (CPW 3:197). The Council of State assigned Milton the task of defending the regime's national interests through his "observations on the complication of interest [the Articles of Peace] which is now amongst the several designers against the peace of the commonwealth," which were to be printed with the Articles and ancillary correspondence.[47] In the Irish commission, Milton welcomed the opportunity to promote war against Irish rebels and wage battle against Presbyterian intolerance. *Observations upon the Articles of Peace with the Irish Rebels* would be preoccupied with what Corns characterized as "a crucial phase of English domestic politics,"[48] however, as shown here, one imbedded in a larger narrative of nationhood that foregrounds questions of toleration, civility, and archipelagic relations.

The early conception of tolerationism within the context of Protestant unity, supremacy, and the advancement of the Reformation – with which notions of anti-Catholicism became entangled – helps explain how the tolerationist Milton could see anti-Irish hostility as congruent with the exercise of liberty of conscience and the true religion. "Even relatively liberal thinkers like Milton" were convinced of the depravity of the Irish people, Christopher Hill reminds us.[49] Miltonists tend to explain – sometimes defensively – Milton's polemical contributions to the Irish crisis as a momentary lapse or compromise of his liberalism and radicalism, or, as David Loewenstein suggests, as confirmation of Milton's "disturbing complexity as a godly revolutionary writer."[50] In our liberal tradition, in which conquest and tolerationism are theoretically worlds apart, Milton's verbal assault on the Irish in *Observations* can hardly be seen as compatible with his heterodoxy, nonconformity, and liberal-mindedness. In the context of early modern England, however, Milton's vision is in line with his colonial republicanism,[51] and, as one might add to Willy Maley's contention, in line with the early notion of toleration as a distinguishing feature of Protestant nationhood.

As indicated, *Observations* did not bear Milton's name and, because it was commissioned, the relationship between Milton's views on Ireland and the content and phrasing of the positions communicated in the tract will remain conjectural. What is apparent is the treatise's contribution to the promotion of national interests, in part through the denial to Ireland of the status, the character, and the rights of nationhood that Milton reserved for Protestant England. The Articles of Peace, which make various concessions to Irish autonomy, are an affront to the "true borne *English-man,*" *Observations* protests.[52] The pamphlet proceeds by creating rifts between English Protestants and Irish Catholics and between Ireland and Scotland.[53] The attention devoted to the attack on the Ulster Presbyterians and Scots becomes at times more extensive than the discussion of the Articles of Peace with the Irish Catholics, as battle lines are redrawn and reasserted. The Ulster Presbytery had itself betrayed English national interests by shifting allegiances from the republican side to Charles's Anglican party and eventually aligning itself with Ormond. As later observed in this chapter, the "complication of interest" that Milton was commissioned to expose was a constellation of interests of Irish Catholics, English Presbyterians, Ulster Scots of Belfast, and royalists opposed to the republican vision of the Commonwealth.

At the outset of his composite pamphlet, Milton secures and defends the English title to Ireland while affirming the right of the English to conquer and govern an inferior, treacherous people. Essentially, he denies Ireland any vestige of national status, which the Articles of Peace, as a quasi-constitutional document, proposed to grant. Of the thirty-five Articles designed to win support against Parliament's army in Ireland, Milton concentrated on those that promised Irish independence. His concern was with threats to England's dominion over its colony that would, under the terms of the treaty, be "grac'd and rewarded with ... freedomes and enlargements ... [and] infranchiz'd with full liberty equall to their

Conquerours" (CPW 3:301). As a people "justly made our vassals," the Irish could not be less deserving of the "Condition of freedome" proposed by the first Article on "the free exercise of the Roman Catholick Religion" (CPW 3:302, 262). Religious toleration in Ireland was for Milton a preposterous gesture given the tyrannical character of popery and given the English state's failure to grant adequate freedoms even to Protestants, a double-edged remark also aimed at the new republican regime itself.

Of the many Articles of Peace that conceded rights to the Irish, articles 2 and 12, which promised an Irish Parliament in which Catholics would enjoy a majority and legislative freedom without the interference of the English Parliament, represented an especially dangerous compromise of England's sovereignty in Ireland.[54] Instituted by Henry VII in the 1490s, Poynings' Law establishes the proper colonial dependence of Ireland on the English crown, Milton decides; the repeal of that Law would undermine the hierarchical relationship (CPW 3:303). The ninth article grants Irish entitlement to a militia, and other articles permit autonomy over legal and political affairs, the upshot of which is the release of "the whole Province of *Ireland* from all true fealty and obedience to the Common-wealth of *England*" (CPW 3:305), in this case the English republican government. An oxymoronic "pernicious and hostile Peace" threatens to weaken the nation's hold on Ireland and thus "disalliege a whole Feudary Kingdome from the ancient Dominion of *England*," Milton reiterates (CPW 3:307). Likewise, the exemption from the Oath of Supremacy, which all members of the church and state had been required to swear, was a betrayal of English authority, a charge Milton directs against the late king. When Milton then condemns Charles for having divided the kingdom and undermining England's ancient and present-day claim on Ireland, he effectively severs kingly power from national sovereignty; and in protesting the king's refusal to answer to the law (CPW 3:308), Milton sharpens his weapons for his next commissioned assignment, *Eikonoklastes*.

Although he had in fact attempted to distance himself from the treaty, Charles I is reviled by Milton for his complicity in its ratification. Charles implicates himself, Milton accuses, in the atrocities committed by the Irish rebels against the now "more then 200000. of his Subjects ... [who have been] assassinated and cut in pieces by those *Irish* Barbarians" (CPW 3:308). As he helps prepare the way for the Cromwellian campaign of avenging the 1641 massacre, Milton also accepts the assignment of retrying the king as a traitor to national interests. Later that year, Milton in *Eikonoklastes* again indicts Charles for "good affection to the Rebels" – the refrain of chapter 12 of the treatise. In holding the Scots more accountable than the Irish rebels, Charles elides the difference between those who fought in self-defence, which Protestantism condones, and those who committed genocide, allegedly without cause.[55]

Ordered to be printed on 28 March 1649 when Milton was given his commission, the March 9th correspondence between Ormond and the parliamentary Governor of Dublin, Colonel Michael Jones, emphasized English interests in Ireland and proclaimed Charles II as king of Britain, France, and Ireland. Ormond's letter summons his supporters by invoking their collective revulsion of the Independents' "atheism" and by declaring allegiance to monarchy, the inverse of which is "a perfect Turkish tyranny" (CPW 3:292), an accusation Milton directs at the late king himself (CPW 3:312, 313). While insisting that only those in league with the papists subvert the true religion, Milton defends the state's policies on toleration by distinguishing the protection of conscience from the practice of indulging "declar'd atheists, malicious enemies of God, and of Christ," from which Milton, like Cromwell, expressly distances himself.[56] The question of toleration and its limits is connected to that of national representation and specifically the relationship of parliament as the assembly of three estates to the nation as a whole, another key issue raised in Ormond's letter to discredit the regime (CPW 3:292). Milton acknowledges that a parliament refers to the "Supream and generall Councell of a Nation, consisting of whomsoever chos'n and assembld for the public good," but then insists on its metonymic relation to the English nation at large.[57] In *Observations*, Milton would in turn challenge Ormond's contentions that Charles's execution and a parliamentary triumph spelled the demise of England and also Ireland. As in the *Defence*s of the English people, discussed in the next chapter (Chapter 3, "Natural Law"), Milton in *Observations* cites models for parliamentary rule that predated hereditary monarchy (CPW 3:314). Histories by de Thou (Jacobus Augustus Thuanus) and Bernard de Girard served as ready sources for defences of the right of the commons in France to intervene in governmental affairs. As for the question of regicide, the Presbyterians themselves did not have to look beyond the recent history of their own nation to be reminded that John Knox, "thir own first presbyterian institutor," had publicly supported the doctrine of deposing and executing monarchs (CPW 3:329).

Although the targeting of the Ulster Scots in the next section of *Observations* seems to sideline the campaign against the Irish, the censure of the Presbytery is designed to expose their complicity with the Irish Rebels and underscore the threat to the English dominion that their collusion entailed. In *A Necessary Representation of the present evills and eminent dangers to Religion, Lawes, and Liberties, arising from the … Sectarian party in England* (15 February 1649), the Presbytery, whom Milton at first distinguishes from the nation of Scotland at large, had become sufficiently confident to intervene in politics.[58] Cited in Chapter 1, the *Solemn League and Covenant*, which represented an alliance between English parliamentarians and Scottish Covenanters – and which Milton himself signed – was designed to establish a federal union between England and Scotland, eliminate episcopacy by instituting a single system of Presbyterian church government, and supply Parliament with a Scottish military force.[59] Reminiscent of the ancient Covenant between God and his people and issued in a period of "covenantal nationalism,"[60] the *Solemn League and Covenant* enjoined all Presbyterians to expose the "Malignants" who had betrayed their nation by obstructing the progress of the Reformation and inciting hatred between king and country and between countries.[61] However, as the opponents of the Belfast Presbytery had maintained, the Presbytery, while acknowledging their dependency on England (CPW 3:297), violated the terms of the treaty through the alliance with the Ormondists and with Charles I while potentially sabotaging English authority over the kingdom of Ireland (CPW 3:317).

A Necessary Examination of a Dangerous Design and Practice Against the Interest and Soveraignty of the Nation and Common-wealth of England, by the Presbytery at Belfast (April 1649) outlines the charge against the Presbyters as the betrayal of England's "interest" in Ireland, which they sought to uproot by transferring English sovereignty to the Scots. The authors also defend themselves against the Presbyters' accusation, detailed in *A Necessary Representation of the present evills*, that the English Puritans (derided as sectaries) had broken the Covenant (Articles 1 and 2) through their embrace of "even Paganisme and Judaisme in the Armes of Toleration."[62] *A Necessary Examination* lashes out at the Presbytery, condemning them for their impudence and deceit: "the Sectaries tolerate all *Religions*? … what *Paganism, Turcism* and *Judaism*? … have not the Priests at *Belfast* heard of a thing called *truth*?"[63] Milton too expostulates on the same line from *A Necessary Representation*: "But we are told, *We imbrace Paganism and Judaism in the arms of toleration*. A most audacious calumny. And yet while we detest *Judaism*, we know ourselves commanded by St. *Paul, Rom.* 11. to respect the *Jews*, and by all means to endeavor thir conversion" (CPW 3:326). In defence of the tolerationists' position, Milton introduces a scale of toleration that allows for the remote possibility of conversion for the Jews while shutting out other non-Christians from the fold and excluding the Catholic Irish entirely.

Anti-Scottish virulence and Scotophobia fuel *A Necessary Examination*, which denounces Presbyterianism and the Church of Scotland (accused of lagging behind the French and Dutch reformed churches), and repeals obligations England has to the Scots by virtue of the Covenant: "We do cordially wish, that there may be a good and *Neighbour-like* correspondence between the Nations of *England* and *Scotland*, but no more *union* we beseech you … little England will ever be better then *great Brittain*."[64] Although there is no love lost for the Scots in *Observations upon the Articles of Peace*, by comparison to *A Necessary Examination*, Milton's pamphlet is more intent on distinguishing between the Belfast Presbytery and Scotland itself – not in order to defend the latter (this being Milton) but to downplay on occasion the representativeness and influence of the former. As he would in *Pro Populo Anglicano Defensio*, Milton in *Observations* defends the parliamentarians against the assertion that they do not constitute the nation. He does so by deflecting the charge at his accusers from the moment he begins his assault on the Presbytery – relegated to a small Ulster town (CPW 3:317) – through to his remarks toward the conclusion of the treatise: "If they say, wee are not all *England;* we reply they are not all *Scotland.*" Milton proceeds to transfer the label of rebel to the Presbytery, reducing them to a splinter group reviled by their own Countrymen "in whose esteem they were no better then Sectarians themselves" (CPW 3:330). The Ulster Scots, however, had close ties with Scotland while also constituting a more heterogeneous body than Milton's polemics allow: Scottish Presbyterianism was divided between those who supported the king and monarchical authority in church government and the moderates who regarded such support as a contravention of the Covenant and who advanced cooperation with Cromwell.[65] Insensitive to or disregarding such distinctions, Milton charges the Presbytery with breaking the Covenant by warring against parliament and betraying the principles of religion and liberty (CPW 3:332), to which the Scottish Commissioners of the Covenant subscribed.[66] The allegation Milton had made against the prelates at the beginning of the decade is now redirected at the Presbyterians in their "Pontificall See of Belfast," the Presbytery having mutated into crypto-Catholics by defying "the sovran Magistracy of *England*," here aligned with the land, people, and nation of England to which they were beholden and "by whose autoritie and in whose right they inhabit there" (CPW 3:333). Milton also dismisses the Presbyterians as "High-land theevs and Red-shanks" – Scottish mercenaries in Ireland – who had been admitted by the "courtesie of *England* to hold possessions in our Province, a Countrey better then thir own" (CPW 3:333–4). In conveying the charges,

Milton boldly reasserts English proprietary, legal, religious, and sovereign interests in Ireland.

Conquest and Settlement

The Order Book of the Council of State, which outlines Milton's tasks from 22 March 1648 to 1649 at the start of his post as Secretary for Foreign Tongues, indicates he was "appointed to make some observations on a paper lately printed, called Old and New Chains," that is, *Englands New-Chaines Discovered* and *The Second Part of Englands New-Chaines Discovered*, impassioned pleas for freedom of speech. Milton, however, did not complete the commission assigned to him by the Council to respond to the Leveller tract.[67] Nicholas McDowell hypothesizes that Milton's sympathy for the Levellers' position on liberty of conscience accounts for his reluctance to undertake the task. Joad Raymond offers a different explanation: Milton's lack of response to Lilburne's *Englands New-Chaines Discovered* may point to "reticence on the subject of the Levellers."[68] Both interpretations serve as a reminder that any exchanges between Milton and the radicals remained largely one sided.

As for the relationship between Milton's and the Levellers' observations on the military campaign against Ireland, there was consensus, although the latter would, by virtue of their opposition to the Cromwellian regime, occasionally express some sympathy for its victims – English and Irish. Still, Levellers did not challenge the assertion that the country of Ireland and its people were a seedbed for dissent, particularly at a time of crisis for the republican nation, and thus they supported in principle a military campaign against the Irish.[69] Continually at war with the Cromwellian government and army, the Levellers are compared with the beleaguered Irish in Mercurius Pragmaticus's 1649 royalist newsbook, in which accounts of Cromwell's persecution of the dissenters and his military preparations for an assault on Ireland are juxtaposed.[70] Cromwell is described as poised to pounce on Ireland to deflect attention from the animosity his government and army had incurred.

The 1649 *English Souldiers Standard* presents a strongly worded response to the Irish expedition while outlining priorities for the nation. These included finishing the revolution, a mission that would certainly meet with failure should the English soldiers be sent into battle in Ireland. In 1642, Milton himself championed the ongoing advancement of the English Reformation over the diversion of resources to English Protestants who had fallen prey to the Irish Rising in 1641 (CPW 1:799–800). However, unlike *Reason of Church-Government* early in the decade, *English Souldiers Standard* not only empathizes with the beleaguered Irish but protests against the reduction of Ireland: "will you go on stil to kil, slay and murther men, to make them as absolute Lords and Masters over *Ireland* as you have made them over *England*?" Would you, accuses the tract's author further, impose tithes on the Irish, fill gaols with disabled Irish prisoners, create a nation of beggars, and ultimately "take down Monarchical Tyranny, and set up an Aristocratical Tyranny?"[71] Several months later, *Tyranipocrit* would develop this last point by exposing the hypocrisy of the assault on monarchical rule by a regime that has itself become tyrannical: "I thinke how worse then barbarians, the *French*-men dealt with the *Waldenences*, and so did the *Spaniards* with the *Moorians*, and how the *English* hunted the poore *Irish* ...."[72] The juxtaposition of the regime's response to the brutal persecution of the Waldensians in the mid-1650s with the English conquest of Ireland would throw into relief the dialectical relationship between toleration and intolerance in the era.

Exposing the depths of his hostility, Cromwell released his longest state paper, *A Declaration of the Lord Lieutenant of Ireland, For the Undeceiving of Deluded and Seduced People ... In Answer to Certaine Late Declarations and Acts, framed by the Irish Popish Prelates and Clergy, in a Conventicle at Clonmacnoise*. The prelates had issued the *Declarations and Acts* in December 1649 to warn the Irish of Cromwell's proposed extirpation of Catholicism from Ireland and the banishing or sequestering of the Irish people.[73] Reiterating a standard claim about the Rising, Cromwell judges the event as wholly unprovoked: "ye hypocrites, Ireland was once united to England ...[The English] lived peaceably and honestly amongst you.... You, unprovoked, put the English to the most unheard-of and most barbarous massacre (without respect of sex or age) that ever the sun beheld."[74] Thomas May, secretary to Parliament, had several years beforehand protested that the Rising was utterly without cause given that "forty years of peace had compacted those two Nations into one body" to the point that they assumed each other's manners: "*Many English strangely degenerating into the Irish manners & customes; and many Irish, especially of the better sort, having taken up the English language, apparel, and decency of living in their private houses.*" May cites as his source for the portrait of this mixed society the *History of the Irish Rebellion*, to which he also directs the reader for more details.[75] Sir John Temple's *Irish Rebellion* (1646), a popular Protestant martyrology that presented a national myth hostile to Irish Catholics, was kept in circulation for many years.[76] The holy war against the Catholic prelates in Ireland is a righteous cause, Temple protests, insofar as it would avenge the massacre of the Protestants by the rebels, whose brutality knew no cause nor bounds. In *Observations*, Milton refers to the "barbarous Massacre of so many thousand *English*" who had a right to the land (CPW 3:301). In *Eikonoklastes*, the number would increase to 154,000 (CPW 3:470). This hugely exaggerated figure, representing likely several times than the number of Protestants living in Ireland in 1641, is taken from Temple and immediately borrowed by Thomas May, who reported in *The History of the Parliament of England* that "persons of above two hundred thousand men, women, and children [were] murthered... within the space of one month."[77]

Also having been influenced by Temple's *History of the Irish Rebellion*, Cromwell warns the Irish prelates about the advance of the English, who come in the name of God "to hold forth and maintain the lustre and glory of English liberty in a nation where," Cromwell insisted, "we have an undoubted right to do it."[78] From August 1649 to May 1650, Cromwell thus led an army against the Irish, allegedly in retaliation for the Rising, anti-Irish hostility and anti-Catholicism having been energized by a tradition of popular culture featuring Irish atrocities.[79] "Ashamed / To see themselves in one year tamed,"[80] the Irish are slaughtered at Cromwell's behest, and England's Gideon returns victorious to England while the campaign continues. Preparations would also begin for the conquest of Scotland (July 1650 to Sept. 1651) by a radicalized parliamentary regime. Months later, Cromwell justified his divine mission to attack an enemy that had betrayed the English state by conspiring with Charles II and the Irish, thus "taking our grand enemy into your bosoms." The war against the Scots reflects English national interests and is reminiscent of the assault on Ireland insofar as it also was "a just and necessary defence of ourselves, for preservation of those rights and liberties which Divine Providence hath ... given us."[81]

As a subjugated country, Ireland lay open for colonization, "ready to have anything writ in it that the state shall think fit."[82] On 12 August 1652, Parliament thus passed "An Act for the Setling of Ireland," which outlined the policies for completing the reduction of the nation.[83] Cromwell displayed what Christopher Hill had shrewdly characterized as "a conscientious enthusiasm for conferring the benefits of English civilization on the natives, whether they liked it or not."[84] Landowners were transplanted to Clare and Connacht between the Shannon and the Atlantic, and Cromwell would give over the Irish lands to Protestants. The conquest and settlement of Ireland represent what John Morrill designates as "perhaps the greatest exercise in ethnic cleansing in early modern Europe."[85] In 1652,

Roger Williams in *The Hirelings Ministry* blamed the bloody saturation of Ireland on the intolerance of Protestants and Catholics alike. Given the claim to Protestant moral superiority, it is telling that much more blood, both English and Irish, was shed during the recent reign of "our *Protestant Princes*" than under centuries of Popish monarchs.[86] The millenarian conversion of the pagan nations awaited and prophesied by the English is hardly imminent, because "who can deny but that the body of this and of all other *Protestant Nations* (as well as *Popish*) are unconverted?"[87]

While James Harrington was recommending in *The Commonwealth of Oceana* that Panopea (Ireland) be "farmed out unto the Jews" for pay[88] – Jews being, unlike Catholics, marginally tolerable – more proposals surfaced for the exportation and transplantation of Catholic Irish. Territorial imperatives and homeland security were used to justify the segregation of the Irish and the English settlement of Ireland. *A Perfect Diurnal* reports that "*Ireland* is hopefull to be shortly reduced and setled," and other entries in the newsbook cite Spenser's work as a guide to disarming, coercing, and civilizing the Irish and taming the land.[89] Irish rebels were also transported to serve in foreign armies, particularly Spain's army, and to English colonies and plantations in the West Indies and Americas.[90] Desperate for settlers, the Council at one point issued an order for the apprehension of "lewd and dangerous persons, rogues, vagrants, and other idle persons" for transportation to English plantations in the New World.[91] Examining these inept expedients, Antonia Fraser concludes that Cromwell lacked anything approaching a "proper practical West Indian policy," much less a global one.[92] Conquest, colonization, and conversion being part of the same mandate, Henry Cromwell, major general of the forces in Ireland, proposed that, upon being transported abroad, Irish girls would have to be restrained but Irish boys could potentially be educated. Corresponding with Secretary John Thurloe about supplies to Jamaica, Cromwell, newly arrived in Kilkenny, remarks:

> I shall not need to repeate any thinge aboute the girles, not doubtinge but to answerr your expectationes to the full in that; and I think it might bee of like advantage to your affaires their, and ours heer, if you should thinke fitt to sende 1500 or 2000 younge boys of 12 or 14 yeares of age to the place aforementioned. We could well spare them, and they would be of use to you; and who knows, but that it may be a meanes to make them English–men, I meane rather, Christianes.[93]

The slippage between "English" and "Christian" reveals the desired effect of the reduction, reformation, and civilizing practices for Henry Cromwell and his contemporaries.

Vincent Gookin, an Irish landowner in County Cork, denounced forced transportations in *The Great Case of Transplantation in Ireland Discussed* ([3 January] 1655) and in *The Author and Case of Transplanting the Irish into Connaught Vindicated from the Unjust Aspersions of Col. Richard Laurence* (12 May 1655).[94] In the place of compulsion, he recommended persuasion through the propagation of Protestant teachings and improved education. "The conversion of that Nation will be a more pious work than their eradication," Gookin advises the colonizers.[95] Arguably, Gookin's proposal illustrates a positive side of English rule,[96] although it was also in Gookin's best interests to discourage transplantation because the Protestants needed a labour force. Far from ensuring the peace of the English nation, the "civilizing" and transplanting of the Irish constitute a "dangerous experiment," Gookin warns, that will jeopardize English national security: "And when will this wild war be finished? *Ireland* Planted, Inhabitants unburthened, Souldiers setled? at this rate who will be able to stir abroad for fear, to live at home for want? … It's a sad thing to fight against men till they are reduced to us, & then to fight against them, because they will not part from us."[97]

Colonial fantasies informed the counter-arguments of English army officer Colonel Lawrence (Laurence), an Oxford-educated English planter in Ireland, who became a major supporter of the ruthless transplantation policies of Charles Fleetwood. Lawrence assailed Gookin while staunchly supporting the segregation and corralling of the Irish in conjunction with the mandate to settle Ireland in *The Interest of England in the Irish Transplantation* (1655) and *England's Great Interest in the Well Planting of Ireland* (1656). As suggested by his discussion of Temple in Lawrence's later work, *The Interest of Ireland* (1682), Lawrence's reading of Anglo-Irish relations was inflected by the authority he invested in the aforementioned *Irish Rebellion* (1646).[98] Homeland security and the defence of English interests serve as refrains throughout Lawrence's works as he recounts in graphic detail the atrocities committed by the Irish, whose transplantation was essential in order that English plantations, designed for "the security of the *English* interest and People there," might be established.[99] In his post-Restoration work, Lawrence described the Irish creation of their own "waste Wilderness," which demanded the presence of an English military order.[100]

Following immediately upon the printing of Lawrence's *The Interest of England*, Gookin's response, *The Author and Case of Transplanting the Irish into Connaught Vindicated*, dissected Lawrence's argument and recommended a more benevolent form of colonization: "We may overspread them, and incorporate them into our selves, and so by an onenesse take away the foundation of difference and fear together; we may breed up their youth, habituate them to our customs, cause a disuse of their Language: we have opportunities of communicating better things unto them."[101] Linguistic and cultural assimilation was proposed as an effective form of civilizing and of rendering Ireland English. The inverse had been achieved when the English settlers habituated themselves to the Irish tongue, notably in their commercial dealings, thus "Irishizing the English colonies," Gookin complained. In the mixed plantations he proposed, the Irish, through their "mingling" with the English, would be "habituated to the English tongue."[102] Transplantation practices, by contrast, would only serve to segregate them and prevent them from learning English, seen as the key to civility and assimilation, ever since the Kilkenny Statutes were instituted. Designed to legislate against cultural integration in order to correct the degeneracy of the English, these fourteenth-century Statutes enflamed tensions between the nations for centuries thereafter.

Among the other social experiments for reforming Ireland in the mid-seventeenth century were those outlined in *Ireland's Naturall History* (comp. ca. 1652). Its authors were the Dutch brothers and natural philosophers Gerard and Arnold Boate, who were Cromwellians and members of the Hartlibean circle. In publishing the tract in 1657, Samuel Hartlib dedicated it to Cromwell as a manual for augmenting the prosperity of the nation of Ireland and expanding its commerce and trade by planting Ireland with English Protestants but also with co-religionists. Arnold Boate writes in his Preface to the Reader that his late brother Gerard had resolved to produce a fourth book detailing the culture and laws of Ireland and the post-Norman Conquest history of the efforts to "civilize" the Gaelic Irish and "improve the Countrie." The fourth book never appeared, and the history of taming Ireland would prove to be anything but straightforward. The infighting of the English, who themselves adopted the "wild fashions [of the 'wild' Irish] and their language," prevented a complete conquest and takeover of Ireland; although of English descent, the inhabitants of the English Pale "conspire[d] with the Native Irish," Boate protested, and thus undermined the interests of the English state and church in Ireland.[103] Having been overly indulgent of Catholicism in Ireland, the English had brought the 1641 rebellion on themselves. Irish rebelliousness becomes again a comment on the failings of the English colonial masters.

Although several decades beforehand, Sir John Davies had recommended mixed plantations, a 1655 petition from soldiers in the occupied counties of Ireland urges the segregation of the Irish in part to discourage intermarriage between Irish and English. Transplantation would prevent the English from uniting with the Irish, a common practice, according to the petitioners, that had resulted of late in the Irish Rebellion (Rising) in which English settlers were complicit. By refusing to isolate the Irish, "we join in affinity with the people of these abominations" through intermarriage, idolatry, and ultimately insurgence. In other words, the English themselves would shamefully and barbarously *go native*. The consequences thereof are illustrated and condemned in Scriptures, and the petition proceeds to quote the Judaic interdictions against exogamy as well as punishments for idolatry and disobedience, outlined in the Book of Judges, a subject explored in Chapter 6, "Exogamy." The intermixing of peoples would in time, the petitioners feared, "permit our own Souldiers to join with the Natives to destroy us once they have been corrupted by debauchery."[104] The Irish Rebellion itself, they determined, was the result of the miscegenation of Protestants with the idolatrous Irish. Intermarriage had brought down God's wrath upon them, engulfed a rebellious people, and shamed the English nation, which had failed to preserve its ethnic purity and exert its colonial dominance. Weeks before the petitioners issued their appeal to Cromwell, Richard Lawrence arrived at the same conclusion about the cause of the Rebellion or the "sad destruction" of the English, namely, "their promiscuous scattered cohabitations among the *Irish*."[105] He strongly urged segregation – or at least a severe restriction of the number of Irish inhabitants in any English plantation – as the solution for preventing further sedition. "Though the *Irish* mixing with the *English* were the cause of their easie perpetrating their bloudy resolutions," acknowledges Gookin in his response to Lawrence, no such danger now exists for the demoralized, conquered Irish.[106] After all, Seneca and Livy themselves had recommended what Gookin identifies as "Communion" between different peoples: "where had been our Empire (sayes *Seneca*) if wholsom Providence had not mixed the conquered with the Conquerours? And *Livy*, The State of Rome was advanc't by receiving their enemies into them."[107] The new Rome, however, would not prove successful in its efforts to assimilate the enemy.

The parliamentary newsbook *The Weekly Post* (1655), in the meantime, reported on the outcome of the mission to subjugate and settle Ireland and congratulated the victors: "By Letters further from Ireland was certified, that the business of setling the Military and Civil Affairs, and Courts of Justice being now well over, the Lord Deputy *Fleetwood* is preparing for *England* with all speed .... great expressions of joy there were at the celebration thereof: *May they not well laugh that wins?*"[108] Even after he returned to London in 1655, Charles Fleetwood's ruthless transplantation policy in Ireland continued to be more influential than the policies of Henry Cromwell and Vincent Gookin. Gookin, for one, had acknowledged the difficulties of colonization: "The unsettling of a nation is an easy work; the settling of a nation is not, it has cost much Blood and Treasure there."[109] There were a few other critics of such cautious and "benevolent" acts of assimilation that Gookin advanced in dealing with Irish Catholics and other religious "detractors." In 1658, Richard Boyle, Second Earl of Cork, a royalist who had patronized Gookin, protested in Henry Cromwell's company against the "wickedness of many of this nation to fetch poor Irish people out of their beds and sell them into the Barbadoes [sic]."[110] During the 1650s, Irish priests, tories, and vagrants were exiled to the colonies, including Jamaica and the Barbados, where planters bought them for less than the price of black slaves.[111] In addition to decrying such practices, Cork was also known to have opposed a fellow magistrate's ruling about the imprisoning of a disruptive Quaker. The plight of the Irish and of English dissenters otherwise generated very little sympathy. The persecution of the ur-Protestant Waldensians in Piedmont, by contrast, would draw the compassion and ire of the English nation and the European international community at large.

The Late Massacre

By the end of Cromwell's Irish campaign, up to forty thousand Irish soldiers had been captured and were sent off to serve in the armies of foreign countries.[112] An Irish regiment did participate in the next conquest that would capture the attention of the continent: Assisted by a communal militia including Irish soldiers, Carlo Emanuele II (Carlos Immanuel II), Duke of Savoy, at the instigation of his mother, Grand Duchess Christina of Lorraine, ordered a massive army led by the Marquis of Pianezza to expel the Waldensians from outside the tolerated limits of the Pellice Valley in Turin. In the name of Louis XIV and Catholicism, Pianezza's troops slaughtered the Waldensians in the Piedmontese Easter massacre of April 1655. Willem Nieuport, the Dutch ambassador in England, reports in a letter dated 4 June 1655 that Cromwell was deeply moved by the tragedy that had befallen the Waldensians and "that the example of Ireland was still in fresh memory, where he told me, that above two hundred thousand souls were massacred."[113] The aforementioned Lord Cork was also distressed by the plight of the Waldensians and compared their tribulations to those of the persecuted Protestants in Ireland.[114] While still stationed in

Ireland in the spring of 1655, Charles Fleetwood and various other officers petitioned Cromwell to reach out to the persecuted Waldensians and to recall the recent massacre of the Protestants in Ireland: "Let the blood of Ireland be fresh in your view, and their [the Catholic perpetrators'] treachery cry aloud in your ears... let not such be left untransplanted here, or unminded in England, whose continuance amongst us do palpably hazard the very being of protestant interest in these nations."[115] In a separate letter to Thurloe, Fleetwood urges the Protector to assist "those poore persecuted protestant in forraine parts" and in the same breath, appeals for aid from England to advance the transplantation or reduction in Ireland, concluding that the Irish possess "a worse spiritt ... than is in those of Savoy."[116]

Cromwell assumed a leading role in Europe in addressing the crisis, denouncing the Duke of Savoy and reaching out to Louis XIV and Cardinal Mazarin, as well as to the rulers of Sweden, Denmark, the United Provinces, Norway, and the Evangelical Swiss Confederation through state letters that appealed for religious toleration. Milton translated Cromwell's letters into Latin, and Cromwell's envoy, Samuel Morland, carried letters to Paris and Savoy and the script of a speech to Carlo Emanuele in Rivale. Milton would be indebted to Morland for his knowledge of the massacre, which became the subject of "On the late Massacre in Piedmont." "Avenge O Lord thy slaughtered saints, whose bones / Lie scattered on the Alpine mountains cold," cries the sonnet's anguished speaker at the outset.[117] The Waldensians were "Slain by the bloody Piedmontese that rolled / Mother with infant down the rocks. Their moans / The vales redoubled to the hills, and they / To heaven" (ll. 7–10), the sonnet continues, reproducing the shared imagery of the testimonies, newsbook entries, and popular accounts of the massacre. The site of the brutality "resound[ed] nothing else but the cries, Lamentations, and fearful Screechings, made yet more pitiful by the multitude of those Eccho's, which are in those Mountains and Rocks," reports the parliamentary *Weekly Post*, echoing the mournful sounds of the dying in the description.[118] In Milton's poem, the rhymes on two vowels – ones ("moans," "bones") and old ("cold," "rolled") in the octave, and ay ("vales," "they") and ow ("sow") in the sestet – produce the same reverberating effect as the "resound[ing]... cries" and "those Eccho's, which are in those Mountains and Rocks."

Milton's reference to the "triple Tyrant" that perpetrated the massacre (l. 12), conventionally glossed by Miltonists as a symbol for the Pope and his three-tiered crown, can also evoke the triple alliance involved in the massacre. The participation of the Irish in the assault committed by the

Italians with the assistance of the French was well documented. Swiss minister and friend of Milton Jean Baptiste Stouppe assembled a popular and extensive set of accounts and depositions of the massacre, *A Collection of the Several Papers…Concerning the Bloody and Barbarous Massacres* (1655), which names in its subtitle the nations involved in the tragedy: "The Bloody and Barbarous Massacres…by the Duke of *Savoy*'s Forces, joyned therein with the French Army, and severall *Irish* Regiments." Joining the Piedmontese army were, "five or six regiments of the French Army … besides the *Irish*." "A Narrative of the bloody Persecution of the Protestants in Savoy" in *The Weekly Post* repeatedly testifies to the assault made on the Piedmontese by the French and Irish.[119] In his dedication to Cromwell in *A Collection of the Several Papers*, Stouppe observes that the slaughter of the Waldensians should enrage the Protector all the more "because this cruell action was chiefly executed by the Irish." (The *complication* that the Irish regiment was reportedly English was disregarded.[120]) The Catholics' revenge involves "*murther*[ing] *the Reformed in* Piedmont, *and clear*[ing] *the State of them, to lodge the* Irish *in their place*."[121] Dated 8 May 1655, Stouppe's testimony encourages Cromwell to insert an addendum in the treaty between France and England that would see the "re-establishment of our Brethren, escaped from the Massacres, which they have caused the Irish to do, as in revenge of their being banished out of their Country, for Massacring the Protestants there."[122] A 22 May 1655 letter to Stouppe from Mr. Antoine Léger, appointed to manage the affairs of the Waldensians, opposes Cromwell's proposal to relocate the exiled Waldensians of the Piedmont valleys to Ireland, given that the relocation would likely prompt their enemies in Italy to root out the remaining Reformed churches. Indeed, there were Waldensian strongholds in the valleys, including some on land that had been reclaimed by "rout[ing] the Irish who had taken possession of it."[123] Milton himself enacts this reclaiming in his adapted Petrarchan sonnet's description of the "bones … scattered on the Alpine mountains" metamorphosing into the "blood and ashes sow[n] / O'er all the Italian fields" where they regenerate (Sonnet XV, ll. 1–2, 10–11).

The final letter in Stouppe's *Collection of the Several Papers* offers a warning to those Protestant heads of state who decline to embrace the cause of the Piedmontese: "Curse ye *Meroz*, curse ye bitterly the Inhabitants thereof because they came not to the help of the Lord, to the help of the Lord with the mighty" (Judges 5:23) in defeating the Canaanite foe,[124] precisely the curse that was uttered to summon English Protestants to the conquest of the Irish, allegedly to seek retribution for the 1641 Rising.[125] Inextricably entangled with the domestic affairs of England, the incursion into and reduction of Ireland involved the English at the most basic level as a Protestant colonial master in a Britain only symbolically unified. A study of English–Irish relations and the debates over Irish transplantation exposes the "complication of interest" implicit in the acts and expressions of civilizing, toleration, planting, and nation formation. For Milton, the writing of the nation becomes an exercise in the justification of expansionism and exclusionism and, by extension, in the negotiation of tolerance and the rhetorical management of internal difference.

CHAPTER 3

Natural Law: Milton's Post-Revolutionary Defences of England

> "If you remove Kingly Government, and set up true and free Commonwealths Government, then you gain your Crown, and keep it … And thus doing makes a War either lawful or unlawful."
> (Winstanley, *Law of Freedom*, 1652)

In *Observations upon the Articles of Peace with the Irish Rebels* (1649), Milton paid tribute to Cromwell for his "eminent and remarkable Deeds" to the Commonwealth during the tumultuous 1640's. He also anticipated in *Observations* Cromwell's victory over the ungodly Irish, in whose company and "unholy alliance" Milton in *Pro Populo Anglicano Defensio* (1651) would locate the late King Charles, Claudius Salmasius, and the Ulster Scots.[1] At the start of the Protectorate, which saw Britain governed by a Lord Protector rather than a Rump parliament, Milton revived his 1652 portrait of "Cromwell, our chief of men," a force of nature, whose military feats in Scotland the poem celebrates. The volta in the sonnet, "To the Lord General Cromwell," which was composed between the two *Defences* of the English people, signals a shift back to internal affairs in England where "yet much remains / To conquer still." The poet appeals for the deliverance of conscience from "the paw / Of hireling wolves," the "new foes" that infest the English church and nation.[2] Cromwell's conquests of Ireland and Scotland were highly acclaimed in England but did not, in the long run, settle conflicts over the direction and agenda of the Reformation nation in the wake of the greatly contested revolution.

The embattled assertions about the justness of the mid-seventeenth-century revolution continued to preoccupy Milton in his Interregnum writings, including *Tenure of Kings and Magistrates* (1649), *Eikonoklastes* (1649, 1650), the 1651 *Defensio*, the 1654 *Defensio Secunda*, and the pre-Restoration *Readie and Easie Way to Establish a Free Commonwealth* (1660). In castigating Salmasius and Alexander More (mistaken for Dr. Peter Du Moulin, the Younger) in his respective *Defences*, Milton himself confronted the haphazardness of the revolution – "conversio" (a turning around) – and the question about the limited representation of the populace in the English nation. While devoting some attention to the political aftermath of the revolution and its textual afterlife, this chapter concentrates primarily on Milton's own privileging of the moral disposition of the Protestant nation over its political, republican character. Of primary concern are Milton's Interregnum *Defences*, which are here situated in literary, legal, and philosophical contexts wherein Milton's engagement with natural law merits special consideration. This approach represents a departure from the main scholarly focus on the treatises' political and republican principles, which have been thoroughly and admirably studied by Blair Worden, Martin Dzelzainis, and Thomas N. Corns in particular.[3]

Because the revolution was not historically fixed, neither were the postwar writings that rehearsed its divergent premises. As material objects, polemics, and studies in the controversialist arts, Milton's *Tenure of Kings and Magistrates, Eikonoklastes*, the *Defences*, and *The Readie and Easie Way* appeared in altered forms in Milton's day, each time inviting a reassessment of the revolution, national self-definition, liberty, and their conjunctions in new politico-historical and philosophical settings. At the same time, Milton's writings rehistoricise the revolution while issuing powerful appeals for a reinvigorated Protestant Reformation. On the eve of the civil war, Milton referred to the translation of the prophesies of the Hebrews, who "liv'd in the times of reformation," into a "more perfect reformation under Christ," culminating in the Reformation of Milton's day (CPW 1:799, 757). As a self-styled prophet on the national and international stage (CPW 4:536–7), Milton in the post-revolutionary period rehearses St. John Chrysostom's explanation of Paul's exhortation to the Romans: "'There was a common report among men of that time which libelled the apostles as traitorous revolutionaries whose every word and deed was aimed at the overthrow of the general laws: Paul stopped the mouths of those slanderers'" (CPW 4:382). Milton's philosophical and legal vindication of the English revolutionaries and their vision of the nation presents what David Loewenstein perceptively describes in reference to *Defensio Secunda*, "a polemical occasion for Revolutionary myth-making."[4]

Defensio Prima

What was the revolution? In the early modern era, the term "revolution" was used in reference to temporal cycles or rotations. Evidence thereof in Milton's works appears in *Areopagitica* (CPW 2:493, 539) and the *History of Britain* (CPW 5.1:1). Neil Keeble confirms this definition while stating that the word did not signify abrupt transformation, as in the modern sense, and thus did not refer to contemporary events like war. David Loewenstein, however, judges that it could have: the seventeenth-century term anticipated the modern political sense, he points out.[5] As for the English civil war, historiographers to this day, including lately John Adamson in *The Noble Revolt* and David Cressy in *England on the Edge*, have yet to settle on a definitive interpretation thereof.[6] Was it ignited by large-scale economic factors and class consciousness? Was it first and foremost a reaction to absolute monarchy? Was it largely the expression of local interests and personal motives? A revolt led by an intimidated nobility and gentry? Was it a reaction to a government exhausted by war, economic problems, and the ineffectual rule of the three kingdoms? Was it a great Rebellion, a proletarian uprising, a war of religions? What is apparent is that the 1640s experienced the atrocities of warfare, the collapse of the personal rule, a major backlash against Laudianism, the temporary overthrow of the bishops, the execution of the King on charges of high treason, the abolition of monarchy and the House of Lords, and a lack of direction for the political nation.

Contemporary scholarship on the English revolution foregrounded political, socio-economic, and class issues, as well as relationships between national and local interests, and the varying degrees of involvement of the commoners, sectarians, and provincial gentry. Progressive, developmental narratives of the revolution, usually designated Marxist and Whiggish, which were advanced by A. S. P. Woodhouse and Christopher Hill, for example, were discredited by "revisionist" historians such as Geoffrey Elton, Conrad Russell, John Morrill, and Kevin Sharpe. The revisionists interrogated the archival (manuscript) evidence for and methodological approaches to the revolution, emphasised regional interests, and maintained the continuities of political events across the three kingdoms. Furthermore, although granting the civil libertarian mandates of the revolutionaries, revisionists qualified Whig historiography by documenting the short-term and avoidable causes of the civil wars. They in turn, however, tended to underplay the shaping role of culture, including print culture, and sometimes fell short in offering persuasive explanations for the outbreak of the war.[7] What is significant for the purposes of this book is the emergence in the revolutionary era of a period of limited toleration – communicated in part through the language and figures of popular representation, rights, and liberties. Equally noteworthy is Milton's identification of the revolution with the championing of liberty of conscience. In this post-revisionist chapter that deals with the immediate aftermath of the civil war era, the term "revolution" does not signal a retreat to Whiggish assumptions or teleology but refers instead to Milton's imagining of socio-political and national *reformation* predicated on the advancement of toleration.[8] Marchamont Nedham's anonymously published *True State of the Case of the Commonwealth* insisted that the revolutionaries were less concerned with political change than with rights and freedoms,[9] and although Milton himself was an employee of the new Republic in the wake of the revolution, and thus a political actor, his self-assigned mission was the promotion of the "*good Old Cause*" of liberty through the work of the pen.

Upon assuming his duties as Secretary for Foreign Tongues in March 1649, as mentioned in Chapter 2, Milton directed his writings largely to international audiences. Following the release of *Tenure*, which promoted the revolution "as a force in history,"[10] Milton was commissioned by the Council of State to compose not only *Observations upon the Articles of Peace* and *Eikonoklastes* but also a response to the anonymously published 1649 *Defensio regia pro Carolo I*. The work was authored by the internationally renowned divine right theorist and Protestant humanist Claude de Saumaise (or Salmasius) at the behest of Charles I's envoy Sir William Boswell. Directed at the future Charles II, *Defensio regia* assailed the new English government. In late 1649 and early 1650, *Defensio regia* made its way from Holland to booksellers in England, and the Council sought the prosecution of the treatise's royalist English printer, William Dugard, who had also printed first editions of *Eikon Basilike*. He would soon thereafter be appointed as printer to the Council of State and be responsible for the printing of Milton's *Pro Populo Anglicano Defensio*, which was authorized on 23 December 1650 and published 24 February 1651.[11] Adapting oratorical models supplied by Cicero, defender of the ancient republic, Milton designed the treatise as an exercise in disputation and an apology for the nationalist agenda of the Purged Parliament.

The *Defensio* became Milton's most famous and controversial work through its multiple editions, translations, and reception in England, France, Spain, Germany, and Holland. Acclaimed as a rhetorical masterpiece, *Defensio*, like its successor, is a declaration of civil, political, and religious rights and liberties – enjoyed by the virtuous, rational "better part" (*pars potior*) or the "sounder" (*sanior*)[12] that bears a synecdochic relation to the nation. Discursively produced, the lineaments of the better nation are represented by "citations from divine law, the law of nations, and the statutes of my country,"[13] which Milton amasses in scripting a constitutional history for England.[14] In the 1640's after counseling his students to study

politics, Milton, in *Of Education*, recommended law, which he characterized as the foundation for a civil society:

> [T]hey are to dive into the grounds of law, and legall justice; deliver'd first,
> and with best warrant by *Moses*; and as farre as humane prudence can be
> trusted, in those extoll'd remains of Grecian Law-givers, *Lycurgus, Solon,
> Zaleucus, Charondas*, and thence to all the Roman *Edicts* and tables with
> their *Justinian*; and so down to the *Saxon* and common Laws of England,
> and the Statutes. (CPW 2:398–9)

In his post-revolutionary *Defences*, the prescribed education in legal
history is supported by the study of constitutional law and natural law
as they inform national identity. The formulations to which Milton subscribes complement (the imprisoned Leveller) John Lilburne's composite
definition of the national law as "the PERFECTION of Reason, consisting of Lawfull and Reasonable Customes, received and approved by the
people: and of the old Constitutions, and modern Acts of Parliament,
made by the Estates of the Kingdome."[15] The "Fundamentall Law of the
Land" must conform, Lilburne insists, to natural and divine law.

Predictably, anti-tolerationists laid claim to the same domains of the
law. Speaking as an adherent of the Reformed Religion in a speech on the
toleration controversy, James Hay cautions the Cromwellian Interregnum
government about the dangers of condoning liberty of conscience, religious pluralism, and a broad toleration. All contribute to the subver-
sion of the key tenets of social and national civility, namely "unwritten
Divine and natural Law," "written Law," "the Scriptures, [and] the Law of
Nations."[16] Milton's own conception of the law during this period is at one
with divine law and the law of nations – international law or the "legal
rules that prevail among, rather than within, political communities."[17]
Unlike Hay's, however, Milton's represents an amalgam and extension of
theories of toleration, Protestant humanism, freedom of conscience, and
moral law – defined as law rooted in "right reason" (CPW 7:479) – as well
as of the aforementioned philosophical "*good Old Cause*" (CPW 7:462).
In his tribute to the free nation, Milton registers the Puritan shift from
legal precedent to the law of nature and from historic to abstract rights. In
upholding the (extra-)judicial process against the late King, Milton develops a defence of nationhood, dependent less on a codified judicature and
legal positivism than on natural law equated with the law of God, thus
confirming Joan Bennett's assertion that "[v]alid revolution tests whether
supremacy is accountable to law, which alone has the power to liberate."[18]

If in the *Reason of Church-Government* Milton ascribes to the nation
"the title of Clergy [that] S. *Peter* gave to all Gods people" (CPW 1:838), in

Areopagitica, he designates the people as "a Nation of Prophets, of Sages, and of Worthies" (CPW 2:554); if in *Eikonoklastes*, iconoclastic readers or the fit though few are cast as "not less then Kings" (CPW 3:542), in the *Defensio*, they are legislators or their "own lawmaker" (CPW 4:479). By accommodating a sovereign people, "the strongest of realms ... is now ... a commonwealth, so much the stronger" (CPW 4:311), Milton declares, as the revolution transformed the kingdom into what he hailed as a free nation whose government was designed "to train up a Nation in true wisdom and vertue."[19] On 4 January 1649, the Commons named the people as the source of power, and authorized its right to represent the nation and to pass legislation independent of monarchical consent. The welfare of the nation rested with the "joynt voice and efficacy of a whole Parlament, assembl'd by election, and indu'd with the plenipotence of a free Nation," as Milton had insisted in *Eikonoklastes* (CPW 3:410). The fickleness of the electorate, consisting largely of the propertied, would, however, call for revisions to his configuration of the revolutionary nation.

Omitting a representation of (a promonarchist) Scotland, the frontispiece of the *Defensio* displays a shield with an English cross and Irish harp, the arms of the Commonwealth.[20] But the polemical warzone Milton designates also comprises an international space. Milton thus selects Latin – the "*common language of Christendom*" (CPW 7:239) – as his medium, while also translating his justifications for the English revolution into the European languages of theology, philosophy, and history. Marshalling his troops and drawing his battle lines, Milton enlists the reformers, "Luther, for example, and Zwingli, Calvin, Bucer, Paraeus" (CPW 4:337–38; also 4:661), and thus subdues the likes of Isidore of Seville, Gregory of Tours, and others – the more obscure figures invoked by Salmasius, a convert to Protestantism. The ancients, whom Milton selectively rescues from *Defensio regia*, come to his aid: among others, Euripides, Sophocles, Horace, Seneca, Aristotle, Xenophon, Polybius, and Pliny the Younger assist with the attack on tyranny (CPW 4:440–2, 446–9, 455). Likewise Tacitus and Sallust, who also supply a psychology of servitude under monarchy.[21] Cicero contributes republican and natural law principles as well as oratorical and rhetorical devices, notably from his *Philippics*, based on Demosthenes's orations against Philip (CPW 4:536). With remarkable agility, Milton proceeds to disrupt unidirectional interpretative practices by demonstrating how incisively the Greeks and Romans, the biblical writers, and the Protestant reformers intervene in early modern controversies over kingship, revolution, and the English constitutional law. The constitutional model Milton develops in the place of the realm's dynastic history is, however, yet tentative. Because he defines the nation not in terms of its (arbitrarily established) political institutions but in terms of the civility and virtue of its subjects, Milton names and compares diverse political models, according to the Aristotelian categorization of forms of government and principles of merit. In the *Defensio*, moreover, diplomacy and internationalism force the concession "all kings are [not] tyrants" (CPW 4:367).

When Milton invoked the *Defensio* in its sequel, he called it "the Defence of liberty and religion" and professed astonishment about its burning in Toulouse, a city he associates for polemical purposes, with a history of religious freedom.[22] *Defensio Secunda* reports that the groundwork for the liberation of the English themselves was laid in the resistance to the episcopate. The full restoration of the nation's liberty depended on what Milton described as the transference of "the discipline arising from religion" to the values and institutions supported by the state (CPW 4:622). Milton's ideas of the nation's religious spirit and moral character dominate and inform matters of political organization.[23] Keith Stavely ascertains that "Milton did not translate his ideals into political terms. If his tracts were the only surviving documents of the English Revolution, we would know little about it as a major political event ... Form embodies abstract ideal to the detriment of concrete political meaning."[24] Applying a politicized theology, Milton cites biblical examples often as historical and legal precedents and compares the revolutionaries' righteous actions with heroic deeds from days of old while investing "with new nobility the laws, the courts, which henceforth were restored to all alike, and above all the figure of justice herself" (CPW 4:330). Judicial principles evolving from moral considerations, reason, deliberation, and self-discipline displace formal legislation.[25] Milton's recourse is ultimately to the law of nature, which Digger-turned-Quaker Gerrard Winstanley called the original language: "to read the *Law* of Nature (or God) as he hath written his name in every body, is to speak a pure language, and this is to speak the truth as Jesus Christ spake it, giving to every thing its own weight and measure."[26] The Independent Arminian minister John Goodwin declares that the law of nature is the law of God, written on the heart and having an "authoritative jurisdiction over all human Laws and constitutions whatsoever."[27] An exasperated Salmasius complains that the English fanatics invoke natural law by default in the absence of written laws.[28]

The philosophical controversy over the revolution revolved around the meaning of divine law and its translation into political theory and practice and, by extension, the king's relationship to the law and nation. Salmasius describes revolution – "*conversio*" or "*mutatio*" (a changing, altering) – as a world turned upside down (Acts 17:6; CPW 4:398), when kings become subjects of the people and the law of nature and the customs and doctrines of Christianity are overturned (CPW 4.2:1006). For the absolutist, natural law models hierarchical arrangements that support sovereignty in the person of the king. Accountable to God alone, kings are above human judgement, which constitutes "the fundamental principle and the basis of this work of kingly defence," Salmasius insists (CPW 4.2:1007). Further, protests Salmasius, by challenging the king's prerogative over the church, as well as over the judicial system including the King's Bench and the army, the English usurp the monarch's position.[29] Sir Robert Filmer would similarly reproach Milton for his theories of kingship and for his promotion of civil liberty that reduced the monarch to the lowest possible social status.[30]

In conjunction with ancient Roman law, divine right theorists emphasised the patriarchal relationship of king and nation.[31] Theories of the supremacy of the sovereign were "perfectly compatible with a strong sense of nationhood,"[32] when the concept of the king's inviolable paternal and political body dominated national imaginings and conscience was wedded to state loyalty. Insisting that elective monarchy was not the original form of government, James I insisted that kingship is modeled on Godly rule. "[T]he stile of *pater patriae* was ever, & is commonly used to Kings," he declared in *The True Lawe of Free Monarchies*, in which he emphasized that the paternal relationship of the king to his subjects accorded with the law of nature and thus with the laws and constitutions of God and humanity.[33]

Availing themselves of scriptural support for the divine right of kings, royalists regularly rehearsed the dictum, "Let every soule bee subject unto the higher powers: For there is no power but of God" (Romans 13:1). The decree was translated into an affirmation of the absolute obedience to the monarch that God's law enjoined, even if the monarch proved tyrannical (CPW 4.2:1030). The Bible had supplied the language in which early modern people thought, communicated, and fought. In his history of the civil war, Thomas Hobbes remarked that "the Interpretation of a Verse in the *Hebrew, Greek,* or *Latine* Bible, is oftentimes the cause of Civil War, and the deposing and assassinating of Gods Anointed."[34] He had offered similar observations about the political dangers of reading anti-monarchical works by Aristotle, Cicero, and others. Fueling the print war over Romans 13:1 – an "early Reformation resistance theorem" – and over the equally contentious decree "be ye Subject to the King as Supreme" (1 Peter 2:13) was Robert Mossom, translator and publisher of David

Owen's *Anti-Paraeus, or A Treatise in the Defence of the Royall Rights of Kings*. Appearing months before the outbreak of the civil war, this printed version of Owen's 1619 speech was a timely reminder of the obedience to magistrates and monarchs required of their subjects.[35] German theologian David Paraeus's *Commentary on Romans* (1609), whose burning James I arranged, had stated that inferior magistrates could resist superiors in self-defence and in support of the nation and true religion.[36] In his *Golden Rule*, John Canne, Baptist minister-turned-Fifth Monarchist, cites authorities, from Augustine on – sometimes overlapping with Owen's sources – who explicate Romans 13:1 but in defence of the lawfulness of revolution against tyranny.[37] The semantic ambiguity of Romans 13:1 meant that the verse would lend itself to competing interpretations, justifying Henry VIII's break from Rome and James I's headship over the English church, as well as the defiance of early modern reformers, radicals, and Milton himself in wrenching the nation from the absolutist monarchy that Henry himself inaugurated.[38] These words of St. Paul, Milton stated in 1649, "Must be understood of lawfull and just power, els we read of great power in the affaires and Kingdoms of the World permitted to the Devil."[39] In conjunction with his view that the law of right reason or natural law – an abstract justice – is "the highest and ultimate power" and trumps the state, Milton reads the verse as a mandate to obey legitimate authorities, those appointed by God, author of the most ancient laws (CPW 4:383). Law, declares Cicero in the *Philippics* – again, a model for the *Defensio* – is "nothing but that right reason derived from divine will which commands what is right and forbids what is wrong" (CPW 4:383), Milton explains, again rooting his theory of law in an ancient source.

In his earlier discussions of natural law, Milton had differentiated between a primary law of nature equated with the unwritten law of God and a secondary law of nature, derived from it. In *Tetrachordon*, Milton develops this distinction in declaring that "prime Nature made us all equall, made us equal coheirs by common right and domination over all creatures," but through the Fall, we "suffer'd ... all that which by Civilians is term'd the *secondary law of nature and of nations*" (CPW 2:661). The fixed and immutable law of nature observed by all nations alike is the basis for the law of nations. In the Roman tradition, international law, founded on custom, differed from the law of nature,[40] but Milton regularly aligns them in defending his position on the monarch's subjection to the law: "Certainly all the best emperors were aware that the authority of the laws and the Senate far exceeded their own: so too in all civilized lands right has ever been the most sacred possession" (CPW 4:382). Reinforcing the connectedness of constitutional law, civil societies, and the Gospel, which "accord[s] with reason and with the laws of nations" (CPW 4:383), Milton buttresses his philosophical defence of the English nation with international precedents that situate political authority in a system of answerability, rational consent, and a spectrum of virtue.

"The Better Part"

In Milton's day, the fraught historiography of the Norman Conquest or Norman Yoke demanded, on the part of advocates of an ancient national sovereignty, a reassessment of William I's imposition of a foreign law on England. In 1649, Milton strategically traced the ancient tenure of kings not to the era of the Norman invasion but earlier to the year 446 CE, when the British elected their kings after the Roman occupation (CPW 3:221). In the *Defensio*, Milton creates a national constitutional history uninterrupted by the Conquest: "those who are most familiar with our history know that the English strength was not so reduced in the one battle at Hastings." Further, William I opted to uphold the ancient laws of England and ratified the law of Edward the Confessor, thereby conceding the king's accountability to the law and nation.[41] Rooting English constitutional history more firmly, Milton here absorbs the Conqueror into a continuous narrative of English nationhood. Salmasius had argued for the validity of Charles I's kingship on the basis of his ascendancy from William I (CPW 4.2:1005). Nonconformists of Milton's day expressed their abhorrence of "the Norman Yoke" that still strangled English liberties. For Winstanley, Charles's succession from the Conqueror established his foreignness, at the same time that his laws represented "the successive Power of that *Norman* Conquest over *England*." On that basis, the revolution of the "Commoners of *England* against King *Charls*" was a just war, Winstanley decides.[42]

As he writes a literary narrative of nationhood grounded in legal theory and history, Milton reviews several constitutions that outline the nation's laws and liberties, which the Commons, in their judicial proceedings against Charles Stuart, had accused him of subverting, thus igniting civil war.[43] Key here was Magna Carta, regarded by early modern tolerationists as a seminal document of English constitutional practice and of the inheritance of liberty and pre-Conquest laws. This charter, along with the medieval *Modus Tenendi Parliamentum* ("Manner of Parliament") and *Speculum Justiciariorum* ("Mirror of Justices") (CPW 4:493–4), formed part of an immemorial law and lent itself to a constitutional historiography extending to the 1628 Petition of Rights and the 1653 Instrument of Government.[44] "When in times past kings refused their assent to acts of Parliament such as *Magna Carta* and the like, our fathers in many cases secured assent by force of arms," Milton states in drawing on an ancient legal precedent for restricting the king's authority and justifying the revolution (CPW 4:497).

John Lilburne had also cited Magna Carta in defence of the restraint of monarchical authority,[45] although nonconformists by no means agreed on the terms that this constitution set out for those not already in possession of fundamental rights. William Walwyn dissented from Lilburne about the charter's principles on tolerance: "*Magna Charta* hath been more precious in your esteeme then it deserveth; for it may be made good to the people, and yet in many particulars, they may remain under intolerable oppressions."[46] The authors of *A Remonstrance of Many Thousand Citizens* – likely, Richard Overton and Walwyn – were equally aggrieved over the disjunction between fundamental rights and the enactment of legislation based on the charter: "common *equity* and *right reason* ... ought to be the Forme and Life of every government. *Magna Charta* it self being but a beggarly thing, containing many markes of intollerable bondage ... made our government much more oppressive and intollerable."[47]

England's constitutional history had betrayed the commoners, although Milton still upholds it in a statement on national identity that targets and alienates the outsider.[48] In addition to being the object of Milton's diatribe that unleashes a battery of vitriolic rhetorical and personalized epithets, Salmasius is reviled as an intruder and meddler in English national affairs, "of which you know nothing," Milton adds (CPW 4:533). He is also berated for citing foreign constitutional models in his defence of divine right, as if the English lacked a legal history. Indeed, the English "were born in freedom, they live in independence, and they can make for themselves what laws they wish," Milton retorts, in a reaffirmation of the people's legislative powers (CPW 4:533). Milton's assaults on Salmasius's alien status are statements on national sovereignty (e.g. CPW 4:306, 336). In *Defensio Secunda*, Milton contests Alexander More's assertion that Salmasius had mastered English laws: "how he played the fool in respect to our laws and was a mere parrot, we have ample proof, in the testimony of our lawyers" (CPW 4:579). He then transfers the charges to More himself, criticizing his ignorance of "our affairs" and his meddling in a foreign state (CPW 4:629, 632, 647). Later Cyriack Skinner, in a work traditionally attributed to John Phillips, reiterates his mentor's characterization of More by denouncing him as "a Forrainer, & grossly ignorant of our

Laws & Constitution (which in all Nations are respective distinguishing Principles of Government)."[49]

The definition of national character through resistance to foreignness is less fraught than the renunciation of internal features that subvert national unity. Among the most vexed issues of the day were the constitution and role of the people in the revolutionary nation. The representation of the people in terms of a qualitative principle rather than a numerical majority is grounded in the Aristotelian political principle of government by the most worthy. The concept of "*sanior pars*" was introduced in canon law in the twelfth century and, in the thirteenth, legist Henry de Bracton applied it to the British kingdom in defending governance by lords and bishops.[50] The distinction that Marsilius of Padua articulated in the following century between the *populus* (the nobles) and the *plebs* (the lower-class masses) resonated through to the early modern era. Populist supporter George Buchanan himself subscribed to the ideal of the qualitative representation of the people.[51] In Milton's time, John Goodwin broached the issue in his remarks on the army's governance of the nation, an arrangement, he determined, that conformed to the law of nature despite being "contrary to the minde and desires of the people or at least of the major part of them."[52] Marchamont Nedham in the following year likewise defended the legitimacy and justness of representative government, particularly in times of national crisis: "our present Governours have no *Call* or *Consent* from the People," but elections are for peacetime: in times of war, government is "decided by the *Sword*" and is entitled to rule "as if it had the Peoples positive Consent."[53] Later he reiterates that "the people" are those "chosen to represent the People *successively* in their Supream Assemblies … the People thus qualified or constituted, are the best *Keepers of their own Liberties*." The identification of the (representative) nation with the preservation of liberty is thus underscored.

Milton's own recourse first to the middling sort – those not corrupted by luxury or encumbered by want – and then to the regenerate over the collective or the majority is a function of the characteristically "restrictive emphasis" of Puritan thought.[54] Yet in a treatise that summons and allegedly represents the interests of the English people at large, it is a practice in need of defence: "why should I not say that the act of the better, the sound part of the Parliament, in which resides the real power of the people, was the act of the people?" particularly, Milton continues, if the minority can preserve the freedom of the commonwealth.[55] The remnant of better citizens and the parliamentary representatives of the people's "real power" resist identification, although their superior rational and sagacious nature is assumed, as is their legal immunity. All are born into a state of natural liberty, but only the "uncorrupted" (CPW 4:332) manage to preserve and exercise it: "I confess that those who long for liberty or can enjoy it are but a few – only the wise, that is, and the brave" and "the larger or more able part" (CPW 4:343, 470).[56] Popular sovereignty for the present extended only to the "well affected," that is, those desirous of liberty and thus entitled to act for the whole people: the propertied, the intellectuals, republicans, Independents, the army, and the Rump, soon to be reconstituted as the Council under the Protectorate.[57] Comprising the "chosen ones," the people with a superior character and intellect have a legal prerogative to judge their tyrannical rulers and condemn those who put themselves above the law (CPW 4:359).

Conflicts over the principles and practices of inclusion and exclusion are central to the debate about the revolution and the constitution of the nation. Royalists and dissenters alike invoked the *Defensio* to gauge the question of popular rule. For his detractors, Milton's qualifications thereof undermined his philosophical and constitutional models.[58] Authority cannot reside in the people if they cannot make laws or create magistrates, and if "the army with their leaders" has delegated judicial power to the lower house, abrogated old laws, implemented new ones, and abused the terms of justice, Salmasius retorts (CPW 4.2:989). Milton concedes Salmasius's point that the revolution was not a majority movement, but in so doing, he upholds the principle of *sanior pars* in the face of national historical exigencies: "If ... a country harassed by faction and protecting herself by arms regards only the sound and upright side, passing over or shutting out the others, whether commons or nobles, she maintains justice well enough" (CPW 4:317). Inferring a distinction between the *populus* and the *plebs*, Milton also acknowledges that the Independents constitute a fraction of the English nation, but rightly so, because the population at large, including the vulgar, deserted the Independents. The concept of the sounder part representing the nation is after all also mirrored in the law of nations: "What is commanded by nature and good sense may best be seen in the case of the wisest nations rather than the greatest number of them" (CPW 4:432). The wisdom of those nations, namely of the Greeks, Romans, Italians, and Carthaginians, is evinced in their resistance to kings, an anti-monarchist position to which the nation's better part also subscribes.

Complementing Salmasius's notion of the law of nature as dictating monarchical absolutism is the divine right patriarchalism of the aforementioned Sir Robert Filmer, whose appraisal of Hugo Grotius precedes his rebuttal of Milton's *Defensio* in *Observations Concerning the Originall of Government*. Herein Milton observes that just as Aristotle never definitively identified the free citizens, so "our modern politicians ... though they talk big of the people ... are content with a few representors (as they call them) of the whole people." Milton exemplifies such inconsistencies and limits of toleration by denying to "the major part of the representors" the status of "people" and condoning "the 'sounder and better part only' of them." The soldiers themselves now stand for the people, Filmer complains.[59]

John Lilburne in the same year of 1652 used the *Defensio* to admonish the Cromwellian regime in his prophetic *As You Were or The Lord General Cromwel and the Grand Officers*. The substantial section from the epilogue of *Defensio* that Lilburne quotes in English resonates with pleas for the preservation of national liberties, although in a critique of the government, to which the author of *Defensio* would have taken exception.[60] Casting his judgement as a lover of his "native Countrey," Lilburne issues Milton's warning to his countrymen and to the Rump to remain vigilant against internal threats to principles of law, liberty, and revolution. Milton advised his own Commonwealth masters "with much faithfulness and Freedome" to conquer ambition and avarice, lest they "prove base and unworthy" in peacetime, Lilburne points out. Surveying English charters and law books, notably Magna Carta, Lilburne catalogues legal precedents for public councils and assemblies since pre-Conquest times, parliaments in particular being "the very Soule and Life of all the Peoples liberties."[61] But in the early 1650s, the republic, although allegedly deriving its power from the people, declined to call new elections, thus violating the nation's constitution, Lilburne accuses. As he interrogates the legitimacy of the increasingly tyrannical republic and laments the shortcomings of the revolution, he turns to Milton's treatise in support of fundamental liberties, having detected a "reproof to the Rump" therein.[62] Milton, however, displayed no enthusiasm for elections at this time and would later compose his own postscript to the *Defensio*. In the meantime, *Defensio Secunda* would negotiate the shifting ideals and limitations of the revolution, toleration, and popular representation.

Defensio Secunda

Much of Milton's first publication on the Protectorate, *Joannis Miltoni Angli Pro Populo Anglicano Defensio Secunda*, was in fact completed by April 1653 and "belongs to the same political environment" as its prequel. The treatise was published in 1654 by Thomas Newcomb, who on 1 September

1649 had been arrested for printing John Lilburne's *An Outcry of the Young Men and Apprentices of London*, to which the printing history of Milton's defence of the English nation and liberty is thereby related.[63] At the beginning of a retrospective account in *Defensio Secunda* of his contributions to the advancement of the Protestant Reformation (CPW 4:622), Milton recalls his commitment to the national cause and what would be termed the "*good Old Cause.*" Often judged as betraying the ideals of the revolution because it was based on single-person rule, the Protectorate remained a republic in Milton's tract (CPW 4:561, 673); as Blair Worden observes, *Defensio Secunda* "fought yesterday's battles." Milton still claimed to be living in a republic, and the treatise is primarily the product of the Rump years, Worden concludes, after meticulously and authoritatively reviewing the stages of its composition.[64] If *Defensio Secunda* is read primarily as a political and topical tract, then it can be judged as dated or outdated, as *The Readie and Easie Way to Establish a Free Commonwealth* (1660) would also seem to be about a time well before the inexorable march to the Restoration.[65] Although composed in a decade marked by "startling shifts of temporality," [66] *Defensio Secunda* is more than the sum of its historico-republican reflections. It is, among other things, a major contribution to what Milton described as a larger program of defending liberty (CPW 4:624) and a powerful literary statement on Protestant nationalism and on tolerationism as a key feature thereof.

"All Europe talks from side to side," Milton boasts in a 1655 sonnet to the aforementioned Cyriack Skinner on the international reception of the 1651 *Defensio*, composed "[i]n liberty's defence."[67] *Defensio Secunda* takes up that key national interest: in a letter to Bremen Envoy to London Henry Oldenburg, Milton refers to the recently completed 1654 treatise as a response to an "unexpected contest with the enemies of liberty."[68] As he sees it, liberty is his to champion, and from that the commission assigned by "the very liberators of my country" (CPW 4:549), he derives his national and international identity and reputation. *Defensio Secunda* is rife with allusions to Milton's recent success that connect the exemplary achievements of Miltoni Angli, as a Ciceronian orator, with the nation itself. "Many good and learned men in all the neighboring countries … are now reading my works and thinking rather well of me," he exclaims in self-satisfaction (CPW 4:611). Of all his works, *Defensio Secunda* best exemplifies the entanglement of self and nation, Barbara Lewalski discerns.[69] The admiring audience in which Milton sees himself and the nation reflected extends from the west of Europe, represented by the Pillars of Hercules or Gibraltar, to the reaches of India, and finds its sentiments completely aligned with his own: "Wherever liberal sentiment ... conceals or openly proclaims itself, ... some in silence approve, others openly cast their votes, some make haste to applaud, others conquered at least by the truth, acknowledge themselves my captives" (CPW 4:554, 555). *Joannis Miltoni Angli Pro Populo Anglicano Defensio Secunda* is an exercise in self-definition, justification, celebration, and self-preservation.[70]

Whereas the 1651 *Defensio* forensically anatomizes Salmasius's defence in order to dismantle it, *Defensio Secunda* takes greater liberties in pursuing its own form and line of argumentation. It includes a character assassination of the author of *Regii sanguinis clamor* (Netherlands, 1652), whom Milton, despite warnings, misidentifies and defames as Alexander More. More or Morris, a French minister of Scottish descent, then a professor at Middelburg, had overseen the printing of *Regii sanguinis* in consultation with the now deceased Salmasius. In the confrontation with More, Milton draws on his earlier *Defensio* in inflecting his pronouncements on political participation with theories on natural law and addressing the disputatious issues of national sovereignty and popular rule. Conceding that the parliamentarians "are themselves now the people" while the commoners constitute an indecisive mob that might have acquitted the king (CPW 4:635), Milton maintains that "nothing is more natural, nothing more just, nothing more useful or more advantageous to the human race than that the lesser obey the greater" – in virtue and wisdom (CPW 4:636). Given the superiority of the Independents "both in law and in merit," they constitute the sounder part or party (CPW 4:636, 648).

Occupying a diplomatic and ambassadorial role as a polemicist on the international stage, Milton at the same time modulates his antimonarchism to forestall the alienation of the Cromwellian regime from Continental states, which were already distressed by the "'parricide,'" Salmasius accuses.[71] Milton summons international examples of the opposition to tyranny, and announces that even French Protestants waged wars against their kings (CPW 4:596). In defending the English revolution against the bishops and papacy, Milton rehearses examples of French resistance movements: the Waldensian defiance of Rome, the fight against feudal taxes in Toulouse, and the French Huguenot uprising against church and state, all of which serve as historical and legal precedents for resisting the despotic Charles (CPW 4:658). But he is also careful to distinguish between the just punishment of a tyrant and the indefensible murder of a lawful king (CPW 4:599). Milton's encomium to Christina, Queen of Sweden – hailed as a patron of the arts, an admiring reader of his *Defensio*, and a paragon of magnanimous virtue – exhibits the differences between tyranny and righteous monarchical rule, differences fortuitously perceived by "Augusta" herself, whom he also credits with banishing Salmasius (CPW 4:603–07). The subsequent panegyric to the Lord Protector – certainly no Augustus[72] – registers the pan-European potential and reach of his appeal by enjoining Cromwell to reflect on and honour England's reputation abroad (CPW 4:673).

During the revolutionary era and the early interregnum, Milton acclaimed Cromwell as the agent of religious and political revolution. Applying his extensive use of the military metaphor for the art of writing, Milton exalts Cromwell's heroism in his own "true history," which constitutes "a second battlefield ... and a space for narration equal to the deeds themselves" (CPW 4:668). The expulsion of the discredited Rump in 1653 was among the "deliverances" of the Puritan revolution that Milton, who continued to work for Cromwell's Council of State, defended.[73] John Hall, like Nedham, had judged the dissolution of the Rump as the most exemplary of "the greatest *Revolutions* ...[that] any memory affords us" because it was nonviolent, occurring "without *contestation*, without *effusion* of blood, and ... without the least resentment of those whom it generally concerns." The dissolution, he assures the reader, is the means of preventing further abuses of national liberty.[74] On 8 February 1654, Nedham's *A True State of the Case of the Commonwealth*, albeit a propagandist piece, maintained that the republicans never took up arms to defend or oppose any kind of government, and that Parliament itself was best suited to protect civil liberties. As noted at the outset of this chapter, Nedham protested that revolutionaries were primarily concerned to further the cause of liberty rather than intervene in political affairs, a premise affirmed by Henry Stubbe's *Essay in Defence of the Good Old Cause*, which testifies that the "Quarrell against the *King*" was about "Liberty, *civill, and spirituall*" and was independent of any intent to transform the constitution of the Commonwealth.[75] Nedham's *True State* supports the expulsion of the Barebones Parliament convened in July 1653 after the Rump's forcible dissolution[76] and, in the face of divided republican support, defends the aforementioned constitution, the Instrument of Government. Milton himself dismissed Barebones: "The elected members came together. They did nothing" (CPW 4:671). The (unelected) Assembly was divided, thus setting the stage for Cromwell's rule.

The tribute that Milton composes for the Lord Protector balances compliment and counsel while keeping criticism largely at bay.[77] Milton defends Cromwell for having "assumed a certain title very like that of father of your country ... and be[ing] forced into a definite rank, so to speak, for the public good" (CPW 4:672). Cromwell is a national saviour, although the apologia also registers some unease with the acclamation as Milton strains to distinguish Cromwell's majesty from regality: "The name of king you spurned from your far greater eminence" (CPW 4:672). Seeking to neutralize the autocratic nature of the Protectorate (CPW 4:674), Milton advises Cromwell to surround himself with counsellors. In addition to celebrating John Bradshaw, who oversaw the trial of the king and who is described as bringing "a liberal frame of mind" to "knowledge of the law" (CPW 4:638), and Thomas Fairfax, whom he cautiously commends for moral rather than political feats (CPW 4:669), Milton elects twelve comrades for Cromwell, republican revolutionaries who represent a combination of Milton's and Cromwell's preferences. In most cases, their positions on toleration had more to recommend them than did their support of Cromwell or his policies. Among the worthies, Bulstrode Whitelocke, like Bradshaw, had in fact rebuked Cromwell for dissolving the Rump; Henry Lawrence, whom Milton praised along with Edward Montague for his patronage of the arts, resisted the proceedings against Charles; Whitelocke, Sir Gilbert Pickering, Robert Overton – parliamentary officer and critic of the Protectorate – were among the practitioners or defendants of religious toleration.[78] Plausibly, the catalogue includes also, by implication or extension, Sir Henry Vane, the Younger, conspicuous by his absence. The list thus accommodates Milton's preferences although they did not always correspond with those of Cromwell, who had in fact forced Vane into early retirement in the previous year. Milton proceeds to admonish Cromwell about his failure to implement disestablishment (CPW 4:678), and Vane was an outspoken advocate thereof.

Milton thereafter modulates the tone of the encomium by rendering the exaltation conditional on the exercise of moral and civic responsibilities designed to further the revolution's cause. The directives to Cromwell include a commitment to self-scrutiny, the implementation of policies on disestablishment, the reform of English legislation and of education, and the protection of freedom of speech and liberty of conscience – for the meritorious.[79] Admonition and the subtle querying of Cromwell's single rule in the tract give way to injunctions on self-rule and on the governance of an inconstant nation. Like its prequel, *Defensio Secunda* is intent on cultivating a climate of toleration, but the advice to Cromwell communicates this message in primarily negative terms as an entreaty to curb intolerance: "*eos autem minimè omnium audieris, qui sese liberos esse non credunt, nisi aliis esse liberis, per ipsos non liceat; nec studiosiùs aut violentiùs quicquam agunt, quàm ut fratrum non corporibus modò sed conscientiis quoque vincula injiciant*" (may you "listen the least of all to those, who never fancy that themselves are free, unless they deprive others of their freedom; who labour at nothing with so much zeal and earnestness, as to enchain not the bodies only, but the consciences of their brethren").[80]

The exhortation to Cromwell to commit to inner reform and secure national liberty[81] is redirected to the people themselves. Milton characterizes the nation in moral and philosophical terms, distinguished by "the acquisition or retention of liberty" (CPW 4:680). The principle of international law derived from Grotius that during a period of civil war, a kingdom comprises two nations – "a single people is considered for the time being as two peoples"[82] – becomes in Milton a crucible of national self-fashioning based on the premise of *sanior pars*. "[N]ation presses upon nation, or the sounder part of a nation overthrows the more corrupt" (CPW 4:681), the healthier part alchemically transforming and constituting synecdochically the free nation. The intranational contest emerges as the venue for the new revolution: "many tyrants, impossible to endure, will from day to day hatch out from your very vitals. Conquer them first. This is the warfare of peace, these are its victories, hard indeed, but bloodless, and far more noble" (CPW 4:680–1).

At the end of the decade, the relationship between the revolution and the free nation was reinforced on behalf of Puritans and dissenters in *Mene Tekel*. George Bishop's admonition to the Council of army officers reinforces the interdependence of the civil, religious, and national liberties: "the *Good Old Cause*, was (chiefly) *Liberty of Conscience*," which the government, Bishop contends, was charged with protecting along with "the *Liberties* of the *Nation*, which with the *Liberty* of *Conscience* were bound up, and joyned together."[83] In fact, the nation's "Common Right and Freedome … hath been the chief subject of our Contest [of war]."[84] But parliament under the Council is now guilty of the King's own transgressions against the cause of liberty and thus against the Reformation. Into this climate, the *Defensio*, although still in circulation in London and Amsterdam, was reintroduced with a coda that could have been meant for both *Defence*s and for the volatile decade of the 1650s at large. The barely revised 1658 edition, printed by Newcomb, who had published *Defensio Secunda*, betrayed the degree to which the Protectorate had by its fifth year deviated from the cause of the revolution celebrated in 1651 and in 1653 to 1654, when Milton located Cromwell in the company of revolutionaries, still clinging to the republic rather than embracing the Protectorate.[85]

Among the additions to the new edition of the *Defensio* was the testimony that civil liberty has never been more valiantly championed than by Milton in this inspired "memorial" (CPW 4:536). Milton both reflects upon and creates an exuberant reception history for his work: the nations and his own country composed of the "best citizens" (CPW 4:537) will recognize his achievement as the Romans had applauded Cicero's oath, with its coda to his single-handed deliverance of the city and state (CPW 4:536). The deliverer, literally, "liberator" of the nation, is hailed as *pater patriae*, a title first bestowed on Cicero, then on Julius Caesar and Augustus. In the early modern era, James I claimed the distinction. When invoking the title in *Defensio Secunda*, Milton confers it on Cromwell (CPW 4:672) before consecrating himself for erecting an immortal "monument ... to those deeds that were illustrious, that were glorious, that were almost beyond any praise" (CPW 4:685). Likewise in the tribute that appears in the 1658 *Defensio Prima*, Milton recalls his own heroic past when he was literally trained up to serve the nation, which, as an ideal, cultivates and exemplifies civic virtues founded on liberty. The philosophical, epic foundation for such a commonwealth had been laid, Milton testifies, by the poet-polemicist whose work is at once a self-defence, national defence, and exemplum. Thereupon he resolves to take on "still greater things" (CPW 4:537), joining "epic vision to revolutionary politics."[86] But while the composition of the national epic was underway, its polemical prequel, the *Defensio*, was burnt by the common hangman and the author incarcerated.[87]

Joseph Washington's 1692 translation of the 1651 treatise confirms its relevance for the Protestant nation in the years following the 1688 Revolution, when the parliamentary right to depose unlawful monarchs was sanctioned and celebrated.[88] One of the more famous owners of a copy of the *Defensio* during this era was Scottish clergyman Gilbert Burnet, a London resident since the year of Milton's death and a key player in the Glorious Revolution. Gilbert was a tolerationist who insisted, as John Locke had also, that liberty of conscience was founded on natural law as "one of the rights of human nature, antecedent to society, which no man could give up."[89] Having been embarrassed by his past obsequiousness to the Stuart monarchy, the Bishop had cut out of his 1692 copy of the *Defensio* the "Advertisement of the Reader,"[90] which features royalist works, including two defences of Charles I's *Eikon Basilike* (1649). The material evidence in possession of this serial tamperer attests to a desire to give Milton rather than the king the final word on the revolution in this treatise.

But Milton himself by no means settled on a definitive reading thereof. In fact, his reappraisals of the revolution's ideals inflect his *Defence*s of the English nation in the Interregnum. The revolution was designed to establish a climate for toleration, inquiry, and the hazarding of truth in a free nation, but Milton's frustrations over the failings of popular self-governance resulted in the subtle, muted transference of legislative and moral authority to an intellectual elite in the 1650s writings. The representation of elected parliamentarians by the regenerate is likewise at variance with the belief in the fundamental law of nature and rights of the majority. Evidenced here is the challenge Milton and his like-minded contemporaries faced in severing the articulation of universal truths from the contingent and particular character and inclinations of the people. That Milton reconstitutes nationhood in the *Defences* in terms of the *senior pars* demonstrates the double-faced nature and contrary impulses of writing the nation in the philosophical and literary afterlife of the revolution.

CHAPTER 4

Disestablishment: Divorce of Church and State

The theme of disestablishment is philosophically and texually bound up with that of law in Milton's articulations of the republican nation. In the Commonplace Book, "Respublica," "Amor in Patriam," and "Leges" constitute the opening entries of the third section of "Index Politicus." Like "Leges," the heading "Respublica" is followed by entries that offer examples of the advancement of liberty in the face of constraint. Among them is a pronouncement from William Camden, "*Inter religionem et rempub. divortium esse non potest*," which is set against a quotation from the politician and tolerationist Michel de L'Hôpital, the sagacious sixteenth-century French Chancellor ("*Galliae cancellarius prudentissimus*"). L'Hôpital, Milton notes, posits a model of toleration and coexistence: "Many, he says, can be citizens who are in no way Christians, and a man who is removed from the bosom of the Church does not cease to be a loyal citizen, and we can live peacefully with those who do not cherish the same faith."[1] Religious conformity and the union of church and state are not requisite for the establishment of a civil society or peaceful commonwealth. Milton's entry of the L'Hôpital reference from the *Historia* by de Thou (or Jacobus Augustus Thuanus) likely dates from the first half of the 1640s, when Milton began formulating principles of disestablishment, as indicated in Chapter 1, "Temple-worke." A formal defence thereof would, however, not appear until his later years when he produced *A Treatise of Civil Power in Ecclesiastical Causes* (1659), *Considerations Touching the Likeliest Means to Remove Hirelings Out of the Church* (1659), and eventually *Of True Religion, Hæresie, Schism, Toleration* (1673).

In recent decades, the critical reception of these treatises has consisted of a small number of studies that situate the works in relation to their historio-political and religious climates and questions of liberty, liberty of conscience, the polemics and poetics of election, and Milton's anti-popery campaigns. This tripartite chapter examines more specifically the conjunctions between toleration and nationhood in the late religious tracts and in related literature by Milton's contemporaries.[2] Milton proposes to the reconvened Rump in 1659 alternative models for the commonwealth, and, in so doing, aligns himself with other abolitionists and advocates of civil and religious liberties in his day.[3] *The Likeliest Means* refers to the appeals for liberty supported by "many thousands," who, Milton states, have the best interest of church and state in mind. Tracts like *Englands Settlement, Upon the Two Solid Foundations of the Peoples Civil and Religious Liberties. Collected out of Divers Petitions* likewise mention the flurry of popular pamphlets directed at Parliament at this time. Such petitions, declarations, and remonstrances include the 1659 *Humble Petition of thousands of well-affected Gentlemen*, printed for Livewell Chapman, who also published Milton's *The Likeliest Means*.[4] In contextualizing Milton's 1659 writings in terms of the pre-Restoration recall of the Rump, Austin Woolrych distinguishes Milton's interest in models of a commonwealth from his preoccupation with ecclesiastical polity.[5] Yet Milton's distinctive contributions to the contentious topical issues of church government, religious settlement, and the exercise of liberty of conscience were in fact central to his imagining of the true nation. Chiefly couched in political theology rather than political philosophy,[6] Milton's late pro-tolerationist tracts highlight these subjects while contesting obstructions to the "freedom" of the church, which forms the basis for an "undisturbd" Christian commonwealth (CPW 7:275, 276).

"Both spiritual power and civil"

Milton's commitment to a disestablishment position evolves gradually during his career and shifts in accordance with historico-political conditions and interventions. Initially Milton had associated the civil magistrate with "the full and perfet reformation of [God's] Church" (CPW 1:928). As early as in *Lycidas*, however, he vilified those herdsmen who served only "for their bellies' sake" in the speech of St. Peter, the prophetic significance of which Milton would highlight in the elegy's second printing, discussed in Chapter 1.[7] *The Reason of Church-Government Urg'd Against Prelaty* contains a passage arguing for separation (CPW 1:831–2) while championing popular participation in church government that would give the regenerate their allotted place "upon the tabernacle as the rightfull Clergy of Christ, a chosen generation, a royal Priesthood" (CPW 1:838). At the end of the 1640s, Milton inserts a paragraph in *Observations upon the Articles of Peace* in which he advocates for disestablishment in his attack on the

Scottish Presbytery.[8] "On the New Forcers of Conscience under the Long Parliament" (1646) anticipates *A Treatise of Civil Power* in imploring the Westminster Assembly to "abjure the civil sword / To force our consciences that Christ set free" (ll. 5–6). Along the same lines, "To the Lord General Cromwell" (1652), responding to the Committee for the Propagation of the Gospel, urges Cromwell to "[un]bind our souls" and, as mentioned in Chapter 3, "save free conscience from the paw / Of hireling wolves" (ll. 12, 13–4). *Pro Populo Anglicano Defensio Secunda* (1654) (CPW 4:678) and the 1652 Sonnet "To Sir Henry Vane the Younger" also take up the cause for disestablishment, with the latter work commending the statesman's awareness of "Both spiritual power and civil, what each means / What severs each" (ll. 10–11). Earlier in his *Doctrine and Discipline of Divorce*, Milton accorded magistrates – still identified as "Christian" at this point (CPW 2:239) – a role in upholding Mosaic Law on matters of divorce. By the end of the next decade, Milton would again question the relevance of Old Testament precedents, particularly as they were used to justify tithing and the magistrate's jurisdiction in ecclesiastical affairs. Although Milton's position on the injustices of the encroachment of civil power on ecclesiastical causes can be traced in the pre-1659 works, it was not fully formulated, as Balachandra Rajan reminded us, until Milton confronted the growing scope and complexity of the crisis over toleration.[9] In the year leading up to the Restoration, Milton also fused for a final time his political ambition to defend the "good Old Cause" of republicanism, as N. H. Keeble has cogently argued,[10] with the cause of reformation and toleration, which he channelled into the anti-Erastian sentiment of the 1659 tracts and thereafter into an aggressive assault on popery in *Of True Religion*.

In this chapter, Milton's theory of toleration in the pre- and early Restoration eras is evinced in a review of the relationship between spiritual and temporal authority as it informs his concept of nationhood. Applying a largely negative concept of toleration (a resistance to constraints), Milton's religious tracts challenge the forced legal, religious, and dogmatic *settlement* of a nation grounded in what he judged as a remnant of Deuteronomic law, upheld by English constitutional law that, as seen in the previous chapter, he rendered answerable to natural law. In conjunction with his polemics on toleration Milton's post-revolutionary tracts on disestablishment advance an alternative foundation, typological narrative, and conscience for a New Testament nation.[11]

The competing interests of the early modern nation included civil, religious, and political liberties, as well as shifting relations between state and church government that ranged from disestablishment to comprehension – an ecclesiastical settlement potentially accommodating divergent opinions on nonessential issues in a single institution.[12] The history of the interconnections between the temporal and religious powers originated in the Old Testament, as Milton and his contemporaries maintained and as the political and ecclesiastical documents of the early modern period underscored.[13] Reassessing Old Testament models of law, nationhood, and the ties between spiritual and secular authority, Milton's late religious tracts exploit the associations between Judaic-papist practices and monarchical tyranny that reformers and radicals first associated with Henry VIII's supremacy over the English Church. The battle had not ended with the demise of the monarchy. Despite the efforts by the mid-seventeenth century Interregnum government to support toleration by condoning practices and doctrines not in violation of fundamental truths deemed essential to salvation,[14] the founding of a national church through the promulgation of Erastian ecclesiology and the settlement of civil and ecclesiastical power was an integral part of Oliver Cromwell's religious and political policy. Consolidation, not mutual respect for difference, delineated national boundaries, and although religious and civil intolerance was often reproved, the terms of toleration were rigorously policed.

Milton's identification of the nation with the fight for freedom of conscience and with the resistance to a settled religion and nation-state not only prompted the production of *A Treatise of Civil Power* – the first tract he devoted to disestablishment – and *The Likeliest Means*, but it also laid the groundwork for the *Christian Doctrine*. His major theological treatise continues the work of distinguishing between ecclesiastical and civil power – the policy of the state towards religious dissent and the authority of the civil magistrate (CPW 6:611–13). At the same time, the writing of the nation entailed for Milton disarming anti-tolerationists who countered the advancement of civil and religious liberties that he envisioned as the building blocks for a free commonwealth. Among the many influential anti-tolerationist documents were the *Humble Petition and Advice* (1657), which demanded a public declaration of faith as confirmation of one's fitness for "any Civill Trust, Imployment or Promotion in these Nations"; the 1658 *Savoy Declaration of Faith and Order* – a settlement between moderate Independents and Presbyterians, which promoted liberty of conscience while granting authority in religious matters to civil magistrates – and the Westminster Assembly's *Confession of Faith*, on which the *Savoy Declaration* drew and which in April 1659 again became the official "public profession of the nation."[15] In *The Likeliest Means*, Milton adds to this repertoire the writings of the indefatigable Presbyterian William Prynne, who grounds his pro-tithing pronouncements in Old Testament traditions, and the work of the Anglican Henry Spelman, who uses the weight of constitutional history to support his agenda. Primacy of conscience led Milton in the religious tracts to refute Prynne and Spelman and to resituate the controversy over tithing in terms of his views on disestablishment, nationhood, and the conditions for toleration.

Occupying different positions on the scale of toleration, the writers of the nation in Milton's day turned specifically to questions of church–state relations and the magistrate's authority. While preaching before the House of Commons in May 1647, Thomas Case decried liberty of conscience on the basis that, set loose from civil power and governmental jurisdiction, it mutates into licentiousness, "improv[ing] it self into *liberty of estates*, and *liberty* of *houses*, and *liberty* of *wives*."[16] In stark contrast, Roger Williams, who divorces church and state in a manner unprecedented at the time, advocates wide toleration and presses for disestablishment. In *Hireling Ministry None of Christs*, Williams protests against any incursion of the state into spiritual affairs by differentiating between nation-states and the elect nation: "The body of a civill State or Nation, and the elect or chosen of God out of each Nation, must be rightly distinguished."[17] Quaker minister Samuel Fisher recommends in *Christianismus Redivivus* (1655) that magistrates protect all men, "without respect to their Religions, whether true or false" and tolerate all whose practice of their principles "is not directly destructive to the true Religion … and safety of the Common-wealth."[18] Among the anti-Baptists whose arguments Fisher refutes is Stephen Marshall, the moderate Presbyterian known to Milton as a Smectymnuuan (Chapter 1). *The Power of the Civil Magistrate*, a posthumous sermon by Marshall, ascribes the moral well-being of the nation to the rule of magistrates on the basis of Isaiah 60:12, "*For the Nation and Kingdome that will not serve thee, shall perish; yea those Nations shall be utterly wasted.*" Quoting the Congregationalist Divine, John Norton (the American Ipswich minister), Giles Firmin, the former New Englander and publisher of *The Power of the Civil Magistrate*, concedes: "It is true what Learned Mr. *Norton* saith, *to Tolerate all things, and tolerate nothing, are both intolerable.*" Applying the early modern definition of toleration as limited permission granted by a temporal authority, Firmin instructs the authorities who legislate the terms of religious toleration to specify "*what they will NOT Tolerate.*" If they fail to delimit the terms of toleration or to "make good fences about the Vitals of Religion," the arising errors and heresies will inevitably endanger the national body.[19]

Central to the debate on toleration was the anatomy of the commonwealth itself, the conventional view of which the anti-tolerationist
English cleric Robert South endorsed and promoted in his illustration
of the relationship between the civil state and ecclesiastical realm: "There
is a great Analogy between the Body Natural and Politick; in which the
Ecclesiastical or Spiritual part, justly supplyes the part of the soul; and
the violent separation of this from the other ... leaves the Body of the
Commonwealth a carcass, noysom, and exposed to be devoured by Birds
of Prey."[20] Particular Baptist Thomas Collier in *The Decision & Clearing of
the great Point now in Controversie* (1659) insisted by contrast that liberty
involves "untwist[ing]" the knot of church and state and resisting religious
settlement.[21] Milton more than agrees; transferring his argument about
divorce from *Tetrachordon* that it is "detestable to joyne that ... which
God hath put asunder" (CPW 2:651) to the question of the magistrate's
jurisdiction, Milton states in *A Treatise of Civil Power*: "If church and state
shall be made one flesh again as under the law, let it be withall considerd,
that God who then joind them hath now severd them" (CPW 7:260).
Indeed, the "mis-yoking" of church and state proves monstrous. In *The
Likeliest Means*, Milton portrays a state-dominated church as a "political head on an ecclesiastical bodie"; the miscreant that emerges is further
transformed "by such heterogeneal, such incestuous conjunction ... into a
beast of many heads and many horns" (CPW 7:308).

Implied in the argument for disestablishment that Milton puts forth
is a new model of the Reformed church. Chapter 1 of this book analysed the relationship between the church and the imagined early modern
nation, which, however, Milton himself had started to reassess by the mid
1640s. The dissenters who advocated church reform and whose example
Milton invokes had conceived of the countercultural, anti-establishment
New Testament community as "an *ecclesia* called out from among the
nations, not a community coterminous with national populations."[22] In
this respect as well, the proponents of the New Testament church challenged the idea of a national church. In his 1650s polemics on the history
and traditions of ecclesiastical polity, Milton insisted on the distinction
between the Jewish temple and the Christian church, a distinction reinforced by the reference to the abrogation of the prescriptive Law of Moses
and the destruction of the temple (CPW 7:289). The true church, unlike
that of the Jews with its "many incomplete synagogues" (CPW 7:292), is
independent of a national identity, to which Milton had still subscribed in
the antiprelatical tracts. In this pre-Restoration moment, the multifarious
corporate Protestant identity Milton imagines differs from the national

church and settled nation-state: "the Christian church is universal; not ti'd to nation, dioces or parish, but consist[s] of many particular churches complete in themselves" as well as by "many particular congregations, subject to many changes" (CPW 7:291–92, 308). As he states in his *Christian Doctrine*, the New Israel, unlike the national or universal church in ancient Israel, features "no national church [but rather] ... a great number of particular churches, each absolute in itself and equal to the others in divine right, and power. These, like similar and homogenous components, joined together by a bond of mutual equality, form a single, catholic church" (CPW 6:602–3). Earlier in the *Christian Doctrine*, Milton points out that the mystical body of Christ that constitutes the church defies temporal and "spatial considerations" insofar as it encompasses people from all times and places (CPW 6:500). The single, catholic church Milton in turn envisages is a product of accommodation and amalgamation, but at the expense of the people who supplied the original model thereof, namely the ancient Israelites, whose commitment to a national church disqualifies them from inclusion in the universal church.

The early forms of English nationhood were derived from a biblical, religious nationalism, one brought about by the "self-identification" of the English people with the Israelites of the Old Testament.[23] But in championing disestablishment, radical tolerationists of Milton's day proposed models based on principles of nature and natural law and resistant to any incursion of civil authorities into ecclesiastical affairs, especially as justified by Mosaic Law. Challenging the applicability of the Israel parallel to the primitive church and present-day church in a larger argument that anatomizes Prynne's proposal for an episcopal government and a national Presbyterian Church, the author of *Certaine briefe Observations and Antiquaeries* (1644) determines that "The Nationall Church of the Jewes cannot be a patterne for us now, because the covenant of the Gospell is not made with any one particular Nation, as with the Jewes, but to all persons that embrace the Gospell." Henry Robinson and Henry Burton likewise observe that "in all the New Testament you finde no Nationall Churches, but severall Independent ones."[24] Rehearsing the premises he outlined in an earlier treatise, Roger Williams concludes in the aforementioned *Hirelings Ministry* that the "The *Civill* state of the *Nations* ... cannot (Christianly) be called *Christian States*, after the patterne of that holy and typical Land of *Canaan*, which I have proved at large in the *Bloudy Tenent*, to be a *Non-such*" or, as Milton judges in *The Likeliest Means*, God "hath now alienated that holy land."[25] The concepts of Protestant nationhood, citizenship, and elect nationalism that distinguish Milton's 1659 religious tracts are founded on a reformulation of the Old–New Israel parallel.

The Anti-Tithe Controversy

Addressed to Richard Cromwell's parliament and repudiating the use of civil power in ecclesiastical causes, *A Treatise of Civil Power* (1659) is an expression and extension of Milton's argument for disestablishment. The service he undertook for his country, notably his censure of Salmasius in *Pro Populo Anglicano Defensio*, is redirected in his tirade against "*Erastus* and state-tyranie over the church" (CPW 7:252). In *A Treatise of Civil Power*, he pleads for Christian liberty – the freedom won from the bondage of the law and the birthright enjoyed by Christians (CPW 7:262; 265) – as distinct from civil liberty, the subject of an earlier discourse (CPW 7:240). Without the separation of civil from religious power, true religion will decay and be overthrown (CPW 7:240). In this tract, which foregrounds religious and philosophical over civil discourses, conscience is described as serving the cause of religion in being answerable to the law of God alone, which trumps human law (CPW 7:242).

Given the threats to toleration, Milton's appeals are often rooted as much in a negative toleration as in an embrace of heterodoxy and involve an assault on error. Thus he admonishes false prophets through "instant and powerfull demonstration to the contrarie; by opposing truth to error, no unequal match" (CPW 7:261) and positions "the right of Christian and evangelic liberty" in contradistinction to "all those pretended consequences of license and confusion" (CPW 7:270). His earlier polemics against custom and conformity are here directed at the settlement of religion by civil power as justified by Old Testament practices. Whereas Old Israel "had a commonwealth by [Moses] deliverd them, incorporated with a national church … so as that the church might be calld a commonwealth and the whole commonwealth a church," the same, Milton asserts, cannot be said of the Christian church "deliverd without the help of magistrates, yea in the midst of thir opposition" (CPW 7:251). Yet the Protestant reformers who adopted the Old Testament model of governance correspondingly proposed the establishment of a national, state church. John Coffey explains that radical tolerationists considered the magisterial reformers' adherence to Old Testament laws a "Judaizing" practice.[26] In *The Likeliest Means*, Milton likewise remarks that the primitive church (until the time of Constantine) did not practise tithing, although "error … miserably Judaiz'd the church" through the reinstatement of the trappings of "priests, altars and oblations" (CPW 7:290). As discussed in Chapter 1 of this book, Milton traced the origins of episcopacy in *Of Reformation Touching Church-Government*, to the forced union of church and state under Constantine (CPW 1:576–7).

As he now advances his argument in *A Treatise of Civil Power*, Milton outlines his objections to the office of the magistrates and their acts of compulsion on the basis that the true religion is founded on charity (*caritas*) "or the love of God and our neighbour, no way to be forc'd, yet the fufilling of the whole law" (CPW 7:256). He thus denounces Deuteronomic laws while nevertheless equating freedom from the law with the law's fulfilment.[27] Restraint of conscience violates an active faith, the principle of toleration, and the oft-rehearsed Pauline dictum from Romans 13:1, which Milton recites as "*Let every soul be subject to the higher powers*" (CPW 7:250), and which, as discussed in Chapter 3, "Natural Law," was commonly invoked by defenders of divine right like Salmasius. Here Milton appropriates the scriptural command for his defence of liberty of conscience. Those who believe that the gospel message is threatened unless it be propped up or "enacted and settled, as they call it, by the state, a statute or a state-religion" fail to understand that obedience cannot be legislated by "thir setled confession" (CPW 7:257–8). Milton's multiple derisive references to "settling" call to mind the *Humble Petition and Advice*, a work that prompted his rebuke of the petitioners' plea that God use Cromwell and the army "in the Setling and Securing [of] our Liberties."[28] Upon chastising the magistrates who insist on settling religion, Milton reclaims settlement for each reasoning individual and "each particular church by perswasive and spiritual means within itself" (CPW 7:271). Membership in the true church is dependent upon the exercise of Christian liberty, defined as a birthright (CPW 7:262; 265) and possible only in a culture of toleration.[29] In turn, Milton presents scriptural proofs that underscore the right to religious freedom by relegating authority to God: Rom. 14.6, Gal. 4.10; Coloss. 2.16, Acts 10.15; Gal 5.13, etc. (CPW 7:263). Scriptural exegesis, distinctions between Christian birthright and state citizenship, and critical engagements with state-issued declarations and legislation underwrite Milton's Christian nation.

Hotly contested in the press and pulpit of the day, the rights of subjects, the authority of magistrates, and the theories of and policies on establishment fuelled controversies over the bounds of toleration in the pre-Restoration nation. Marshall's aforementioned *Power of the Civil Magistrate* (1657) ascribes the health of the nation to the magistrates' role: "They are to look to the preservation and restauration of Religion: as

the Physitian either aimes at the preservation, or restauration of health."
Correspondingly, magistrates are morally and legally entitled to what he
calls "publique provisions" that include "Glebes, Tythes, and such publike
stipendia already setled by law."[30] Giles Firmin, who takes the liberty of
glossing Marshall's sermon, cites "*Deut.* 17:18. a text commonly brought
to prove that the Magistrate is *keeper of both Tables*" and insists that "The
Duties of the second table [are] the sinews of Commonwealths" – the second table constituting commandments 6–10 and prohibiting social and
civil transgressions.[31] Milton, by contrast, reminds Parliament of the differences between the state of religion under the gospel and under the law
(CPW 7:259). In the fourth section of *A Treatise of Civil Power*, which
prohibits compulsion (CPW 7:265), he thus rejects the teaching that the
magistrate is "*custos utriusque tabulæ*, keeper of both tables" (CPW 7:271).
The jurisdiction of civil authorities does not extend to what Milton refers
to as the "inward man" or to conscience or religion, on which he bases
his arguments for tolerance (CPW 7:255). Milton, however, is less radical than Roger Williams in still conceding a function for magistrates as
civil authorities, specifically in the exorcising of a politicized popery and
idolatry.

The fight for toleration and disestablishment and the corresponding
resistance to the settlement of the national church and ministry take the
form of an anti-tithe argument in the sequel to *A Treatise of Civil Power*. As
mentioned at the outset of this chapter, *Considerations Touching the Likeliest
Means to Remove Hirelings* was published by Livewell Chapman, who also
issued petitions in support of the anti-tithe movement[32] and would at his
peril publish the first edition of the *Readie and Easie Way*. *The Likeliest
Means* appeared in August 1659 following Richard Cromwell's abdication
and the reconstitution of the Long Parliament, the Rump, when the ethical and legal question of tithing again came to the fore in the disputes
over church–state relations. That the *Likeliest Means* is a response to the
crises over toleration is evidenced in a reminder to Milton by a Hartlib
circle member, Moses Wall, about Milton's own complaints on "the Non-
progressency of the nation, and of its retrograde Motion of late, in Liberty
and Spiritual Truths." Wall urges Milton to fulfill the promise made in
A Treatise of Civil Power to write a companion treatise on the injustices
of hire in the church, on the assumption that economic reforms were
most needed to alleviate oppression and further national progress. Fearing
that England's leaders may "lead us back to Egypt," he recommends the
"improving of oᵣ native Comodities, as our manufacturers ...[which] wold
give the body of the nation a comfortable Subsistence and ... breaking

that cursed yoak of Tythes wold much help y^{r}to."^{33} Although commercial interests and justifications were, along with the biblical, legal, and historically based arguments, central to the anti-tithe movement, Milton steers clear of economic concerns. Instead, he broaches the question of toleration in terms of the difference between Old and New Testament models of nationhood and the degree of liberty enjoyed by the subjects thereof. As the Old Israelites had subjected themselves to Egypt, so are the New Israelites enslaved by tithing, Milton judges. John Hale recognizes that Milton in 1659 "could expect his fellow religionists to resent the return to an 'Egypt' of monarchy, bishops, and tithing." Accordingly, the "sincere tolerationist" dismissed the prospect of reserving the designation of "New Israel" for England exclusively. Hale is also justified in noting that for Milton, disestablishment itself is "too moderate a doctrine to affirm the only parallel."^{34} Nevertheless, the Israel–England analogy remains relevant for Milton, although from here on it is used to illustrate how much the intolerant, backsliding English had deviated from their original peculiar status and pattern of the ideal commonwealth.^{35}

Given the inflexible state policy on the practice, Milton resigns himself to proposing ways of limiting the number of hirelings in order that hire in the church may be rendered "least dangerous" (CPW 7:280). Milton's argument is further founded on negative toleration, as underscored by its three parts, in which he contests the recompense due to church-ministers, then considers the question of who is responsible for the maintenance of ministers, and finally reviews the administration of the recompense. His strategy throughout involves driving a wedge between the model of the national church based on an Old Testament type and the Christian community of the New Testament. Present-day ministers "being neither priests nor Levites" have no right to exact taxes, Milton judges, thus invalidating the Mosiac law that awarded a tithe or tenth to the Levites (CPW 7:284). Reproaching those contemporaries who still support "old Papistical tithes" and the "Judaical or ceremonial law" that licenses tithing, Milton invokes gospel law, which is founded not on Mosaic law, particular to Israel, but on the principle of "moral, and general equitie, given us instead: 1 *Cor.* 9. 13, 14" (CPW 7:289). Rather than sanctioning a legal right to tithes, gospel equity establishes "a rule of common equitie" designed to regulate the practices of hire in the church (CPW 7:290).

Anti-tithe advocates like Milton drew on jurist John Selden's 1618 history of English law and natural law, *The History of Tithes. That is, the Practice of Payment of Them*, which argued against the clergy's claim that tithing was ordained by *jure divino*, thus by extension separating ecclesiastical from state law. At the same time that Milton leans on Selden's legal history, he channels his energies into discrediting historically rooted arguments for tithing which influenced state policy on the subject. Among the pro-tithe defences was Spelman's 1639 *Concilia, Decreta, Leges, Constitutiones, in re Ecclesiarum Orbis Britannici*, which grounds tithing practices in a period beginning with pre-Conquest Britain. Further, Milton refutes Prynne's 1653 *A Gospel Plea ... for the Ancient Settled Maintenance and Tithes* and his 1659 *Ten Considerable Quaeries about Tithes*, which appeared in the month he began composing *The Likeliest Means*. Milton proceeds by challenging justifications for tithing grounded in the laws of Saxons and kings whose ancient constitutions date back to Athelstan (CPW 7:294). He continues by exposing the fallacies of "our new reformed English presbyterian divines" who betray the Reformation by ransacking and contorting the authorities they reference – Mosaic laws and "Romish" canon law – in order to glut "a covetous clergie" (CPW 7:295).

Prynne, who in 1653 uses Spelman as an authority to argue that the maintenance of the ministers was instituted by religious Christian kings and by divine and civil right, accuses anti-tithe supporters of betraying the public faith and the nation-state. The motives of the opposition, he determines, proceed not from matters of conscience but from a "designe to subvert and ruine our Ministers, Church and Religion" and thereby "our Nation."[36] He complains further that these "Anabaptists" along with their popish supporters attack tithing as "Jewish and Antichristian." To illustrate his point, Prynne cites a "new Voice from the Alehouses" by the aforementioned John Canne, whose *Second Voyce from the Temple* appeared in August 1653.[37] *A Second Voyce* locates the origins of tithing in popery and decries the present-day vesting of tithing in ecclesiastical officials by English common law.[38] "To retein tythes, is to keepe up and give honour to the Jewish shadowes, which by Christs death were taken away,"[39] Canne asserts, in line with those who condemned tithing in support of the New Testament ascendancy over the Old. In his characteristically bombastic retort that features Canne as one of many targets, Prynne brands the opposition as treacherous to the nation. The Pope too, Prynne warns, hopes "to see England perfectly reduced to her former obedience to the See of Rome"; he and his home-grown supporters, the "professed Enemies of our Church, Religion, Nation," must be prevented from sowing their "seeds of ruine and desolation amongst us."[40] That Prynne's indictment of Canne might be extended to Milton is suggested by Prynne's attack, several months before the publication of *The Likeliest Means*, on "Melton," whose seditious writings condoned "the very highest, worst treasonablest ... tenents," including the "subverting of Kingdoms," "the altering of all setled Laws," and the breaching of the commandments of the second table.[41]

In *A Treatise of Civil Power*, Milton in contrast attributes national upheaval to the betrayal of national election. Peculiar status becomes for him not a confirmation of England's Old Testament nationalism but a condition for the health of the true church comprised of voluntary members in a New Testament covenant (CPW 7:245). In *The Likeliest Means*, the argument for the establishment of the new covenant is overshadowed by an emphasis on the abrogation of the Mosaic Law. National election is thus negatively defined as a rejection of tithes and Old Testament types: "1 *Pet.* 2.5 signifying the Christian true and *holy priesthood, to offer up spiritual sacrifice*; it follows hence, that we are now justly exempt from paying tithes, to any who claim from *Aaron*, since that priesthood is in us now real, which in him was but a shaddow" (CPW 7:283). Peter razes the social and ecclesiastical hierarchy: "we [are] now under Christ a royal priesthood, 1 *Pet.* 2.9, as we are coheirs, kings and priests with him" (CPW 7:286), a reference that underscores the principle of New Testament equity. However, that chosen status has been misappropriated ever since the days of the early Church by ministers who "affected to be calld a clergie" and who become "a peculiar tribe of levites, a partie, a distinct order in [and at the expense of] the commonwealth" (CPW 7:319). The present-day English commonwealth has been defiled by the compulsion of hirelings, who falsely declare "that if ye settle not our maintenance by law, farwell the gospel" (CPW 7:318). By failing to exercise its birthright and Christian liberty, the nation at large has become "as lay-papists are to their priests" (CPW 7:320), Milton laments, as he confronts the prospect of the imminent settlement of the church and state.

Debates on the terms of toleration and national stability continued through the eve of the Restoration. Parliament declared a fast day to appease a God outraged by the heresies that were plaguing the kingdom and by the civil magistrates' failure to enforce the law.[42] In contrast, *Englands Settlement, Upon the Two Solid Foundations*, attributed the divine wrath visited upon the nation to intolerance, compulsion, and the violation of religious and civil liberties: "*foul Tyranny* or Coercive power over Mens Consciences, is the principall sin that has drawn down these judgements from Heaven."[43] The settling of the state demands the securing of "just Civil Liberty," which has, however, been obstructed by the installation of the magistrate, by the miscarriage of justice resulting in many unwarranted imprisonments, and by excessive taxation.[44] The other pillar

upon which the nation rests according to *Englands Settlement* is "spirituall liberty," protected by "an innocent Toleration," or an "in-offensive
Toleration in matters of Religion."[45] A nation-state that contravenes the
terms of spiritual liberty is in danger of collapse. The author acknowledges
Henry Vane, H. S. (Henry Stubbe), and the aforementioned Thomas
Collier, whose argument for opposing the office of the magistrate is
grounded in the repeal of the Old Testament model of a national church
and, correspondingly, of "Priesthood-government, and that whole minis-
tration," which he judges as equally oppressive.[46]

Englands settlement identifies the "Good old cause" as that of toleration,
as do George Bishop in *Mene Tekel* and the physician and philosopher
Henry Stubbe, disciple of Selden and author of various 1659 tracts, including *The Common-wealth of Israel* and *An Essay in Defence of the Good Old
Cause*.[47] The latter is a meticulous historical and philosophical survey in
which civil and spiritual liberty is hailed as the "GOOD old cause" and in
which "all *true power*" is said to be derived from the people.[48] Containing
transcriptions from Selden's *De Jure Naturali et Gentium juxta Disciplinam
Ebraeorum* (see Chapter 6, "Exogamy"), Stubbe's *Essay* discusses religious
toleration among Romans and Hebrews and, in turn, urges "an universal Toleration … the basis upon which our Common-wealth stands."[49]
Having been invited to comment on the work by Stubbe, John Locke
only really took exception to Stubbe's proposal for toleration for Roman
Catholics.[50] There is yet further evidence that Stubbe's terms of toleration
are less restrictive and his notions of popular sovereignty considerably more
inclusive than Milton's. The pre-Conquest narrative of popular sovereignty
in the *Essay in Defence of the Good Old Cause* reaches back to emperors like
Constantine, who is shown to have tolerated heathens.[51] Despite arguing
that the office of the civil magistrate has no basis in biblical history, the life
of the primitive church, or natural law, Stubbe proposes coexistence with
a present-day episcopacy prepared to condone freedom of conscience and
also with Catholics loyal to England rather than Rome.[52]

Throughout Stubbe's tracts, the exercise of coercion over conscience is
a bad old cause, one that disqualifies the oppressor from the category of
the "people." The author of *Englands Settlement* designates religious persecution as "a Bad new Cause," one *not even* practised by Turks.[53] Milton
likewise frames the question of toleration in terms of negatively evinced
models of the nation: Erastians who support the exercise of state power
over ecclesiastical matters and cases of conscience betray their nation and,
by their example, rightly incur the judgement of foreigners, notably Turks,
about compulsion and abuses of liberty by the English (CPW 7:318).

The competition over the conditions and dangers of toleration generated an immediate and blunt retort to *Englands Settlement*, titled *Englands Settlement Mistaken*, which accuses the author of the former of inciting sedition. The confuter insists that magistrates be charged with the responsibility of permitting only the true religion to be practised, given that diversity in religion will "unsettle the peace of the nation."[54] Because there is only one true religion, dissent is intolerable. Implied disputations between Erastians and proponents of disestablishment are integrated into both of Milton's 1659 religious tracts, with the exchange in *A Treatise of Civil Power* focused primarily on countering the arsenal of biblical support for Erastian arguments and that in *The Likeliest Means* on the practice by magistrates of exacting fees for weddings and funerals (CPW 7:298–99). As for generating actual dialogues, there is little evidence that *The Likeliest Means* or its prequel had any impact in its day, although James Harrington refutes some of its key tenets in contending that a commonwealth, in conjunction with its Old Testament type, must have a national religion, tithes, and an endowed clergy in order to guarantee liberty of conscience.[55] On the eve of the Restoration, Harrington maintained the inseparability of civil and religious liberty or liberty of conscience as the basis for national security.[56]

Of True Religion

The Restoration saw the re-establishment of the Church of England, the reinstatement of the Book of Common Prayer, and the reinforcement of the civil magistrate's role in securing obedience to the law and the ecclesiastical hierarchy. In 1662, the Commons legislated outside of monarchic jurisdiction adherence to the Act of Uniformity that identified "the settling of peace in this nation" with "the honour of our religion and propagation thereof."[57] The discourses of uniformity served as sutures for a Restoration nation resistant to policies on religious toleration and accommodation. Roger L'Estrange, Surveyor of the Press, maintained in his 1663 *Toleration discuss'd* that religious union was "the Ciment" that bound the religious and civic societies together; "Take That away, and the Parts drop from the Body," he warns. "Uniformity if it were carefully maintained, and diligently looked after," as Thomas Tomkins declared several years later, would restore the nation's ancient unity.[58] In February 1668, Parliament voted to enforce laws against nonconformists to prevent anyone from bringing an act for comprehension or indulgence before the House. A comprehension bill was, however, in great demand by a majority, remarked Samuel Pepys at the time.[59] In the same year, Charles II, who was again approached about the matter, promised to fight for the comprehension of nonconformists but failed in those efforts.[60] Having been in effect between 1644 and 1667, the Conventicles Act was renewed in 1670.

The argument for ecclesiastical settlement was tied to the question of citizenship and national loyalty. In 1669, Samuel Parker justified the "severe government over men's consciences and Religious perswasions" on the basis of national order, security and prosperity.[61] Moderate Independents including John Owen, Philip Nye, and John Humfrey proposed a balance between the subject's liberties and the civil and ecclesiastical jurisdiction of magistrates.[62] Committed to his disestablishment position, Milton persists in advocating a divorce between temporal and spiritual power, although his last major prose tract, *Of True Religion, Hæresie, Schism, Toleration* (1673) redraws the battle lines through conciliatory maneuvers that include a profession of allegiance to the universally held tenets of the "true Religion" (CPW 8:420). The pamphlet further seeks to galvanize the Protestant community by extending the terms of toleration, liberty of conscience, and nationhood to nonconformists and by waging an anti-popery campaign.[63]

In the early years of the 1670s, the controversy over toleration reached another climax: Shortly before the outbreak of the Third Anglo-Dutch War in which the King allied himself with France, Charles issued the 15 March 1672 Declaration of Indulgence, the first such declaration having failed a decade beforehand (26 December 1662). Citing the futility of the twelve-year-long suppression of religious dissent, the King's Declaration called for the suspension of "Penal Laws in matters Ecclesiastical, against whatsoever sort of Non-Conformists or Recusants." The 1672 Declaration was designed for "Quieting the Minds of Our good Subjects ... for Inviting Strangers in this Conjuncture, to come and Live under Us, and for the better Encouragement of all to a Chearful following of their Trade and Callings." Although encouraged by the prospect of comprehension, Nonconformists were, like Church of England authorities themselves, alarmed and outraged by the King's proposed summoning of "Strangers in this Conjuncture," viewed as tantamount to welcoming "French caterpillars ... and swarmes of Romish locusts."[64]

Finally unacceptable for its indulgence of Catholics, the Declaration was voted down by the Parliament, which still continued to navigate the minefield of accommodation for nonconforming Protestants. The debates resulted in the implementation of the 1673 "Test Act," which came into law on 29 March. The Act was intended to protect the state, quiet the minds of the king's "good subjects," and enforce uniformity by requiring office holders to demonstrate publicly their allegiance to the Established Church, thus shutting out Catholics and secondarily nonconformists.[65] Milton stepped into the fray, seeking to reconcile the interests of the state with those of the Protestant coalition he conceptualized as the nation while reacting to the incursion of civil power in ecclesiastical causes. In *Of True Religion*, Milton decries Anglican policies toward Nonconformists, which violate liberty of conscience, an offence against "the Clemency of the Gospel, more then what appertains to the security of the State" (CPW 8:431). His appeal for toleration in the tract is in turn built on biblically grounded claims of conscience (CPW 8:423), and takes the form of a rhetorically modulated stance on the jurisdiction of magistrates and an assault on popery, "the greatest Heresie" (CPW 8:421).

For much of his career, Milton classified many of his published views as unorthodox or at odds with convention and he derided the "irrational bigots" who branded as heretical any views that departed from their conventional beliefs.[66] In *Of True Religion*, he balances occurrences of "true" with "heretical" to register rhetorically a clash of opposites. Milton also introduces a nuanced (latitudinarian) distinction between error and heresy, the former being an involuntary – and thus not outright condemnable – deviation from scriptural truths. In contrast, heresy, etymologically derived from the Latin *haeresis* and the Greek *hairesis* (choice), represents for Milton a conscious rejection of the Word of God. In *Of True Religion*, the different definitions of error and heresy are used to distinguish Nonconformity and popery. Error is heretical only when aligned with popery, which is itself synonymous with "heresy." The Papist and popery are thus characterized by the juxtaposed epithets *"Mother of Error, School of Heresie."* Only heretics would denounce the sectarians as heretical, and in so doing, they imitate the papists (CPW 8:423). In accordance with the "main Principles of true Religion" and "the Rule of true Religion," the Papist is consigned to the outer bounds of a civil Protestant nation (CPW 8:420). Janel Mueller rightly observes that Milton in *Of True Religion* "jettisoned" his persistent efforts to redeem the concept of heresy and surrendered to "the influential precedent of strongly opposed opinion in Pauline and post-Pauline Christianity" that supported the mutual exclusivity of heresy and the universal Christian church.[67]

Citing a politicised popery as the worst example of the enmeshing of secular and religious power, Milton conceded to the magistrates a role in resisting the Roman authority as a national threat: "supported mainly by a civil, and, except in *Rome*, by a forein power," Catholicism is "justly

therfore to be suspected, not tolerated by the magistrate of another countrey," Milton stated in *A Treatise of Civil Power* (CPW 7:254). In *Of True
Religion*, magistrates are likewise assigned the task of uprooting popery,
given the danger it poses to king and parliament, as evidenced during the
repeatedly invoked Gunpowder Plot. "I submit . . . to the consideration of
all Magistrates" the conditions for tolerating Catholics, Milton declares.
As for the matter of condoning the practice of Catholicism, I answer in
the negative, Milton adds; "Toleration is either public or private; and
the exercise of their Religion, as far as it is Idolatrous, can be tolerated
neither way" (CPW 8:430). The intensified hostility to Catholicism in
Milton's Restoration treatise is apparent in the differences between this
statement and his earlier remarks on the policing of Catholicism: "a magistrate can hardly err in prohibiting and quite removing at least the publick and scandalous use" of idols (CPW 7:254–5). In *Of True Religion*,
papists have relinquished their right not only to public but also private
worship because in both spheres, they have indentured themselves to
external, foreign authorities. Milton simultaneously seizes the opportunity to decry Charles II's 1672 indulgence of Catholics "in the common
Exemption from the execution of the Penal Laws, and the Exercise of
their Worship in their private Houses."[68] Translating what he calls "state-
tyranie" in *A Treatise* (CPW 7:252) into an attack on popery in *Of True
Religion*, for which he imagined nationwide support, Milton reins in toleration as a tactical manoeuvre to argue from a position of authority as
an English Protestant nationalist.

A contrast between the New Testament church and the Jewish
state church becomes the basis for the distinction between a catholic
Protestantism and a parochial Roman principality: "Catholic in Greek
signifies universal: and the Christian Church was so call'd, as consisting of
all Nations to whom the Gospel was to be preach't, in contradistinction to
the Jewish Church, which consisted for the most part of Jews only" (CPW
8:422). In the case of *Of True Religion*, the universality of the Christian
Church is thus specifically established through its opposition to "the common adversary" (CPW 8:420) and through its differences from Judaism,
which is what this tract shares with the other late religious writings as well
as with the early antiepiscopal treatises.

Among the expressions of comprehension and solidarity in *Of True
Religion* are appeals to a shared Protestant faith and concessions to a
theological reductionism that identifies commonalities among the co-
religious and that institutionalizes the faith.[69] Milton's uncharacteristic
and surprising defence of the Church of England's Articles of Religion

(CPW 8:419) – which contrasts with his rebutting of scriptural proofs in the Articles' previous dogmatic and confessional incarnations – can be explained by his efforts to align nonconformist religious principles with the national religion largely by contrasting them with Catholic dogma. Recourse to scripture and scriptural authorities provides the platform from which he lashes out at popery and pleads for toleration of the sects: "Another means to abate Popery arises from the constant reading of Scripture, wherein Believers who agree in the main, are every where exhorted to mutual forbearance and charity one towards the other, though dissenting in some opinions" (CPW 8:435). Milton reminds his readers in *Of True Religion* that "Our Church ... hath proposd [the Bible] to all men, and to this end translated it into English" (CPW 8:434), an extension of his declaration in *The Likeliest Means* that Protestantism "make[s] more easie the attainment of Christian religion by the meanest: the entire scripture translated into English with plenty of notes" (CPW 7:304). His diatribe in *The Likeliest Means* (CPW 7:302, 320) against Protestants who fail to practise an active faith is likewise registered in *Of True Religion*, in which the remissness of such "heretick[s] in the truth" (*Areopagitica*, CPW 2:543) has national implications and consequences: complacency, subservience, and scriptural ignorance which supports popery threaten to ruin the Reformation nation as a moral and political entity (CPW 8:435).

What are the outer limits of toleration for Protestants? "If it be askt how far they should be tolerated? I answer doubtless equally, as being all Protestants ... For if the *French* and *Polonian* Protestants injoy all this liberty among Papists [of public speaking, writing, and printing], much more may a Protestant justly expect it among Protestants" (CPW 8:426–7). Toleration is commanded by the gospel, Milton avers, and yet as he concedes at the heart of his pamphlet, "some times here among us, the one persecutes the other upon every slight Pretence" (CPW 8:427). An overview of policies and practices on toleration gives way to an exhortation to purge popery among the natives, with the weight of judgement falling on English Protestant intolerance and a compromised national election: "it is a general complaint that this Nation of late years, is grown more numerously and excessively vitious .... no wonder if Popery also grow a pace" (CPW 8:438–9). "[T]he heaviest of all Gods Judgements, Popery" (CPW 8:440), Milton prophesies, will be visited upon the nation for its moral degeneracy, exacerbated by the intrusion of state authority into ecclesiastical causes.

This chapter has sought to assess the competing and correspondent relationships of toleration and nationhood in the pre- and early Restoration years, as negotiated in Milton's late religious tracts. At a time when the majority supported establishment and the reinstatement of a national religion, Milton upheld a minority, oppositional position that rendered Christianity and national election discontinuous with a Jewish past. The marriage of crown and church had once been imaginable when the Church constituted the nation in Hebrew society (CPW 7:292) and when the civil magistrate could ensure the "reformation of his Church" (CPW 1:928). But disestablishment emerged as the only conscionable solution in a climate of intolerance and corruption. Justification for disestablishment had less to do with complaints about the Judaizing practices of officials – which reformers nevertheless cited since the days of John Foxe – than with the betrayal of elect nationalism.

The sinews for the regenerate commonwealth Milton imagines are reasoned, biblically based arguments founded on New Testament values, gospel equity, and freedom of conscience and expressed in the vernacular in a consciously unadorned style. In turn, Milton identifies the subject and architect of the nation as answerable to spiritual authority independent of temporal power. Furthermore, in the midst of the crises over toleration, he envisages a disembodied nation in contradistinction to the body politic and settled nation-state.[70] During the Restoration, a turbulent era of national self-fashioning, the polemicist modulated that antithetical relationship into an argument for the comprehension of all Protestants, including nonconformists. At the same time, *Of True Religion* is the product of a period of intense anti-Catholic agitation. Milton's program of national reform, as scripted by his polemics, is founded on a dialectical model of politicized anti-popery and religious toleration: By adhering to God's Word alone and renouncing their implicit popery, Protestants would prevent schism and persecution and thus "unite against the common adversary" (CPW 8:420). Indeed, as Milton declares, in another negatively formulated pronouncement on toleration, "no true Protestant can persecute, or not tolerate his fellow Protestant, though dissenting from him in som opinions, but he must flatly deny and Renounce these two his own main Principles, whereon true Religion is founded" (CPW 8:420–1).

CHAPTER 5

Geography: Spatial Poetics

"Space may produce new Worlds." (Satan in *Paradise Lost*, 1.650)

"The study of geography is both profitable and delightfull." (Milton, *Brief History of Moscovia*, 1682)

"Nation is a moral essence, not a geographic arrangement." (Edmund Burke, 1796)

"Milton defines the nation not so much by geography, shared language, religion, or even culture as by a kind of national character." (Laura Lunger Knoppers, 2008)

The final third of this book offers, largely from the perspective of Milton's poetry, different formulations of the relationship between the nation and the international community. To begin, the outer limits of a civic society described in Chapter 4 assume geographical, poetic, and ethical dimensions in this chapter and in "Exogamy" (Chapter 6), both of which show Milton to be as regular a traverser as a reinforcer of national boundaries. The present chapter, "Geography," studies the forms of nationhood and national interests, not as internally defined by principles of natural law, intra-national politics, or church–state relations, but in terms of a global formulation and mapping of place and space. A discursive, material, and imaginative construction, the early modern nation was increasingly conceptualized as a geographical entity. Originally subsumed under cosmography, the focus of which was the globe and its relationship to the heavens, geography – the delineation of the land or earth-writing (Gk *geōgraphia*) – was subject to historical narration (chorography). As he reconstitutes nationhood by charting England's sea voyages ("navigations"), the major English geographer Richard Hakluyt figures "Geographie and Chronologie" as "the Sunne and the Moone, the right eye and the left of all history."[1] Also reflecting on the comprehensiveness of the discipline, Johannes Leo de Medici (alias Leo Africanus) determined that geography was as much concerned with ancestry, political and dynastic history, wars, culture, religion, and civil government as with longitudes, latitudes, and topography.[2] When Milton, for whom geography was a science second in importance only to astronomy,[3] compiled the geographical treatise he called his *Brief History of Moscovia: and Of other less-known Countries lying eastward of Russia as far as Cathay*, he likewise proposed to concentrate on Russia's "Manners, Religion, Government and such like, accounted Geographical."[4] His explorations, however, caused him to stray from his subject and from his account of Anglo-Russian trade, which had been documented by voyagers and geographers and built up by English merchants drawn to Russia as they sought the northeast passage to Cathay.

In conjunction with geopolitics – "an organized set of determined relations between geography and politics"[5] – geographical terms designated sites of power that delineated the frontiers of the nation.[6] Geographic categorization also literally mapped international and intra-national relations that furthered religious, political, and economic ambitions. In the case of early modern England, geography sanctioned the identification of the dominant Protestant nation as distinct from other nations, thereby generating both a national and imperial sentiment of "the knowability, controllability, and inferiority of the wider world."[7] In the seventeenth century, atlases and globes continued to be part of the "general mapping impulse," but maps emerged along with tables, divisions, and treatises as key mediums of geographical representation.[8] By synthesising cultural and historical information, maps and geographical writings offered cognitive modes of authority. Catalogues emerged as popular figures and instruments in geographical discourse, which in turn constituted a language of nationhood.[9] As seemingly encyclopaedic, even comprehensive inventories, prose and verse catalogues promoted applications of historical and geographical knowledge that helped establish national supremacy and conveyed imperialist sentiment.

A review of Milton's descriptive geography and poeticised cartography reveals his indebtedness to biblical and classical geographical sources and to early modern cosmographies, geographic compendiums, and travel narratives. The literary evidence displays Milton's awareness of the philosophical, educative, and moral purposes of geography, as well as the exploitative uses thereof, and of the possibilities for poetic space to reconstitute geographic place. Michel de Certeau suggestively distinguished between "place," representing a set and ordered location, geographic or otherwise, and "space" or a "practiced place," a place put to use.[10] The conversion of place, including geographical places, into a charged space is a common practice among historical geographers, but more compellingly the achievement of poets like Milton, whether through the epic catalogues of place names specifically or the stanza form more broadly. Building on the early findings in Allan H. Gilbert's *Geographical Dictionary of Milton* (1919/68), George Wesley Whiting's discussion of "The Use of Maps" in *Milton's Literary Milieu* (1939/1964), and Robert Ralson Cawley's *Milton and the Literature of Travel* (1951), this chapter surveys Milton's geographic imaginings in key passages from the *Brief History of Moscovia* and from *Paradise Lost* and *Paradise Regained*.[11] In the epics, the poetic and spatial assembly of place names delineates the parameters, status, and history as well as the moral character of the nation, while also designating the literal and political contours of global relations. Milton underscores the epic genre's authority in compartmentalizing and managing knowledge while conceptualizing the forms of empire and nationhood through a poetics of temporal and spatial representation, which, in Foucauldian terms, "gives on to the analysis of related effects of power."[12]

Theatrum Mundi

In his preface to Euclid's *The Elements of Geometry*, magus and philosopher John Dee affirms that geography – among the many arts constituting the branches of geometry – "teacheth ways, by which, in sundry formes (as *Sphaerike, Plain*, or other), the Situation of Cities, Towns, Villages, Forts, Castles, Mountains, Woods, Havens, Rivers, Creeks, and such other things, upon the out-face of the earthly Globe … most aptly to our view, may be represented."[13] Likewise an offshoot of geometry, cosmography is defined by Dee in his *Mathematicall Preface* as "the whole and perfect description of the heavens and also elementall part of the world," an art that "matcheth Heaven, and the Earth in one frame, and aptly applyeth parts correspondent: So, as, the Heavenly Globe, may (in practise) be duly described upon the Geographicall and Hydrographicall Globe."[14] About a century after Dee, Milton's nephew and student, Edward Phillips, identified astronomy and geography as branches of the science of cosmography, defined as "a Description of the visible World."[15] The vision of an orderly universe that emerges from the application of these interwoven philosophies simultaneously contributed to a national consciousness. In the early modern era, the imperializing element too became a regular component of geographical representation, a science subject to exploitation by Europeans.[16] Dee used geographic texts in promoting the national as well as imperial and mercantile ambitions of the Elizabethan court.

As geographical expansionism and historical legitimation went hand in hand, Dee also traced an Elizabethan title to the empires of Brutus and Arthur.[17]

Both Dee and the aforementioned Richard Hakluyt owned copies of Abraham Ortelius's *Theatrum Orbis Terrarum* (theatre of the earthly globe), originally published in 1570.[18] The later editions of *Theatrum* differ from the 1570 original, although the work was not updated after 1589. *Theatrum* was a distinctly Renaissance cosmographic project representing the world's unity and diversity, and it was partly an example of the use of globes and world maps as icons and subjects of meditation and contemplation. Ortelius's adoption of the cosmographic vision of the *theatrum mundi* as a moral space relied on a commonplace for the comprehensiveness and vastness of the knowledge contained and arranged within a great theatre.[19] Various cosmographers and geographers, including Ortelius, drew upon the alternative figure of global space and thereby developed a more liberal and tolerant approach to global knowledge itself. The global understanding conveyed by the geographic representation was designed to promote the quest for wisdom and foster toleration for difference, but also potentially provide a stimulus for imperializing feats.

Ortelius's *Theatrum* unfolded as a narrative through space that moved from the whole world and its continents to individual states and principalities. Such a narrative was a characteristic mode of knowledge creation in the later sixteenth century. The journey undertaken by the reader "like unto a travailer or a Pilgrime" is epic in nature, as he ventures off to many nations before at last returning to the starting point of his journey.[20] The compendium contains numerous maps, each accompanied by a description on the verso side of the page. Mapped out textually and visually are the journeys of Abraham, St. Paul, Aeneas, Ulysses, Alexander the Great, and Jason, leader of the Argonauts, thus aligning the classical and biblical traditions. In the years Ortelius produced his atlas project (and Dee his *Mathematicall Preface*), Luis de Camoes composed *Os Lusiadas* (*The Lusiads* [1572]) in celebration of Portuguese imperialism[21] and Alonso de Ercilla y Zúñiga wrote *La Araucana* (1569, 1578, 1589) in honour of the Spanish empire. Both are travel narratives, modeled on the voyages of Aeneas. Each contains both geographical descriptions of newly discovered lands and scenes featuring visions of the cosmos, thus connecting imperial missions with a manifest destiny.

English trade and colonization were also conceptualized by early geographers and venturers on the basis of their encounter with earlier Latin editions of Ortelius.[22] A correspondent of Gerrard Mercator and Ortelius,

Hakluyt, quoted at the outset of this chapter, was, along with William Camden, a major contributor to the knowledge of history and natural and social sciences in his highly influential study of the imperial English nation. The first edition of *The Principal Navigations* was published in 1589 and was followed by an enlarged edition in three volumes between 1598 and 1600. Geographic research and knowledge accumulation were nationalist undertakings conducted by way of travel as travail, primarily represented as textual examination and engagement: "how many long & chargeable journeys I have traveiled; how many famous libraries I have searched into; what varietie of ancient and moderne writers I have perused; what a number of old records, patents, privileges, letters, &c. I have redeemed from obscuritie and perishing ... [for] the honour and benefit of this Common weale."[23] Hakluyt proceeded to legitimize English nationhood not only on religious and international grounds but also notably on economic ones. In seeking to increase mercantilism, he added "Traffiques" to the title of his later edition of the history. *Principal Navigations* featured Hakluyt's own translations of key works and influenced the production of other translations of geographical writings and descriptions. John Wolfe's translation of Jan Huygen van Linschoten's *Discours of Voyages* was among key writings of the time that showed how the heroic ventures of other nations were appropriated to bolster English supremacy.[24] A related example was the aforementioned Leo Africanus's *Geographical Historie of Africa*, translated in 1600 by John Pory, who was well-known by Hakluyt and in fact encouraged him to translate it.[25] The translation of descriptive geographies and travel literatures and narratives was a practice designed to advance knowledge about other European nations' discoveries and rhetorically stake a claim to the described lands, a later illustration thereof being the translation by John Phillips, nephew of Milton, of Bartholomé de las Casas's *Brevíssima relación de la destrucción de las Indias*.[26]

Following the death of Hakluyt in 1616, the Essex minister Samuel Purchas compiled his highly popular geographical history, one that drew on many hundreds of authors by the time of the final edition in 1625. Purchas had secured Hakluyt's source materials in preparing *Hakluytus Posthumus or Purchas His Pilgrimes*, which he described in his dedication to Prince Charles as an act of divine creation, the framing of "Historicall world ... out of a Chaos of confused intelligences."[27] Purchas's various editions of *Pilgrimes* served in turn as geographies and natural histories of non-European regions. His primary agenda in assembling the narratives was self-evident: He sought to buttress English expansionism with a "philosophical statement of purpose,"[28] by furnishing information and the impetus to further imperial ambitions. From the start of his project through to his condemnation of Spanish atrocities in the New World – recounted in the final chapter of the *Pilgrimes* with its translation of Las Casas's *Brevíssima relación* – Purchas legitimized the Protestant claim to empire. His contribution to a tradition of English geography that promulgated Protestant sovereignty especially over Catholic dominions was substantial.[29]

That tradition included the work of John Speed, who was influenced by the geographic imagining of a British national identity in Ortelius's aforementioned *Theatrum Orbis Terrarum* (1570). A version of Ortelius's project appeared in English in 1606 during this formative period of English exploration and mercantilism and inspired Speed's *The Theatre of the Empire of Great Britaine* (1611), the titular term "theatre" having been derived from Ortelius's *Theatrum*. The maps of England in Speed's *Theatre* helped delineate the political geography of the nation and the British kingdom. Milton's own engagement with Speed is evidenced by the dozens of citations of Speed's works in the Commonplace Book.[30]

The discipline of geography was also integrated into the university curriculum and contributed to the fashioning of English nationhood, as Milton himself emphasized.[31] *Of Education. To Master Samuel Hartlib* credits the study of geography with the advancement of the nation's health and also the formation of national subjects – the "stedfast pillars of the State" (CPW 2:398). As an art and science (or philosophy), geography constitutes an integral part of a Humanist educational model. After recommending the study of law in *Of Education*, Milton advances his theory of pedagogy in a catalogue of key disciplines, of which geography is one, but one that intersects with all Humanistic learning. In outlining what is a Herculean undertaking, Milton encourages the reading of works on agriculture by Cato, Varro, and Columella before turning to "the use of the Globes, and all the maps first with the old names; and then with the new" (CPW 2:388, 389). The study of maps and globes prepares students for engagement with natural philosophy, which, along with the classical languages and grammar, facilitates comprehension of writings on historical physiology by Aristotle and Theophrastus. Geographical descriptions of the continents and of the known world produced by Pomponius Mela and Gaius Julius Solinus, among others, become accessible as well. Together with the study of geometry, astronomy, and physics, geographical learning opens the door to an education in trigonometry and leads to the mastery of such arts as architecture and navigation. The reading of maps with old and new place names in the curriculum Milton outlined melded philosophical and cosmographic study with imaginative and historical narration, to which scientific and factual knowledge gave way.

"[N]either do I care to wrinkle the smoothness of History with rugged names of places unknown, better harp'd at in *Camden*, and other Chorographers," Milton later asserts in his *History of Britain*.[32] Milton's writings nevertheless exhibit a scholarly attentiveness to geographic knowledge and accuracy. The oft-rehearsed anecdote about his material interest in geographic works features the blind poet in 1656 inquiring of his travelling European correspondent Peter Heimbach about the cost, correctness, and number of volumes in the enormous and recently produced *Novus Atlas, sive theatrum orbis terrarum*. The "New Atlas" was based on *Atlas sive Cosmographicae meditationes de fabrica Mundi et fabricati figura* (1595) by the cartographer Gerrard Mercator, and translated into English by Henry Hexham.[33] *Novus Atlas* itself was published by the major Dutch cartographer, Jan Jansson/Johannes Janssonius.[34] Milton wondered about its accuracy compared with the issue produced by W. J. Blaeu, the rival Amsterdam publisher and official cartographer for the East and West India Company.[35] Blaeu's *Atlas Major*, the most expensive book published in the century, appeared in eleven volumes (1647–62) and twelve by 1663. Complaining to Heimbach about the prohibitive cost of the atlas, Milton puns on atlas/Atlas Mountain: "You say that they ask one hundred and thirty florins. I think it must be the Mauritanian Mount Atlas, not the book, that you say is to be bought as such a steep price."[36] Seemingly unbeknownst to Milton was the identification of "atlas" with the mythical African king, philosopher, mathematician, and astronomer who purportedly produced the first celestial globe.[37] Gerard Mercator's use of the term "atlas" after 1569 to designate an assembly of maps[38] invests the project – and its designer – with a heaven-bracing power. Oxford geographer Peter Heylyn, who ascends with the reader to the great heights of Mount Atlas in his magisterial *Cosmographie: In Four Bookes*, combines the mythological, historical, and geographical significances of "atlas" in his explanation that the mountain in North Africa derives its name from Atlas, a king of the African coastal country of Mauritania. On his shoulders the heavens rest, together with an "extraordinary knowledge in *Astronomy*," reports Heylyn, underscoring the interrelationship of geography, cosmography, astronomy, and knowledge advancement and accumulation. Heylyn then reverts to Vergil's description in the *Aeneid* of the Titan Atlas, which gives way in the *Cosmographie* to geographical surveys of the African countries bounded by the mountain range.[39]

Milton himself contributed to the literature on geography in producing a work of travel writing. Theodore Haak reported to Samuel Hartlib that Milton was preparing "an Epitome of all Purchas volumes" around 1648, which would become his *Brief History of Moscovia*.⁴⁰ This geography is the product of Milton's nationalist vision, geographical and poetic imagination, and historical investigative methods. Lewes Roberts, merchant and Captain of the City of London, names Moscovia among the nations to which Englishness was dispensed and exported, a feat accomplished not by conquest but rather commerce:

> [I]t is not our swords, but our sayls, that first spred the English name in
> *Barbary*, and thence came into *Turky, Armenia, Moscovia, Arabia, Persia,*
> *India, China*, and indeed over and about the world; it is the traffike of
> their Merchants, and the boundlesse desires of that nation to eternize the
> English honour and name, that hath enduced them to saile, and seek into
> all the corners of the earth.⁴¹

The northernmost country of Europe (*Ultima Europú regio*) was the most popular subject of English geographic descriptions because its northern parts were, as Milton notes, "first discovered by English Voiages" (CPW 8:475). The Company of Merchant Adventurers of Sir Richard Chancellor, who along with Sir Hugh Willoughby went in search of the northeast route to Cathay, wound up in Russia, where the former would establish trade relations with Russia's first tsar Ivan IV. In the last and longest chapter of *A Brief History*, which describes England's encounter and diplomatic relations with Russia in the latter half of the 1500s, Milton proudly proclaims his nation's discovery of Russia. By extension, he justifies his choice of Russia for the para-colonial geography he produces⁴²: The country offers testimony of English prowess in commerce and nation building.

In assembling his *Brief History of Moscovia*, Milton immersed himself in the writings of the cosmographers Hakluyt and Purchas, travel writing consisting largely of episodes from historical narratives, which Milton here compiles, as Hakluyt himself did, "to save the Reader a far longer travaile of wandring through so many desert Authours."⁴³ Milton's "national pride" is on display in his condescension to the Russians, Cawley determines, equating English self-definition with intolerance.⁴⁴ In negatively formulated articulations, Milton does, however, concede Russian liberties in a couple instances when they complement his own interests and principles. Russian men were justified in divorcing unsatisfactory (or unsatisfying) wives, a "Liberty no doubt they receiv'd first with their Religion from the *Greek* Church, and the Imperial Laws" (CPW 8:493–4), Milton surmises without citing a source. Further, Russians were not subjected to forcers of conscience (CPW 8:499), a condition for toleration for which Milton himself had campaigned in England in the 1640s and throughout his career. Milton leaves Russia to venture off to the Far East in the company of the travel writers who "drew me after them, from the eastern Bounds of *Russia*, to the Walls of *Cathay*," a phrase that will also resonate in *Paradise Lost*.[45] Excerpts taken from Purchas's travel literature include an account from 1618 to 1619 about the first Russian trade mission to China. The information about the Chinese that Milton gleans and records underscores the concern of geographers with "customes, religions, and civile government," as the aforementioned Leo Africanus had stated,[46] and exhibits even more obviously England's fascination and preoccupation with economic prosperity of the East: "The People are Idolaters; the Country exceeding fruitfull ... Next to the [Great] Wall is the City *Shirokalga* ... [which] abounds with rich Merchandize, Velvets, Damasks, Cloth of Gold and Tissue, with many sorts of Sugars ... [In Beijing] the People are very fair, but not warlike, delighting most in rich Traffick" (CPW 8:509–10). The cultural, material, and nationalist interests that had attracted Milton as intellectual traveller and his English contemporaries as venturers and merchants to Russia drew the Russians and the English alike to each other, and to the Far East.

"Capital Seat"

Exported from *A Brief History of Moscovia* to his national English Protestant epic, *Paradise Lost*, are various place names, including Astracan, Cambaluc (for Peking), Caspian, Cathay, Lapland, Mosco, Nagay, Ob, Pechora, Russia, Samoedia, and Tartaria. Demarcating the journey undertaken by an enterprising, imperialistic Satan, and comprising geopolitical epic catalogues featured in the account of the aftermath, the place names from *Moscovia* lose any neutrality or purely descriptive function they may have had in Milton's geographical writing. Poetry facilitates or completes the conversion of place into space. In epics, which are encyclopedic vehicles for the transmission of history, prophecy, epistemology, creationist narratives, and scientific learning, the roll call of names, particularly in catalogue form, is an expression of mapping and knowledge assembly but also cognitive and philosophical reflection. Because geography as a discipline is embedded in Humanistic study, the poeticized geographic allusions in the epic are thickly contextualized, and the tightly wrought catalogues of sonorous place names put a wide range of learning, mastered by the English epic poet, on full display.

In composing *Paradise Lost*, Milton seizes the opportunity to explore imaginatively the origins and farthest reaches of the globe, an act that begins with God's circumscription of the universe and the world at the heart of the poem (PL book 7). The creation account is presented as the subject of the distinctly English literary composition. The poet's global consciousness and the arrangement of place and space in *Paradise Lost* render the world accessible for Milton's readers while exposing the distortions that the art of mapping and both geographic and chorographic representation can engender. Descriptive geography featured prominently in English narratives of exotic and distant peoples and places, and Milton would use geographic specificity as a marker of national identity and foreign relations.

Comparisons between east and west, for example, had cultural, moral, and ethical implications that could be activated to justify subordination and reinforce supremacy. In book 9 of *Paradise Lost*, the elision of east and west implicates Adam and Eve in fallenness. Milton imports images of corruption from the feminized East and the New World; reduced to a fallen and primitive state, the lapsed couple covers itself with leaves from the (feminized) Indian fig or banyan tree "as at this day to Indians known / In Malabar or Decan." Despite their actual small size, the leaves acquire mythic proportions when compared with the broad shields of the legendary Greek Amazons (PL 9.1102–3, 9.1111). Superimposed is then a description of the postlapsarian couple as Amerindian: "Such of late / Columbus found the American so girt / With feathered cincture, naked else and wild" (PL 9.1115–7). In Eden, nudity – innocent and noble – is distinct from American nakedness, discovered "of late" in the New World, a land originally mistaken for India. The descriptions of the "pillared shade" of the tree under which the Indian herdsman shelters himself and of the "feathered cincture" used by the Americanized Adam and Eve to cover themselves rely on an architectural trope that bridges and binds the worlds of the Indian and the Amerindian.[47] Geographic dislocations and the conflation in the stanza of western and eastern place names and states of degeneracy register the high point of the tragedy.[48] The aftermath of original sin gives rise to a permeable fenceless (defenceless) world (PL 10.303), one joined to hell by Sin and Death's causeway, which entraps humanity as the Persian Xerxes, who "over Hellespont / Bridging his way, Europe with Asia joined," trapped the Greeks (PL 10.309–10).

As a prelude to the postlapsarian history recounted in books 11 and 12, Michael ascends with Adam to "a Hill / Of Paradise the highest" (PL 11.377–8) to view a panoramic "prospect." The revelation thrusts Adam into geopolitical and temporal awareness. The privileged perspective he is afforded anticipates Moses' vision upon Pisgah and Ezekiel's "visions of God" whereby the prophet was brought to Israel and "set upon a very high mountaine" (Ezek. 40:2). The prospect reinforces, as Purchas states, the Israelites' association of holy places with "high hils," and the Rabbis' conception of the "land of Israel . . . [as] the highest of all lands," as William Greenhill reminds the reader.[49] Thomas Fuller describes the transference of divine favour from the Jews to the Christians (and converted Jews) throughout his lengthy treatise, in which the Christian reader occupies a position of authority: "May the reader now conceive himself standing on the top of mount *Pisgah*." Whereas the contemporary reader must "content [himself] with a narrower compass, then what *Moses* discerned," he now enjoys the true vantage point and the sense of entitlement it affords. The same applies to Fuller's account of Ezekiel's "Visionary Land of Canaan," characterized as "no *Geography*, but *Ouranography*, no earthly truth, but mysticall predication."[50] The expansive vision of the Christian writer discovers a role for the Jews in the fullness of time, but, again, one that requires their conversion. In the present day, the prophesied gathering of the Jews and the temporal restoration of the New Jerusalem are indefinitely deferred, however, while the Hebraic tradition is rendered "serviceable" to Christians in the scripting of their foundational providential narratives and peculiar status.[51]

The geographic site of Michael's revelation to Adam is also overlaid with classical significance. The mountain on which Adam stands is likely the legendary Mount Niphates in the Taurus range on the Assyria–Armenia border, source of the Tigris in southwestern Asia. Relying on such sources as Strabo, who was immensely indebted to Homer, and Jordanes, author of *Gothic History*, Milton invests the site of the prophetic revelation with mythic and literary value at the expense of geographic accuracy. According to Jordanes, Niphates marks a convergence point of various place names and nations: "The Indian calls it Imaus and in another part Paropamisus. The Parthian calls it first Choatras and afterward Niphates; the Syrian and Armenian call it Taurus. . . ."[52] At this ancient location, Adam momentarily regains the "capital seat" he had lost (PL 11.343), although his global perspective is a geopolitical prophecy of corrupted power, anticipated by the sight of passion featuring a "disfigured" Satan on what Milton describes in *Paradise Lost* as an Assyrian Mount (PL 4.126–7). The geographic location links Milton's two epics both textually and symbolically: Niphates is destined for another display of worldly power, one that will feature the tempter's offer of "all earth's kingdoms and their glory" to "Our second

Adam" (PL 11.384, 383). The geographic positioning and tragic episodes of the human drama that unfold for Adam in *Paradise Lost* thus foreshadow the scene in *Paradise Regained* (PR 3.252–65) staged at the tip of a horn of land representing the Assyrian Empire at the height of its glory. The ascent affords opportunities for the communication of knowledge about the history of imperialism, punctuated by poetically and spatially configured anti-imperialist pronouncements, which take the place of defences of toleration in the postlapsarian world.

As a scene of contemplation, the book 11 revelation has ancient antecedents that featured the globe as a vast stage upon which the drama of human existence was played out. Such scenes commonly featured philosophers like Democritus and Heraclitus transported above the theatre of the world (*theatrum mundi*) to reflect on human nature. The process whereby ordinary mortals could attain a global vision was at once intellectual and revelatory. The Ciceronian contemplation of the earth's surface from afar generates awareness that promotes self-knowledge. In Cicero's well-known episode on the "Dream of Scipio" that concludes his *Republic*, Scipio encounters Publius Cornelius Scipio Africanus the Elder, who counsels him about his destiny and duty. Scipio's father, Paulus, who rests among the ranks of heroes, offers various directives to his son that include imitating his grandfather and father and embracing justice and duty as owed to parents and kinsmen, "but most of all to the fatherland. Such a life is a road to the skies" ("*ut avus hic tuus, ut ego, qui te genui [j]ustitiam cole et pietatem, quae cum magna in parentibus et propinquis, tum in patria maxima est; ea vita via est in caelum...*").[53] From his vantage point attained through his elevation to the starry spheres, Scipio recognizes the insignificance of the earth and empire: "Indeed the earth itself seemed to me so small that I was scornful of our empire, which covers only a single point, as it were, upon its surface" ("*iam ipsa terra ita mihi parva visa est, ut me imperii nostri, quo quasi punctum eius attingimus, paeniteret*").[54] Moved by the spirit that constitutes the true self ("*sed mens cuiusque is est quisque*"), those who participate in the higher good of defending their country will be rewarded with immortality.[55]

The tenet of duty to the fatherland (*pietas*) is championed in Vergil's national epic, in which the individualism that marked the Homeric epics is converted into a patriotic *pietas*.[56] *The Aeneid* also represents the inauguration of what would become a commonplace: the use of the epic mode to communicate a nationalist and imperialist ideology, thus departing from the ancient Greek narrative of world history. The epic's celebration of Roman glory was inspired by Vergil's patron, Emperor Gaius Octavianus

(Augustus), who had united Rome after generations of civil war. *The Aeneid* pays tribute to the new imperium, that is, to Rome as conqueror and civilizer. The epic prophecy of Rome shown to Aeneas in book 6 (756–885) would serve a classical model for the episode in *Paradise Lost*, but Milton transforms the original epic prophecy into a cosmographical vision. In his criticism on Milton's epic, Joseph Addison acknowledges the indebtedness of Adam's visions to the prophecy of Aeneas's descendants in the *Aeneid* but maintains that Milton's rendition of the scene is superior insofar as it applies not just "to any particular tribe of mankind" but "to the whole species."[57]

Milton's retelling of Mosaic history in the final books of *Paradise Lost* reflects a politically and morally charged geographical imaginary in a catalogue of worldly civilizations and empires. Cawley, whose thesis in *Milton and the Literature of Travel* develops from an analysis of *Paradise Lost* 11.385–411, underscores the significance of the vision in impressing Adam with the long-term consequences of sin and the betrayal of the divine plan.[58] Bruce McLeod compellingly ties the world-encompassing prospect to Milton's nationalism, which invests the poet with the confidence to possess and display a "global consciousness"; Milton's capacity and tenacity is "nowhere better exemplified" than in the book 11 episode on top of the Mount of Paradise.[59] The catalogue prophetically displays an anti-Christian world through the Eurocentric "visions of God" (PL 11.377) – the visions sent by God.[60] McLeod's brief summary of the account concludes with the remark that the scene exhibits the "heroic … adventurer and his often overreaching pursuit of an ideal, which ultimately is for his country."[61] This observation certainly applies to the classical epics, arguably more so than to *Paradise Lost*. The prophecy Vergil describes in the *Aeneid* tells how Aeneas's descendants will rule first Italy and then the known world while avenging themselves on the Greeks for the fall of Troy. Also predicted are the events leading up to Augustus's reign and the expansion of the Roman Empire.[62] In the course of the prophecy, Augustus's ascendancy from Aeneas is established, marking the culmination of millennia extending from Greek history through to Roman history, represented by a catalogue of heroes of Roman lineage. Vergil builds on but diverts the Homeric model: Apollo, the favoured deity of Augustus, prophesies Aeneas's settlement of Italy and his founding of the Roman Empire. "[W]e will raise your children to the stars," the gods tell Aeneas, "And give the wide earth to your city … / … / … / … / There is a place Greeks call Hesperia, / An old land, strong in war and rich in loam. Oenotarians lived there, whose descendants take / Their name, it's said, from Italus the king.

This is our own home."[63] The westward journey to Rome in the Western land of Italy, Aeneas's destination, will involve a *translatio imperii*.

Genealogy is a key component of national imagining and self-fashioning, and in book 6 of the *Aeneid* the late Anchises describes the future to his son, Aeneas: "Now turn your eyes here, see this clan – your Romans: / Caesar, and all of Julus' offspring, destined / To make their way to heaven's splendid heights" (788–90). Augustus then is hailed as the destined emperor who will extend Roman rule "past the solar pathway / That marks the year, where Atlas hefts the sky" (6.794–5). Michael's prophecy in *Paradise Lost* subsumes and reworks that of Apollo: Whereas Vergil extols the Princeps, establishing Augustus's lineage from Aeneas, Milton inserts proleptic Roman imperialism into a geopolitical history, which, in turn, is intregated into a longer providential narrative. Further, *Paradise Lost* becomes less specifically about the founding of a nation than about the founding and falling of the human race.

In the poem's final books, Adam becomes privy to the poetically, spatially configured transcontinental reaches of Asia, Africa, Europe, and America. Having mounted the hill of speculation with Adam, Michael presents the earthly kingdoms and rulers from – as the incantation begins – "the destined walls / Of Cámbalu" (future destination of European merchants)[64] to India and Malaya (in Southeast Asia), Persia, Russia, and to the Ottoman Empire, where the "Turchestan born" Ottoman sultan ousted the Byzantines. The prophecy of the empires then moves across the African continent, from Abyssinia (north Ethiopia) to Mombasa ("Mombaza"), Kenya and Kilwa, to "Sófala thought Ophir" in Mozambique, sometimes identified with the biblical "Ophir," and to the west coast – "the realm / Of Congo, and Angola farthest south" (PL 11.387–401). The vision of the Niger River flowing to the Atlantic – to the Atlas mountains (or perhaps to the Mauritanian Mount Atlas) – then transports Adam to various Muslim kingdoms in northwestern Africa. The incantation and the political imagination map state authority territorially. The wide prospect, which enables a navigation from the extra-biblical history of antiquity through to the geopolitical history of Milton's time, creates a charged space, one that implicates kingdoms and rulers in acts of imperialism, which are shown here to originate, at least in the era before Columbus, in the East rather than the West.[65]

In mapping out the world in this regard, Milton walks in the footsteps of Leo Africanus, as well as of George Sandys, who in *Relation of a Journey* lent a sense of contemporaneity to classical geography.[66] Likewise, Peter Heylyn's aforementioned compendium commemorates "the heroick Acts

of my native Soil, and … the Gallantrie and brave Atchievements [sic] of
the People of *England*"[67] and sanctions a globe-consuming vision of geographic descriptions of the continents. Heylyn supplies a model for reading the relationship of history, geography, and religion that could have
served Milton's needs here. Although decidedly royalist, Heylyn's work,
according to most commentaries on Milton and geography, may have
influenced Milton's geographical surveying, both in terms of the information it supplied and the philosophy that underlay it.[68] The impressive
publication history of *Cosmographie: In Four Bookes* included six editions
between 1652 and 70, after its original appearance as *Microcosmos: A Little
Description of the Great World*, eight editions of which appeared between
1621–39. Passages could have been read to Milton in the period of his failing eyesight, and the encyclopaedic chorographical project *Cosmographie*
may have enabled a surveillance "with blind eyes [of] the actual globe of
the earth," as Milton attested.[69]

In *Theatrum Orbis Terrarum*, Ortelius supplied a "briefe and short declaration and Historicall discourse" on the "backsides" of the leaves containing the maps, each of which was folded and impressed with letterpress text
descriptions on the verso.[70] In the unfolding map of the book ii vision in
Paradise Lost, global coordinates are represented in the form of a catalogue,
the "omnipresent figure in geographical discourse."[71] A poetics of spatial
orientation in the inventory, which is encapsulated in the epic catalogue,
establishes global relations: The naming and symmetrical alignment of the
kingdoms, capitals, and rulers of the Far East, Asia, and Russia comprise
the first eight and a half lines. The second principal clause of the Baroque
sentence surveys Africa and its rulers and moves westward to Rome (PL
11.396–405), with the appositional relationship between the place names
of Bizance [Byzantium] (PL 11.395) and Rome (11.405), pointing to what
Alastair Fowler calls "an uncomplimentary analogy" between the Ottomans
and Catholics. From Russia and Turkey, next mentioned, the mental traveller is transported south, to "The empire of Negus to his utmost port /
Ercoco and the less marítime kings / Mombaza and Quiloa, and Melind, /
And Sófala thought Ophir" (PL 11.397–400). The anatomising and spatial
arrangements of the kingdoms occur in circular patterns: Along with their
unspecified rulers, the golden Chersonese (located east of India and known
for its riches) and the Portuguese East African port of Sofala – visited by
the author of the *Lusiads* and identified with Ophir (where Solomon pro-
cured gold for his temple) – strategically occupy the central positions in the
catalogue.[72] The poetic structuring of geographic space therein redraws the
lines of power, building in a geopolitical critique.

Upon gesturing toward a Rome-dominated Europe, Milton moves further to the west, to lands lying beyond the ecliptic, beyond the circle on the celestial sphere representing the sun's annual journey. The spectacle conjures up what is for Adam a distant future and what is for Milton's readers recent history, when the dream of a "yet unspoiled / Guiana" had already vanished. "Guiana" refers to the fabulous city named *El Dorado* by the Spaniards.[73] Milton's allusion to the Spaniards (PL 11.410), "Geryon's sons," inserts into the historical and geographic panorama the fabulous and mythological, as is the case with "Ophir," among other examples.[74] The catalogue of empires encodes an anti-imperial, anti-monarchist reading of history, which unfolds before the viewer who is interpolated in the drama that he helped stage. In that regard, the prophecy shown to Adam differs from the scenes of contemplation described by detached philosophers and poets who featured the globe as a theatre in which the drama of human existence was acted out.

Milton in turn numbers among the defenders of a Judeo-Christian narrative of the fall who recounted the demise of the ancient pagan empires. George Sandys outlines the succession of empires, and maps their decline: What once were "the most renowned countries and kingdomes: once the seats of most glorious and triumphant Empires; the theaters of valour and heroicall actions … are now through vice and ingratitude, become the most deplored spectacles of extreme miserie."[75] Heylyn likewise attributes the desolation experienced by the "mighty Empires" of the Mediterranean and Middle Eastern regions with "their crying sins," namely, "the pride of the *Babylonians*, the effeminacy of the *Persians*, the luxury of the *Greeks*, and such an aggregation of vices amongst the *Romans* (or *Western* Christians) before the breaking in of the barbarous Nations, that they were grown a scandall unto *Christianity.*"[76] In *Paradise Lost*, the prospect of the worldly civilizations and monarchies sets into motion a visual and verbal narrative that will culminate in an apocalypse – Revelation supplying what Claire McEachern characterizes as "a narrative pattern for the internal unity so instrumental to the nation."[77] The narrative of the poem's final books, however, unsettles any unified representation of the nation. A series of vignettes positions the reprobate chosen people politically, morally, and historically while exposing the corruption inherent in its subjects. Launched by the vision of the world that Michael presents to Adam, the ensuing episodes in the epic concentrate less on the dynamics of power than on the tension between a coherently patterned globe-encompassing vision and a fraught nationhood with its liberty-abusing peoples. The shift in the prophetic narrative of book 11 from a global geography to a national chorography distinguishes the episodes from their counterparts in Du Bartas's *Divine Weeks* while complicating what becomes a participatory narration of national, biblical history interspersed with Adam's often misguided remarks.[78] Epic catalogues also drop out in books 11 and 12, signalling not only the change to an unadorned style but also the consequences of disobedience and corruption of knowledge. The global and temporal journey that Adam undertakes culminates in the creation of a conceptual space, a "paradise within" – the antithesis of what constitutes in *Paradise Regained* the ultimate temptation – the empire of the mind (PR 4.221–4).

Paradise Regained

The catalogue is used with the same frequency in *Paradise Regained* as in its prequel, and the language of the catalogues in the brief epic is likewise elevated through the skilful and strategic amassing of resonant proper names and place names.[79] The poetic catalogues survey the historical and geographical panorama: book 3, 269–93, for example, features the various ancient kingdoms comprising the Parthian Empire; book 3, 316–21 lists places from where the Parthian horsemen came; and book 4, lines 67–79, name the near and distant places that are now tributary to the Roman Empire. Catalogues serve as devices that reinforce the all-consuming nature of imperial power. The accounts of the worldly kingdoms in the brief epic complement those in the major epic, although more directly critiquing the forms and language that epic and empire have engendered.[80] In a parallel/parallax vision that constitutes the temptation scene of book 3 in *Paradise Regained*, Satan, likely on Niphates, displays to the Son the ancient empires "in a moment of time" (Luke 4:5). Stephen Greenblatt identifies "wonder" as the primary and quintessential human reaction to first encounters.[81] Milton's Satan is intent on inducing the Son's wonder as he invites him to survey the wide prospect: "here thou behold'st," he motions to Jesus, directing his gaze at the empires (PR 3.269). The descriptions of kingdoms identified in succession – Assyria, Babylon, Persia, and Emathia or Macedonia, which is subsumed in the Parthian Empire that extends, as Assyria did in ancient times, from "*Indus* East, *Euphrates* West" (PR 3.272) – are indebted to Ptolemy's maps in *Geographia* (1605), "the touchstone" for early modern cartographers.[82] The references to the geographical sites derived from ancient, heroic, and biblical sources and compressed in a compendious catalogue (PR 3.267–385) conjure up images of decadence and decay as a reminder of the corrupt foundations that lie beneath power and splendour.

In the opening book of the brief epic, a soliloquy in which Jesus rehearses his genealogy, interpolates his mother's testimony of her son's divine paternity: "For know, thou art no Son of mortal man, / Though men esteem thee low of Parentage, / Thy Father is the Eternal King, who rules / All Heaven and Earth" (PR 1.234–7). But the divine imperium passes the power of dominion to Satan, at whose own disposal *translatio imperii* becomes a demonic device:[83] "For God hath justly giv'n the Nations up / To thy Delusions; justly, since they fell / Idolatrous" (PR 1.442–4). At the start of book 4, Satan displays the panorama of the Roman Empire composed of the "Kingdoms of the world, and all thir glory" (PR 4.89) in order to whet Jesus' appetite for imperial might: "glorious *Rome*, Queen of the Earth / So far renown'd, and with the spoils enrich't / Of Nations; there the Capitol thou seest" (PR 4.45–7). The expanse of empire reaches from Rome to the Adriatic, to the extreme south of the empire in Africa: Syene/Assouan and Meroe, a city on the Nile; then Asia, the golden Chersonese, Malacca, and the Indian isle of Taprobane; thereafter to Europe, west to France, Gades/Cadiz in Spain (the westernmost city of the empire), and Brittany. Finally it incorporates Germany, ancient Scythia and Sarmatia, and the Taurick pool or Sea of Azov representing the northern boundaries of the empire. The middle of the catalogue contains references to embassies from prominent nations like India and from Chersonese and Taprobane or Sumatra. Yet despite Satan's claims that "All nations now to *Rome* obedience pay" (PR 4.80), Indian envoys, although they apparently sought peace with the first Roman emperor, seem not to have come to Tiberius; nor did Chersonese or Taprobane embassies venture to Rome.[84] The satanic tempter employs his imperial imagination to extend the device of *translatio imperii* far beyond the reaches of the historical Roman Empire.

Milton's epic narratives of the founding of a nation nevertheless complicate associations between nation and empire.[85] Milton thus distinguishes *Paradise Lost* and *Paradise Regained* from their Vergilian antecedent. *Paradise Lost* reinforces the identification of nationhood with liberty in Michael's warning to a postlapsarian Adam about the loss of inward liberty by future nations (PL 12.97–101). *Paradise Regained* also surveys the history and knowledge of the ancient worlds and navigates the empires that replaced them. At the same time, the brief epic renounces globe-consuming visions, the temptations of empire, and the classical values of glory, fame, and duty while exposing the tyranny that resides within. In book 3, Satan proposes that the Son secure his kingdom by applying Parthian against Roman military might. Indeed, the survey of empires in *Paradise Regained* is intended to evoke the liberationist compulsions, to which the Son confessed his attraction in the opening soliloquy. In response to the temptation to deliver the Jews, the chosen race, the Son protests, however, that liberation must start at home: "no, let them serve / Thir enemies, who serve Idols with God" until they prove themselves "repentant and sincere" (PR 3.431–2, 435).

In book 4 it is the victor people, the Romans, Satan indicates, who require liberation from the "servile yoke" of the tyrant Sejanus, the "wicked Favourite" of the lascivious old Roman emperor Tiberius (PR 4.102, 95). Once again, the Son resists on the basis that liberation by force is futile for a people that has, as Balachandra Rajan perceived, "surrendered to the other within itself,"[86] a condition that paralyses Israel and Samson himself in *Samson Agonistes* (Chapter 6, "Exogamy"). The global geographic displays and exhibitions of the worldly power in the concluding book of *Paradise Regained* diminish as the site of contestation is internalized: "What wise and valiant man would seek to free / These thus degenerate, by themselves enslav'd, / Or could of inward slaves make outward free?" (PR 4.143–5). The Son predicts that the end of time will bring about not the establishment but the destruction of all monuments to power. The spiritual Jerusalem will then rise up from the centre of corruption or ruins of the "Mightiest Empire[s]": "when my season comes to sit / On *David's* Throne, it shall be like a tree / Spreading and over-shadowing all the Earth / Or as a stone that shall to pieces dash / All monarchies besides throughout the world, / And of my Kingdom there shall be no end" (PR 4.146–51). In the *Aeneid*, Jove prophesies to Venus that Romulus "will then lead the race and found / The walls of Mars for Romans – named for him. / For them I will not limit time or space. / Their rule will have no end."[87] For the Christian poet, the endless kingdom is not Roman but providential.[88]

In an epic in which alternatives to the extension of imperial dominion are evinced, the *translatio studii* is also modified. Upon descending the mount of speculation, Michael in *Paradise Lost* offers Adam the following injunctions: "This having learned, thou hast attained the sum / Of wisdom; hope no higher ... only add / Deeds to thy knowledge answerable, add faith, / Add virtue, *patience, temperance*, add love, / By name to come called charity, the soul / Of all the rest" (PL 12.575–85; emphasis added). Michael's scale of virtues renders worldly knowledge and imperial power under "one empire" (PL 12.581) inferior to self-governance, so that *sapientia*, trumps *scientia*. In *Paradise Regained*, the Son's response to Satan's temptation to fame and glory rehearses Michael's lesson, using the same metrical conjoining of "patience, temperance": "But if there be in glory aught of good, / It may by means far different be attained / Without ambition, war, or violence; / By deeds of peace, by wisdom eminent, / By patience, temperance" (PR 3.88–92). Like *Paradise Lost, Paradise Regained* will ultimately rehearse the transference of authority from *scientia* to *sapientia*.

At Satan's instigation, *translatio imperii* becomes *translatio studii*: The instrument for the imperial expansionism serves as the tool for intellectual control and conquest of "all the world" (PR 4.223). Milton's account of the temptation in the wilderness is unique in its inclusion of the test of knowledge in book 4. The westward glance that Satan prompts – "Look once more, e're we leave this specular Mount / Westward, much nearer by Southwest" (PR 4.236–7) – reveals Greece, the seat of ancient intelligence, arts, and eloquence. In his 1652 letter to the Athenian-born politician and scholar Leonard Philaras, Milton confesses his temptation to use eloquence in the service of the Greek nation, enslaved by "the Ottoman tyrant" (CPW 4:853). He then, however, reminds Philaras of his duty as their spokesperson to "ignite the ancient courage, diligence, and endurance in the soul of the Greeks" in order that they might effect their own liberation. Rehearsed in the epics, Milton's warning redefines the conventionally oppositional relationship between the subjected self and the imperial other. Winning the Greeks over necessitates the mastery of their learning and culture, Satan insists in the temptation of *translatio studii*. "Be famous then / By wisdom," Satan prods the Son, "as thy Empire must extend, / So let extend thy mind o'er all the world, / In knowledge" (PR 4.221–4). The prospect of expanding the kingdom of the mind – a commonplace in Renaissance thought[89] – is one that Satan entertained in *Paradise Lost*: "The mind is its own place, and in itself / Can make a heaven of hell, a hell of heaven" (PL 1.254–5). The place the mind occupies becomes a space – a "practiced place" – and a new locus of power.

The international spaces Milton maps have philosophical, ethical, and epistemological dimensions and connotations.[90] The renderings of global space in the epic are variously construed, and Satan's readings certainly differ from God's and Adam's. The reductiveness of geographic investigation as an imperialist undertaking or as a science yielding empirical representations of the world was already being communicated in Milton's day.[91] An alternative engagement with the world and knowledge thereof arises from the philosophical tradition of locating knowledge (*scientia*) and specifically geographic knowledge within a more self-reflective moral project, the primary goal of which is wisdom (*sapientia*). The distinction between the aforementioned terms "*scientia*" and "*sapientia*" was acknowledged by

Platonists and Stoics and had been adapted for the Christian tradition by Augustine. "What dost thou in this world?" a frustrated Satan asks of the Son in a poem in which the shift from place to space epitomizes the mental odyssey (PR 4.372). From the start, "all the world" is aligned with and literally situated between Satanic strength and sinful flesh: "His weakness shall o'recome Satanic strength / And all the world, and mass of sinful flesh," God announces (PR 1.161–2). *Scientia* acquired through empirical observations of the *world*, which Satan repeatedly invokes to define and test the limits of power, contrasts with *sapientia*.[92] Whereas Satan's understanding of worldly engagement is based on power relations, the Son's is grounded in self-reflection. The Son's experience of the world recalls Milton's early experience of his ascent to the spheres, a feat accomplished through knowledge, reason, and art: Milton in "Ad Patrem" – a verse epistle to his father about his chosen profession – describes the power of poetry to order the constellations and disburden "Mauretanian Atlas" from "the weight of the stars" ("*Stellarum nec sentit onus Maurusius Atlas*").[93] The atlas that Milton had inquired about, whose prohibitive price led to his comparison of the book with the "Mauritanian mountain *Atlas*," is now deemed of lesser value than self-knowledge, acquired as an embodied being in the world.

Paradise Regained is about the constant redefinition of place and space and the distortion and restoration of vision. Milton and Milton's Satan anticipated questions about the optical illusion and "strange Parallax or Optic skill / Of vision multiplyed through air, or glass / Of Telescope" (PR 4.40–2), which enabled the spectacle of all the world's theatre of empires. Equally perplexing and compelling is the oracular experience of Satan's "Aerie Microscope" (PR 4.57) that literally narrows one's perspective while allowing simultaneous inside and outside views. Like *Paradise Lost*, however, *Paradise Regained* signals a shift from *scientia* to *sapientia*, as Milton redirects the search for knowledge from place to space, away from physical locations to various loci where spiritual truth (or error) resided. The study of Milton's repertoire of spatial ideologies and of his figures, discourses, and poetics of cosmography, geography, and empire illuminates the significance of literary evidence in the cultural history of early modern English nationhood and geopolitics. At the same time, the poetic redefinition of geographic place as space divests nation and empire of their geopolitical and territorial denotations.

CHAPTER 6

Exogamy: "Entercourse" with Philistines

"It is a grave irony ... that Milton left us his thoughts on marriage primarily in four pamphlets advocating divorce." (Annabel Patterson, "Milton, Marriage and Divorce," 2001)

"Some of these passages manifestly shew *Sampsons* weaknesse and sins, and his unwarrantable entercourse w[it]h the Philistines." (Thomas Hayne, *The General View of the Holy Scriptures*, 1640)

"As if [the Jews] had learned from their River of *Jordan*, running through the *Galilean Sea*, and not mingling therewith, daily to pass through an Ocean of other nations, and remain an unmixed, and un-confounded people by themselves. A comfortable presumption ... that they, once *Gods peculiar*, are still preserved a *peculiar people*." (Thomas Fuller, *A Pisgah-sight of Palestine*, 1650)

Ancient Israel was marked by assertions of exclusiveness and gestures of incorporation and assimilation. Prohibitions against intermarriage and injunctions to crush the enemy confirmed the Israelites' chosen status, but the interdictions and models of retaliation were counterbalanced by examples of the accommodation and the acculturation of outsiders (strangers).[1] Although toleration is conventionally among the casualties of elect nationhood, in Milton's *Samson Agonistes*, in which Israelite chosenness is interrogated and divisions within the peculiar nation exposed, the terms of inclusion and exclusion are redefined. Significantly, any negotiation in the poem occurs along legal, philosophical, and ethical more than ethnic lines. *Samson Agonistes* is not an allegory of nationhood, and yet the poem invites comparisons between Samson's contest and ancient Israel's turbulent history of nation formation as represented by the encounters with national and trans-national differences and feminized otherness and paradoxically by the struggle for reintegration in the midst of defeat.

Historically and biblically, the Israelites shared a geography, etymology, and genealogy with the Philistines. "Palaestinus" denotes Hebrew, Milton implies in "Ad Patrem."[2] George Sandys refers to the biblical Philistines as "Palestines" from whom the "whole Land of Promise" or Palestine derived its name.[3] Genesis 10 notes the shared ancestry of the Hebrews and Philistines, although *Samson Agonistes* is set in a time long after the common genealogical line of the Philistines and Jews was severed with the founding of Israel, beginning with Jacob (Israel). During the period of the Danite Samson's judgeship, Israel, along with Judah, was subject to the Philistines as well as being internally fractured. Milton's Greek tragedy, which features Samson, "this great Deliverer now … / … / Himself in bonds under *Philistian* yoke" (SA 40, 42), focuses on the aftermath of the Israelites' overthrow by what is otherwise a "little nation," namely, Philistia.[4] *Samson Agonistes* in turn conceives the nation out of dislocation and in "entercourse" with foreignness, which the poet repudiates, occasionally recuperates, and eventually relegates to the interior world of the self.

The reception history of *Samson Agonistes* is steeped in regenerationist readings that have advanced typological or antinomian interpretations of the dramatic poem. Critics thus have largely reinforced the poem's dichotomies – Hebrew and Philistine, Samson and Dalila, God and Dagon, Old Testament and New Testament law.[5] In this chapter, the treatment of the poem's complications of those binaries is mediated by discussions of Milton's formulations of natural law, the law of nations or international law, and Hebrew Law – on which the poet and polemicist leans very heavily. Conformity to the national law (or "National obstriction" [SA 312]) is a marker of identity and a means of delineating the contours and character of the nation: "the Law is the *Israelite*" and will "*make no cov'nant with sin the Canaanite*," Milton repeats in his *Doctrine and Discipline of Divorce*, in which the unwritten law of divorce is commensurate with natural law and the law of nations (CPW 2:288, 2:343). A study of *Samson Agonistes* in relation to Milton's unorthodox theories about marriage, "not only its proper contraction, but also, if need be, its dissolution" or divorce (CPW 4:624), demonstrates how ethnic and religious differences within both the domestic and public realms are channelled into debates about psychological, mental, and moral compatibility and finally translated into a (closet) drama of self-estrangement.

The Bondage of Canon Law

Milton's writings on marriage, a subject largely confined to his divorce tracts,[6] support his broader agenda to advance domestic liberty, which, along with ecclesiastical liberty, characterizes his program for the Reformation nation in the first half of his career. Recalling in 1654 his early contributions to public discourse, Milton emphasizes that his defences of marriage and divorce were formulated fully "in accordance with divine law," which was upheld by Christ, who in turn never endorsed any law in civil life "more weighty" than Mosaic Law (CPW 4:624). The promotion of a monist conception of the Law implied here situates Milton in a tradition of political theorists and natural law philosophers that, in the seventeenth century, included Hugo Grotius (*De Jure Belli as Pacis*, 1625) and John Selden (*De Jure Naturali et Gentium juxta Disciplinam Ebraeorum*, 1640), Selden representing for Milton on the national stage what Grotius stood for internationally – the pinnacle of learning.[7] In that line-up of legal and philosophical writings also belong James Harrington's *Oceana* (1656) and *The Art of Lawgiving* (1659), Samuel von Pufendorf's *De Jure Naturae et Gentium* (1672) – which engages Grotius, Selden, and Thomas Hobbes and also offers a lengthy critique of Milton's *Doctrine and Discipline of Divorce*[8] – John Locke's *Letter Concerning Toleration* (1689), and later, Jean Barbeyrac's editions of Grotius and Pufendorf (1738, 1749).

Curiously, Milton's discussions of law, including natural law – and, paradoxically, his meditations on charity – are primarily reserved for the notorious divorce tracts and the anti-monarchy *Defence*s (Chapter 3, "Natural Law"), which justify rights that have an uneasy or strained relationship with conventional interpretations of the law. Throughout his defences of ecclesiastical, domestic, and civil liberty and reform, Milton broadens the parameters of the law and not infrequently turns exceptions into new standards and rules. To name but a few examples thereof relevant to this book: Milton builds his church of one[9] from stones laid in contiguity (Chapter 1, "Temple-worke"; CPW 2:555); he recommends indifferency as a principle of toleration (and of marriage); his tracts on domestic liberty refuse to reduce divorce to a transgression, prohibition, or dispensation (in fact, he champions divorce as an exercise in natural law and as an act of Godly sufferance and beneficence). Furthermore, he converts the regicide into an expression of civil and natural law; he substitutes the *sanior pars* for the nation (Chapter 3); he sanctions the controversial performances of Gideon, Jephthah, Jael, and Samson, among others, while entertaining that of Dalila. Finally, Milton portrays the displaced Samson "[e]yeless in *Gaza* at the Mill with slaves" as the chosen nation of Israel (SA 41), and he imagines himself as "a nation unto himself."[10]

In a fallen world, the embrace of law and liberty entails for Milton a release from bondage in the domestic and public spheres. The national program he outlines is intended to bring about a present-day Reformation and the renewal of the Church and commonwealth (CPW 2:433–4). In his address to Parliament in *The Judgement of Martin Bucer* (1644), Milton compares the act of temple-work, that is, the construction of the Reformation nation discussed in Chapter 1, to the establishment of healthy domestic relations: "the constitution and reformation of a com-mon-wealth, if *Ezra* and *Nehemiah* did not mis-reform, is, like a building, to begin orderly from the foundation therof, which is mariage and the family" (CPW 2:431). Interrelated figures of a nation diseased by a tyran-nical government and of a husband emasculated by a dysfunctional mar-riage pervade Milton's divorce tracts, which feature the domestic sphere as a microcosm of the state and nation: "as a whole people is in propor-tion to an ill Government, so is one man to an ill mariage" (CPW 2:229). In his divorce tracts and the outlines for his tragedies, including *Samson Agonistes*, Milton compares marriage to affairs of government,[11] but he also observes that spousal relations affect one's civic and national commitments: A man imprisoned in a bad marriage will, on the one hand, be impotent, that is, "unactive to all public service, dead to the Common-wealth" and, on the other, "unprofitable and dangerous" or a burden and detriment to the commonwealth. Correspondingly, the prohibition against the reform of divorce legislation denies human liber-ties and represses human nature, thus rendering the trapped, enslaved parties "vitious, useless to friend, unserviceable and spiritless to the Common-wealth."[12]

First published in 1643, *The Doctrine and Discipline of Divorce: Restor'd to the Good of Both Sexes, From the Bondage of Canon Law* – a defence of the Mosaic law of divorce – was Milton's anonymous but hardly incon-spicuous re-entry into the arena of theological controversy, church disci-pline, and the polemics on liberty, notably domestic liberty.[13] At the time, Protestant reformers maintained a fervent commitment to the doctrine of the marriage contract as an indissoluable bond.[14] The terms for licensing marriage in Milton's day were outlined in the *Constitutions and Canons Ecclesiasticall*, and the conditions for divorce, including the edict against remarriage, followed thereupon.[15] Reinforced by the Established Church, which retained its jurisdiction over the rite of marriage, divorce *a mensa et thoro* (from table and bed) was condoned, but remarriage after divorce (divorce *a vincula*) was not. Although there were numerous exceptions to the rule, remarriage was legal in seventeenth-century England only for the innocent partner of an adulterous marriage or one who had been deserted. As in the case of his ineffectual campaign for disestablishment on the eve of the Restoration, discussed in Chapter 4, Milton remained at odds with a stubborn ecclesiastical and legal system.

In addition to citing the ancient precedents for the practice of divorce in Moses' time and in the Roman and Byzantine empires of Constantine and Justinian, Milton declares that divorce is legitimate according to the terms of natural law and liberty of conscience. Canonical tyranny – as Milton characterized divorce legislation at the outset – condemns trapped marriage partners to a life of drudgery, that is, to the demeaning labour of "grind[ing] in the mill of an undelighted and servil copulation" (CPW 2:258). To such a fate is the tragic hero in *Samson Agonistes*, the figure of a subjected but also self-enslaved Israel, sentenced at the hands of Dalila and the Philistines (SA 41, 415; Judges 16:21). In the *Doctrine and Discipline of Divorce*, Milton radically reinterprets Christ's prohibition of divorce and uses scriptural exegesis and reason to test and dismantle rigid thinking on the subject. Divorce law is not a concession to hardheartedness, Milton insists, and does not license sin, which he distinguishes from law, sin being "an eternal outlaw, and in hostility with law past all atonement." Indeed, sin and law are "*diagonal* contraries" (CPW 2:288). In the Second Book of the *Doctrine and Discipline of Divorce*, Milton ascribes "a hatefull hard-hearted[ness]" to those who forbid the dissolution of a bad marriage (CPW 2:328–9). In a strategy he applies in various polemical writings, Milton lines up the magistrates, clerics, and other opponents of divorce behind the "Canon Doctors." Through their "papal encroachment," the enforcers of canon law appropriate divine authority and meddle in private, domestic affairs by "pluck[ing] the power & arbitrement of divorce from the master of family, into whose hands God & the law of all Nations had put it" (CPW 2:342, 343). In *Tetrachordon*, Milton not only enlists Christ in the validation of Mosaic Law, as noted at the outset of this section, but simultaneously casts the canon makers as lawbreakers in Christ's eyes. "Our Saviour was by the doctors of his time suspected of intending to dissolve the law," but Christ turns the tables by condoning divorce in support of "the equity of this particular law against the foreseene rashnesse of common textuaries, who abolish lawes, as the rable demolish images ... perceiv[ing] not how they abolish right, and equall, and justice, under the appearance of *judicial*" (CPW 2:639, 640). Specifically designated as preservers of the Law, the Pharisees, that is, the "separated ones," become the transgressors of the Law, a designation Milton applies to the ecclesiasts of his day. In turn, he campaigns for the transference of the church doctors' power into matters of conscience, and he defends divorce as an exercise in reviving liberty.

Milton's argument for the legalization of divorce is founded on principles of toleration, which take the form of sufferance throughout *Tetrachordon*. In an extended discussion of the definition of "sufferance," Milton maintains that the term refers to legal obligation and permission, so that "to *suffer* is but the legall phrase denoting what by law a man may doe or not doe" (CPW 2:660). He also strategically ties divorce and God's sufferance of divorce to the law of nature and of nations, deemed secondary to divine law. Although all were originally made equal and entitled to common rights, as mentioned in Chapter 3, "Natural Law," God condoned divorce "as a remedy against intolerable wrong and servitude" in a fallen world (CPW 2:661). To forbid divorce is to abolish the "whole law of nations, as only sufferd for the same cause," that is, for the restitution against injustices (CPW 2:662). Milton then shifts to a positive toleration: "this law of divorce hath many wise and charitable ends" (CPW 2:663). Not only is divorce a moral law "altogether conversant in good or evill" (CPW 2:642), but it is an act of benevolence and generosity of spirit. Milton maintains that by implementing legislation in support of divorce, the civil leaders would be heeding "the greatest, the perfetest, the highest commandment" (CPW 2:667), namely that of charity, a term that unexpectedly reverberates throughout divorce tracts – ninety-two times, in fact.[16] Law must be conversant with ethical considerations, although arguably extra-legal. In what would otherwise be a contravention of marriage laws, a woman may take "the Law of God and Conscience" into her own hands, and, in the name of self-defence, "secure her Person from his [her husband's] violence by absence (though that ordinarily be against the Law of Marriage, and the end of it)," states Presbyterian minister Herbert Palmer, who would, however, denounce Milton as a divorcer.[17] Although subscribing to traditional assumptions about gender relations in his day, captured in such expressions as "woman was created for man, and not man for woman," Milton recognizes that civil and natural law tolerates certain qualifications of male domination in marriage: "particular exceptions may have place, if she exceed her husband in prudence and dexterity, and he contentedly yeeld, for then a superior and more naturall law comes in, that the wiser should govern the lesse wise, whether male or female" (CPW 2:324; 2:589). As one might expect of an early modern thinker, any adjustment to the male-dominated gender hierarchy is an exceptional and temporary measure. In his broader argument for liberty in the domestic sphere, however, divorce, intended for the "good of both sexes," emerges for Milton as a rule and charity becomes its impetus, justification, and consequence.

In support of his bold claims about divorce, Milton turned to the philo-semitic work of the legal historians and Christian Hebraists.[18] As announced in the heading of the Preface to Book 1 of *The Doctrine and Discipline of Divorce* (CPW 2:234), Milton enlists Hugo Grotius, biblical exegete and father of the science on international law, in the cause. Grotius opened up a subject, namely that of divorce, that canon makers had foreclosed debate on: Recalling his reading of Matthew 5 in Grotius's *Annotationes in Libros Evangeliorium* (1641), Milton announces that the biblical expounder "excites the diligence of others to enquire further into this question, as containing many points that have not yet been explain'd" (CPW 2:238). Milton himself will develop Grotius's argument for the purposes of advancing temple-work, that is, the "generall labour of reformation."[19] Upon completing the *Doctrine and Discipline of Divorce*, Milton declares in the *Judgement of Martin Bucer* that he understood Grotius as "inclining to reasonable terms in this controversie" by implying that the law of charity is "the true end of wedlock" (CPW 2:434). In his internationally renowned treatise *De Jure Belli as Pacis* (1625), a copy of which Milton also had in his library, Grotius observed that God intended marriage to be permanent; the possibility of dissolution, however, is not completely ruled out: "it is not … proved that God had then commanded that this bond should not be broken for any cause whatever."[20] Divorce is within the parameters of the Law, and given that the moral code of the Hebrew Bible was commensurate with natural law, it was also relevant for Christians: "All that was enjoined by the law of Moses with reference to those virtues which Christ requires of His disciples, is just as much … to be required of Christians now."[21]

If Milton's antiprelatical tracts and the late religious tracts promote the separation of Old Testament legalism from New Testament truths, as Chapters 1 and 4 respectively sought to demonstrate, the divorce tracts support a conception of Judeo-Christian law as continuous. To back up his central contention that Jesus did not abrogate Mosaic teachings on divorce, Milton turns to Puritan theologian William Perkins, although he in practice opposes him on such issues as remarriage for reasons other than adultery.[22] "*Perkins* must needs grant," decides Milton, "that somthing then is left to that law which Christ found no fault with; and what can that be but the conscionable use of such liberty as the plain words import?" (CPW 2:320). Milton pushes for a liberal, monist reading of the Law and, despite Perkins's insistence to the contrary, he protests that Christ did not restrict divorce to cases of adultery.

The matter of religious incompatibility between marriage parties enters the discussion in *Christian Oeconomie*, in which Perkins cites Ambrose, Lombard, and Augustine in defence of his gloss on I Corinthians 7:15, which tolerates the separation of the unbeliever from the believer. "It is far better," explains Perkins, "that the covenant should be dissolved, that man and wife have made each with other, then ... the Covenant which man hath made with God." He finds support for his position in the Hebrew Bible, notably the Book of Ezra, whose author was the scribal priest instrumental to the reform of Judaism and the establishment of the Torah as the constitution. Aiding the work of Nehemiah, the governor of Judah, Ezra outlawed mixed marriages that defiled the fragile community in the postexilic period. "The people of Israel being in affliction, were constrained to break the former made with strange women, that they might keepe the latter, Ezra 10.11.19," Perkins notes.[23] Thereafter Perkins inserts into his commentary a non-Pauline clause that licenses the dissolution of the marriage bond given the unlikelihood of the conversion or penance of the unbeliever.

According to Milton in the *Doctrine and Discipline of Divorce*, the Second Epistle to the Corinthians likewise lends itself to a lesson on the doctrine and discipline of divorce. Again the Pauline exposition of the Deuteronomic dictate on intermarriage is made to conform to Milton's radical argument for divorce as consistent with the law of nature: "Therefore saith the Apostle 2 *Cor. 6. Mis-yoke not together with Infidels, ...* *what concord hath Christ with Belial? what part hath he that beleeveth with* *an Infidell?*" In expanding his analysis, Milton asserts that Paul confidently and zealously defended "a generall divorce between the faithfull and unfaithfull seed" (CPW 2:262; Deut. 22:9–10). In chapter 10 of the divorce tract, Milton has Paul expounding again on the Deuteronomic injunction against cross-contamination and "mis-yoking"; however, as Milton notes, Paul's illustration is restricted to one example of "mismatching with an Infidell." As usual, Milton takes the liberty to extrapolate, and in so doing, diverts the discussion to mental and psychological inconsonance: "what can be a fouler incongruity, a greater violence to the reverend secret of nature, then to force a mixture of minds that cannot unite," a violation, then, of the law of nature (CPW 2:270). When Milton appealed to Parliament and the Assembly for the reform of divorce legislation, he advanced the nebulous concept of spiritual, psychological, or emotional incompatibility in order to promote a more charitable application of the Christian tradition by virtue of its relation to rather than departure from the Law. Incompatibility in marriage is unnatural, and neither God nor nature would condone the consorting of "unmingling natures" or discordant parties, Milton argued, seeking to prevent the restraint of "honest liberties" (CPW 2:272; 2:229). The compulsory enforcement of marital bonds under any condition is more detrimental to marriage and Christianity than is the joining of ethnically diverse persons (CPW 2:280, *Colasterion* CPW 2:731). Represented in the Hebrew Bible as marriage between Jews and Gentiles, exogamy – the conjunction of domestic, national, and international relations – becomes for Milton a metaphor for the "fouler incongruity" and "greater violence" of the forced union of mixed minds (CPW 2:270).

Milton's vocal critics were outraged. As surveyed in Chapter 1, his tracts on divorce were "implacably hounded" by anti-tolerationists in the 1640s.[24] Herbert Palmer, William Prynne, Robert Baillie, and Presbyterian cleric Thomas Edwards were among Milton's detractors, accusing him of Anabaptist and antinomian fanaticism, and, in Edwards's case, of licensing adultery.[25] In the year after Milton published the first edition of the *Doctrine and Discipline of Divorce*, Prynne, in the name of a Presbyterian government, a national church, and a "setled Reformation," vilified the Independents for the "dangerous divisions" they created between the Church and state. Represented in its extreme by the likes of Roger Williams, the notorious defender of liberty of conscience for "*Jew, Turk, Pagan, Papist, Arminian, Anabaptist,*" the licentiousness of the Independents and dissenters gave rise to heresies, the "many *Anabaptisticall, Antinomian, Hereticall, Atheisticall opinions, as of the souls mortality, divorce at pleasure, &c.* lately Broached, Preached, Printed in this famous City."[26] In a sermon later printed, Palmer confronts the Westminster Assembly about appeals for what he characterizes as an "ungodly Toleration" made "under the pretence of Liberty of Conscience": "If any plead Conscience for the Lawfulnesse of Polygamy; (or for divorce for other causes then Christ and His Apostles mention; Of which a *wicked booke* is abroad and *uncensured*, though *deserving to be burnt*...) ... will you grant a *Toleration* for all *this*?"[27] The following month would see the Stationers' Company complaining to the Lords about Milton's "scandalous books," although shortly thereafter (1645), the *Doctrine and Discipline of Divorce* would be reissued. Less than a decade later, the Nominated Assembly's *Act Touching Marriage* (1653) gave the Justice of the Peace jurisdiction over what Milton characterized as a "civil ordinance, a houshold contract, a thing indifferent and free to the whole race of mankinde."[28] Milton credits the Assembly with the recovery of "the civil liberty of marriage from th[e] incroachment" of ministers (CPW 7:300), although the justices were not granted authority over divorce procedures.[29] That year, in the early stages of the debate about the Jewish readmission, Alexander Ross aligns Anabaptist convictions with ancient heresies, denounces the alleged Anabaptist position on divorce, whereby "a man may put away his Wife, though not for adultery," and reviles the sectaries for their shameful imitation of the customs of the Jews – here labelled "old Hereticks."[30] Despite the backlash from his defence of the doctrine and discipline of divorce, Milton remained invested in the cause and would, near the end of his life, return to render it into verse.

"Mingling shall be his destruction"

The interdictions against exogamy, for which the books of Ezra and Nehemiah (and Deuteronomy) remained touchstones, demarcated national identities and boundaries. In Milton's day, the argument for the segregation of the Irish was urged as a means of preserving the purity and integrity of the English. In the wake of the Irish Rising, Protestant minister Daniel Harcourt compared the Irish to the Philistines and called for holy violence against the Rebels, given that "the sonne of *Hagar* now abuses the heire of the Promise, now is disoculated *Sampson* that grindes his abused soule more then their meale brought forth to make pastime to the Philistims."[31] He ends his diatribe with an exhortation against exogamy: As he calls the English to arms, Harcourt reminds them about the Israelites' oath at Mizpeh, "none of us shall give his daughter to the Benjamite, to wife."[32] A decade later, following Cromwell's bloody Irish conquest (Chapter 2, "Reduction"), officers in the occupied districts of Ireland issued an appeal for the transplantation of the Irish to prevent fornication by prohibiting the English settlers from "becoming one with those Irish, as wel in affinity as Idolatry." The 1655 petition continues with citations of Judaic interdictions from Ezra and proof texts from Deuteronomy, Numbers, and Judges of the visitation of God's wrath on the "unclean Land" for the "corporall and spiritual fornication" of its mingled people. Another pressing reason for the transplantation urged by the officers is the threat faced by the colonizers, it being consistent with the natural law principle of self-preservation to retaliate by "destroy[ing] the Enemies of their holy Faith ... and lawfull[y] ... war[ring] against Hereticks (which they conclude us to be) since, say they [the Irish], such a war tends to the defence and amplification of Faith."[33] The petitioners acknowledge the natural inclination of a conquered and barbarous people to exercise charitable hatred. It is this intersecting narrative of the Hebrews' "entercourse" with strangers in marriage and in holy war that is played out in *Samson Agonistes*, in which the position of the other, although treated *disparagingly* (literally, "as an unequal marriage partner"), is also accommodated.

In his edition of Milton's dramatic poem, John Carey states that no scriptural prohibition seems to bar marriage with Philistines, and that marriage with Gentiles was not considered unclean until the time of Ezra.[34] Ezra and Nehemiah, however, merely reinstate the ordinances set out in Deuteronomy (e.g., Ezra 9:1 repeats Deut. 7:3). That intermarriage with Philistines was forbidden is implied in the denunciations of Canaanite uncleanness and paganism in Genesis 28:6–7, Exodus 34:12–6, Deuteronomy 7:3–4.[35] In *Samson Agonistes*, the Philistines are cast as "Sons of *Caphtor*" (SA 1703), Caphtor being identified with Crete, the Delta of the Nile and Cilicia[36] – from where the Philistines were thought to have gone to Canaan, which they conquered. Among Samson's numerous epithets for his wife, Dalila, is "A *Canaanite, my* faithless enemy" (SA 380), and both the Chorus and Manoa question Samson about his exogamous marriages.

Thomas Taylor in *The Progresse of Saints* admonishes his Christian readers to "abstaine from idolaters in the nearest society, which is marriage; for this hath a manifest appearance of evill." He cites the expected biblical glosses, 2 Cor. 6.14: "Be not unequally yoked"; 2 John 10: "Receive not such into thy house: much lesse into thy heart or bosome"; and Exod. 23: "the Lord wisheth the Israelites to forbeare marriage with those seven Nations of the Heathens, for feare of seduction." The objector in the treatise's rhetorical exchange notes the provision in scriptures of "approved examples" of exogamy, including Samson's marriage to the woman of Timna. Granting the allowance for exceptions, the respondent states,

> Some of these examples were of women converted, as *Rahab* and *Ruth*: now what they had beene, was no hindrance, the case being that of the captives taken in warre, who might be married, Deut. 21. but conditionally, if they betooke them to the true religion .... Some of them were women not converted, as *Sampsons* wife, but he married her by diuine instinct, that there might be occasion taken of reuenge against the *Philistims*, Iudg. 14.4. Now we must *walke by the rule*, not by an exception from it (Gal. 6.16. 3).[37]

In *Tetrachordon*, Milton takes up the example of Rahab, the harlot of Jericho who protected Joshua's spies, in reference to a larger argument about the terms of marriage and divorce for Israelites and between Israelites and "strangers" or foreigners. Admittedly, Rahab was not a Hebrew, Milton acknowledges, but foreigners like Rahab, "not beeing *Canaanites,* and they also beeing Converts might bee lawfully maryed" (CPW 2:628). Milton uses the example of Rahab to steer between the worlds of the chosen and the infidel in order to make the larger point that divorce between Israelites was as permissible and straightforward as divorce from a stranger in an exogamous marriage. Seeking to naturalize divorce by recourse to Hebrew legal precedents, Milton turns an exception into a rule, one not answerable to institutional authority. *Samson Agonistes* will see him wrestling with the same issues in the portrayal of the marriage between Samson and the woman of Timna, as well as in the depiction of Samson's exogamous marriage with Dalila, a Canaanite whose conversion, unlike Rahab's, is *not* "heer suppos'd" (CPW 2:628). As Rachel Trubowitz perceptively notes, Milton in *Samson Agonistes* permits Dalila's foreignness,[38] which turns out to be the lesser impediment in the marital relationship, as was also the case in the divorce tracts.

In reference to their son's marriage choice, Manoa and his wife in the Book of Judges ask, "Is there never a woman among the daughters of thy brethren or among all my people, that thou goest to take a wife of the uncircumcised Philistines?" (Judges 14:3). Confronted about his insistence on intermarriage, Milton's Samson pleads divine prompting: "what I motioned was of God; I knew / From intimate impulse, and therefore urg'd / The Marriage on; that by occasion hence / I might begin *Israel's* Deliverance" (SA 222–5). The corresponding biblical source text (Judges 14:4) reads, "It was of the Lord, that hee sought an occasion against the Philistines." The poem is more troubled than is the biblical book by Samson's exogamy. God is entitled to dispense with the law, that is, with "National obstriction," surmises the Chorus, in an effort to explain what could have "prompted this Heroic *Nazarite*, / Against his vow of strictest purity, / To seek in marriage that fallacious Bride, / Unclean, unchaste." The Chorus, however, reverses its verdict: "Down Reason then, at least vain reasonings down, / Though Reason here aver / That moral verdict quits her of unclean."[39] In the *Christian Doctrine*, Milton had observed that the right to divorce was abused in Moses' time by many "merely on the pretext of uncleanness, without any just cause" (CPW 6:373). The Chorus itself rashly and mistakenly pronounced the uncleanness of the woman of Timnah "without any just cause." Having determined that "vain reasonings" contrived the unjust accusation, the Chorus moves to acquit the woman of Timna (SA 324), and, by extension, vindicate the "Heroic *Nazarite*" Samson from the charge of violating Hebrew marriage laws.

When Delilah is introduced in Judges 16:4, she is identified as the subject of Samson's next attraction and by the place of her origin: "And it came to passe afterward, that he loved a woman in the valley of Sorek, whose name was Delilah." The valley of Sorek separated the Land of Judah from the Philistines, and its liminal geographic location reinforces Delilah's own marginality – geographic, national, and moral. In the Book of Judges, her nationality is left unspecified: She may have been an Israelite or a daughter of the Philistines, to whom Israel was subject. Likely she was the latter because she served the Philistine Lords, according to Jewish exegetes, including Levi ben Gerson (Gersonides) and Isaac ben Judah Abrabanel. For Josephus and Philo, Delilah is a harlot, although according to the latter, Samson marries her. In their respective works, *Jewish Antiquities* and *Biblical Antiquities*, Samson's intercourse with foreignness is described as his curse and cause of his downfall. Samson transgressed against the laws of his ancestors and tarnished his Nazarite identity by imitating "foreign usages," Josephus judges. In Philo, God accuses Samson of "mingl[ing] with the daughters of the Philistines," and in contrast to Joseph, who refused to "afflict his seed," Samson's "mingling shall be his destruction," God judges.[40] In medieval and early modern literature and homiletics, Delilah would be cast as a figure who rendered men religiously and patriotically disloyal.[41]

Since ancient times, chosenness was aligned with an "unmixed, and unconfounded" condition, whereby no "mingling … with … other nations" occurred. Such a status is no longer enjoyed by the Jews, Thomas Fuller judges, chastising them for their presumption.[42] Samson's own "mingling" was a controversial subject. Exegetes, especially those who affirmed the Nazarite's heroism, struggled with his attraction to Philistine women, and Samson's courtship with Dalila is particularly vexing in this regard. Dominican Cardinal Cajetan, who with rabbinical assistance prepared a literal translation of the Bible, inferred Delilah's Hebrew identity from his scriptural explication: "*Nescitur, an mulier ista fuerit Hebraea, an Pelistina*" ("It is unknown whether that woman was Hebrew or Philistine") raises the question on the matter, although Cajetan's position is hardly neutral: "*ista*" invests the word "*mulier*" with a pejorative meaning. "*[E]x eo tamen, quòd non scribitur Pelistina, innuitur, quòd non erat alienigena, sed Hebraea*": because the text does not explicitly call Delilah a foreigner, Cajetan observes, one presumes she was Hebrew.[43] F. Michael Krouse determines that Cajetan is the sole exegete who defended Delilah,[44] although Cajetan's hypothesis that Delilah was Jewish is primarily intended to restore Samson's integrity. Other scriptural commentators, including Gersonides, Moses Maimonides, and later John Selden, decided that Samson's wives must have converted to Judaism before he married them.[45]

As for Milton, he opts for the untraditional identification of the biblical Delilah as Samson's wife,[46] although one unsuited to a "meet and

happy conversation" (CPW 2:246), thus Manoa's complaint: "I cannot praise thy Marriage choises, Son, / Rather approv'd them not" (SA
420–1). Samson himself admits to choosing Dalila from among his foes
rather than from "the daughters of my Tribe / And of my Nation" (SA
876–7; also 1192). The verses continue with a lament of how he loved
Dalila "too well … / Too well" (SA 878–9), thus duplicating and dou-
bling the sin of Shakespeare's Othello. Samson's explanation for the
marriage choice in this exchange with Dalila differs from his previous
declaration that he sought to infiltrate the Philistine forces through
access to her and thus "oppress / *Israel*'s oppressours" (SA 232–3). Manoa
recalls that Samson defended his decision to marry Dalila on the basis
that he might "Find some occasion to infest our Foes" (SA 422). At the
same time that Samson bemoans his ill-fated match, the poem at large
registers ambivalence about the exogamous marriage and, by extension,
about interracial compatibility and the toleration of otherness in the
realm of the elect.

From Grotius's *De Jure Belli ac Pacis*, Milton might have learned that
foreigners in England, including Catholics, were "Privileg'd by the Law
of Nations," as Milton concedes in *Of True Religion, Hæresie, Schism,
Toleration* (1673).[47] At the centre of *Samson Agonistes*, Samson arraigns
Dalila and finds her guilty of transgressing "the law of nature, law of
nations."[48] Here in the poem, the dispensation or exemption granted to
the foreigner gives way to marriage laws. By virtue of marriage and the
gender hierarchy, wives are admitted into their husbands' families, Grotius
explains.[49] Although the laws given to and by Moses to the Jews did not
fully accord with the universally applicable Adamic and Noachide commandments, in the case of marriage, the international law is joined with
Hebrew Law:

> [W]hen God said through Adam, or through Moses, that so strong was the
> bond of marriage that the husband ought to leave the family of his parent
> in order to establish a new family with his wife, he said almost the same as
> is said to the daughter of Pharaoh in the eleventh verse of the forty-fifth
> Psalm: "Forget also thine own people and thy father's house."[50]

If a Grotian lens is applied to an interpretation of *Samson Agonistes*,
Samson has a legal claim on Dalila when he reminds her of her obligation "to leave / Parents and countrey" (SA 885–6). The ethical nature of
the country to which Dalila professes allegiance is also at issue: Dalila's
complicity with what Samson characterizes as "an impious crew / Of men
conspiring to uphold their state" (SA 891–2) allegedly invalidates her piety
and patriotism.

Samson Agonistes does allow space for a more nuanced reading of the Samson–Dalila relationship and the character of Dalila herself. Although critics like Stanley Fish have reduced the character of Dalila to "an object of [the Philistines'] interpretive desire," it is noteworthy that no one before Milton accorded Delilah/Dalila as much agency as she demonstrates in *Samson Agonistes*.[51] Dalila eventually succumbs to Philistine compulsion but not without first exercising masculine resolve to fend off the authorities, a feat reflected as well in her muscular verse style[52]: "Hear what assaults I had, what snares besides, / What sieges girt me round, e're I consented; / Which might have aw'd the best resolv'd of men, / The constantest to have yielded without blame" (SA 845–8). Dalila unsettles the victim testimony and passivity that her speeches also exhibit through her shrewd and strategic use of legalisms, expressed in internally balanced verses that communicate a deliberate assent to the authoritative dictum "to the public good / Private respects must yield" (SA 867–8). Although guilty of "breaking marriage-faith to circumvent" Samson (SA 1115), she concludes that sacrifices in the name of patriotism are signs of a higher calling, a classical precedent for which is discussed in Chapter 5. This is also Samson's defence when confronted about his controversial exogamous marriages.[53]

It is the "impious crew" of Philistine officials that bribed Dalila with gold, Samson repeatedly accuses (SA 390, 831, 849, 959, 1114), but here, in the middle of the poem, he alters the charge against her by judging, "zeal moved thee; / To please thy gods thou didst it" (SA 895–6). In so doing, Samson converts Dalila's temptation into one worthy of Jesus' trial: In *Paradise Regained*, the companion poem to *Samson Agonistes*, Satan tests the Son with an opportunity to exercise authority in the cause of liberty: "let move thee Zeal, / And Duty; Zeal and Duty are not slow; / ... / ... / Zeal of thy Fathers house, Duty to free / Thy Country from her Heathen servitude" (PR 3.171–6). It is a temptation by which the Son earlier confesses himself moved (PR 1.215–20). As for Dalila, she seeks to legitimize the acts for which Samson divorces her: Fated to be vilified by the Israelites for treachery, Dalila aligns herself with celebrated biblical women, patriotic wives, who surrender "private respects" in the name of a nobler cause.[54] More specifically, she scripts for herself a history that recounts sacrifices made in the line of duty for *her country*, a phrase she utters repeatedly in the poem to underscore her national subjecthood (SA 975–94). At the same time, justification of her valorous deed involves an embrace and appropriation of an Old Testament model of deliverance: "Not less renown'd" is she, boasts Dalila,

> then in Mount *Ephraim*,
> *Jael*, who with inhospitable guile
> Smote *Sisera* sleeping through the Temples nail'd.
> Nor shall I count it hainous to enjoy
> The public marks of honour and reward
> Conferr'd upon me, for the piety
> Which to my countrey I was judg'd to have shewn. (SA 988–94)

The salience of the prosodic "Smote *Sisera* sleeping," with its alliteration and elision ("Smote Sis'ra sleeping"), supports the identification of the Philistine deliverer with the Hebrew champion, Jael.[55] "It is only because the victim is on the other side," Mieke Bal says about the account of Sisera and Jael in Judges, ch. 4, that the latter "gets away with less – even if not so much less! – contempt than Delilah."[56] In the seventeenth century, the example of Jael was cited, among many others, by Katherine Chidley. In *The Justification of the Independant Churches*, Chidley, in anticipation of Milton's accusation that canon makers are lawbreakers, denounced canon law as "the Discipline of Antichrist" and championed separation from the Church of England as a condition for toleration. As noted in Chapter 1 ("Temple-worke"), Chidley invited a comparison between herself and the champion, Jael, who "smote [a] naile into his [Sisera's] temples"[57] in defence of Israel.

Critics have regularly remarked on the compelling nature of Dalila's discourse and valiant defence of a national cause. Norman T. Burns, who acknowledges the potency of Dalila's speech – "it is characteristic of Milton to give strong arguments to his unsympathetic characters" – nevertheless determines that no discerning reader will fail to distinguish Dalila's treachery from Jael's righteous deed of violence performed in the service of God.[58] John Shawcross credits Dalila with broaching the key question about "whose nation is right, whose god is true god?" and recommends that she be recognized as "a verisimilar character to be understood as herself." He insists, however, on reading the poem as confirmation of the deliverance of those who, like Jesus, keep the faith or who, like Samson, undergo renovation.[59] Attentive to the various pressures in the poem caused by the antinomy of nationalism, Victoria Kahn explains that in assigning powerful discourse to Dalila, Milton hopes to "clarify ... by contraries, the true idea of the nation"[60] – a significant insight about a work that provocatively sets up comparisons between Samson's and Dalila's commitments to their marital bond and national obligations.

Dalila's self-testimony does not lack dismantling features, which, for example, connect the "double-fac't" and "double-mouth'd" nature of the

fame she seeks to her own and Dagon's duplicity (SA 971).[61] In a classical tragedy featuring a Hebrew combatant, the memory Dalila creates for
herself heightens the Greek irony. "It is her infamy that will be imparted
to the ages, since her story is to be told by Hebrews, not by Philistines,"
Gordon Teskey states in a reminder that history is produced and documented by the winners.[62] Moreover, after being divorced by her husband
(SA 955–9), Dalila is dismissed and generally glossed over in the poem's
reception history, partly conditioned by the Chorus's derisive remarks.
From Samson's perspective and that of the chosen nation, Dalila's arguments are spurious, and her testimony about the rewards of self-sacrifice
for a perfidious nation is reprehensible. Tellingly, however, Dalila's words
are etched into Samson's/the nation's historical memory[63] and present a
different side of the conflict and, correspondingly, of national commitment. Her self-defence ultimately participates in a process, albeit inconsis-
tently and haltingly enacted throughout the tragedy, of de-orientalizing,
whereby the position of the orientalized other is brought to the fore.
Milton inserts "cultural and historical relativity" in the narrative through
the portrayal of Dalila, whose prowess and national loyalty are destined
to be acclaimed and rewarded by her people.[64] The poem accommodates
additional glimpses of the Philistines from alternative perspectives. Samson
acknowledges the rehearsal of his tragedy by non-Jews: He anticipates the
condemnation of his "sin" by "Gentiles in thir Parables" (SA 500). The
Philistines are portrayed as acting in accordance with "legal and civilized
considerations in trapping …[as Harapha would have it] a murderer and
a common enemy."[65] Manoa himself admits to discovering among the
Philistine lords one "More generous far and civil, who confess'd / They
had anough reveng'd" (SA 1467–8).

   In a chapter in the *Christian Doctrine* on "Special duties towards
one's neighbor," Milton surveys different types of dissimulation, including acceptable and defensible acts thereof that are as necessary in times
of peace as in war (CPW 6:762). Previously invoked in reference to the
argument about intermarriage, conversion, and divorce, the Canaanite
Rahab appears here among the examples of biblical figures who "lied
nobly and not dishonestly" (CPW 6:764). The Commonplace Book entry
on Sophronia's "noble lie" in Torquato Tasso's *Jerusalem Delivered* anticipates the reference to Rahab's deceit, which, in helping to defeat God's
enemies, is an act of "holy violence" of the kind discussed in Chapter 2,
"Reduction."[66] In conjunction with the religious and national duty to exact
vengeance against the "enemies of God and violators of hospitality,"[67] Jael,
too, in an act of "inhospitable guile" (SA 989), legitimately "enticed Sisera

to his death when he sought refuge with her, Judges iv. 18, 19, though he was God's enemy rather than hers" (CPW 6:764). This example in the *Christian Doctrine* is intended to support a nuanced understanding of the art of deception. Milton's parenthetical explication of an annotation on Judges 4:20 in *Testamenti Veteris Biblia Sacra*, uses the description of Jael's shrewdness to illustrate and defend sanctioned fraudulence.[68] Along with the other references in the *Christian Doctrine* catalogue to exceptional personages from the Hebrew Bible, the examples of Jael and Rahab can be seen as setting up the arguments about Dalila's and Samson's dissimulations in *Samson Agonistes*. The tragic poem in turn invites comparisons of alternative examples of national allegiance and of standards of judgement that multiply in the recollection and interpretation of Samson's dissembling final performance.

"Horrid spectacle"

In the *Doctrine and Discipline of Divorce*, Milton cites Josephus, the Septuagint and the Chaldaean versions of the Hebrew Bible, as well as David Kimchi, and likely Gersonides and Rashi, in support of his contention that "fornication," for which divorce is warranted, refers not only to adultery but also to "stubbornnes and rebellion against her husband."[69] Samson divorces Dalila on these grounds, a tragic and surprising outcome for a marriage purportedly lawful, at least according to Samson's protests (SA 231, 949). An added complication is Samson's own complicity in the ill-fated relationship and thus in his downfall: Samson testifies,

> I my self have brought ... on [evils],
> Sole Author I, sole cause: if aught seem vile,
> As vile hath been my folly, who have profan'd
> The mystery of God givn me under pledge
> Of vow, and have betray'd it to a woman,
> A *Canaanite*. (SA 375–80)

Although the character of Dalila calls forth the disgrace and degeneracy of the blinded Samson, who partakes of the identity of the other he now resists, the "foulest contagion" that threatens, weakens, and divides the peculiar nation is ultimately *internal* foreignness or estrangement. As Samson bitterly recalls, Dalila "sought to make me Traytor to my self" (SA 401), and then reflects again on his own frailties: "nature within me seems / In all her functions weary of her self" (SA 595–6). Dalila later discerns, "E're I to thee, thou to thy self wast cruel" (SA 784). When Milton discusses divorce in the *Christian Doctrine*, he argues for the legality and charitableness of deliverance from "an evil so distressing and so deep-seated" as a soul-destroying marital incompatibility, which God, who "joynes not unmachable things," would never have sanctioned (CPW 6:372, 2:651). In *Samson Agonistes*, Milton figures that evil as a "thorn / Intestine" (SA 1037–8) from which the tormented Samson longs to be freed, just as he seeks healing from his melancholia, characterized by "tumors of a troubl'd mind," "a lingring disease," "wounds immedicable," and "black mortification" (SA 185, 618, 620, 622).

Given the physical and psychological nature of his affliction, the divorce from Dalila that Samson decrees inevitably fails to restore his former self. Jason P. Rosenblatt asserts that the dissolution of the marriage affords the peace promised in the divorce tracts (e.g., CPW 2:328), but the poem's textual evidence suggests otherwise. Dalila readily observes that all passion has not been spent by Samson's dismissal of her: "Thy anger, unappeasable, still rages, / Eternal tempest never to be calm'd" (SA 963–4). Ironically, the release from a marriage in which his exogamous partner is guilty of "wedlock-trechery" (SA 1009) does not liberate him; rather, Samson must confront his own estrangement in a contest that continues even after Dalila leaves the stage.[70]

F. Michael Krouse, Joseph A. Wittreich, and R. W. Serjeantson have surveyed the early modern literature on the Judges story and uncovered a vast array of religious, moral, didactic, philosophic, and nationalist interpretations, which generally bestow sainthood on Samson.[71] Many of the commentaries are mediated through Paul's Epistle to the Hebrews ch. 11.[72] God turned Samson's weakness and frailty to Israel's good by investing in him the power to exact revenge against Israel's oppressors, explains Thomas Hayne, for example, who reads the Judges account in relation to Paul's canonizing of Samson.[73] Whereas Paul unconditionally exalts Samson, Milton troubles his heroic status while also highlighting the strained or broken relationship between the unworthy elect nation and its deliverer. Further, Milton deviates from the Pauline reading of Samson and that of early modern commentaries on Judges by showing little interest in either his prose or verse in christening Samson. *Samson Agonistes* reflects on the elect nation's infidelity through the Chorus's reference to Israel's betrayal of Gideon (Judges 6–8) and Jephtha(h) (Judges 11–12) (SA 277–83). "Of such examples adde mee to the roul," Samson responds, fully cognizant of his doubly ironic role as the champion of the Israelites, whose vices have led them to "love Bondage more then Liberty" (SA 290, 270).

At the central moment in the tragedy as Samson struggles to come into his own, his separateness must be affirmed through his conformity to the Law. Bondage associated with a bad marriage results in self-alienation and alienation from God, which paradoxically demands separation (CPW 2:260, 2:681). In an essay on the tragedy's "excluded middle" as a site for the virtually indistinguishable Samson and Dalila, John P. Rumrich observes that in the denouement, Samson defiantly asserts himself in the face of an enormous "dereliction of identity."[74] Personal and national salvation depend on the renunciation of the other self, an act carried out all the more aggressively when the self, like the nation and as the nation, is divided. Samson simply should have divorced earlier, Thomas Luxon surmises.[75] But in this case, when the divorce is pronounced, Samson remains aware of his own humiliation: "God sent her to debase me, / And aggravate my folly," he concedes after Dalila's departure (SA 999–1000).

Summoned to perform before the Philistines, Samson refuses at first to "stain [his] vow of *Nazarite*" (SA 1386) by entering their playhouse, which Milton distinguishes from the "house" where the biblical Samson was led from his "prison house" (Judge 16:25–6). Given his separate or consecrated identity as a "Nazarite" (Hebrew *nazar*) (Num. 6:2–5) – a figure "separate to God, / Design'd for great exploits" (SA 31–2) – Samson's acquiesence to the Philistine lords and specifically to their command to enter the theatre appears out of character. "The *Philistian* Lords command. / Commands are no constraints. If I obey them, / I do it freely," Samson explains in self-justification (SA 1371–3). Of course, it was also the "command[s]" of the Philistine lords "[a]djur'd by all the bonds of civil duty / And of Religion" that propelled Dalila into the political arena and compelled her to "consent" in the conspiracy against the rebel Samson (SA 852–4, 846). In Samson's case, he refuses compliance with anything "Scandalous or forbidden in our Law" (SA 1409) and, in a speech act that rehearses the re-integration of his separate identity as a Nazarite and nation, Samson pledges not to dishonour his God, his Law, his nation, or himself (SA 1425). Samson's protestation complicates Norman T. Burns's assertion that Samson's participation in the Dagonalia "*contradicts* his commitment to do nothing unworthy or dishonourable."[76]

In much of the best and most influential criticism on the subject, including that by the aforementioned Burns, scholars have introduced Pauline and antinomian readings to explain the stage appearance of the Nazarite, whose "faith or his proleptic Christian liberty" is said to "free[] him to suffer indignity."[77] In an astute and cogent essay, Catherine G. Martin, for example, explicitly calls Samson a lawbreaker and compares the supplanting of Israelite law by Samson's motions to the supersession of canon law by Christian liberty.[78] In this case, Samson subscribes to antinomianism, which denied the authority of positivism, the theory of the validity of laws as social rules, by appealing instead to the indwelling spirit. In Milton's day, this belief was widely condemned as an expression of libertinism and enthusiasm, as the reference to antinomianism in *Doctrine and Discipline of Divorce* indicates, despite Milton's qualification thereof.[79] Christian supersessionism and typological readings of a christened Samson cannot account for Samson's avowed commitment to the Law; nor do they satisfactorily resolve the problems opened by the poem, including those raised by the different characters' interpretations of the catastrophe.[80]

Just as *Samson Agonistes* confounds readings of the motives for Samson's exogamous marriages, so does it invite speculation about his motions in the final scene. Before hearing the report on the catastrophe, Manoa and the Chorus are caught up in questioning (SA 1508–40). Haunted by the images of the "horrid spectacle" experienced at a distance and translated by his "dire imagination" (SA 1532, 1534), the Messenger cannot fully appease their longing for answers. Whatever prompted the Messenger's return to Manoa and the Israelites to recount Samson's last act remains elusive, "whether providence or instinct of nature ... / [o]r reason though disturb'd, and scarse consulted," and foreshadows his remarks on the ambiguous source of the tragic hero's own promptings (SA 1535–6).

Natural law validates vengeance enacted against wrongdoers. According to Grotius, the burning of the Philistines' crops by the biblical Samson in Judges 15:3 is warranted: Samson justly defends himself "*by this law of nature* against the Philistines ... who had first wronged him."[81] The validation of Samson's brutal massacre of the Philistine foe in the final act of Milton's tragedy is founded on the same principle. Subject to varying interpretations, the substance of Samson's interior drama, however, renders the scene controversial. The omission in *Samson Agonistes* of the biblical Samson's prayer (perhaps in consonance with Josephus's account)[82] is among the curiosities in the poem's internally issued report on the (self-) sacrificial slaughter. Traditional interpretations of Samson's prayer in the temple reinforce his mission as God's agent. Thus the aforementioned Thomas Hayne decides that Samson prayed to the Lord, "yea prayed to him in faith: for he is recorded as famous for his faith," as Heb. 11 confirms.[83] In Milton's account, however, the Messenger describes Samson "as one who prayed, / Or some great matter in his mind revolved" (SA

1637–8). The conjunction "Or" leaves the question of Samson's motivation open-ended. Samson's oath, "of my own accord" (SA 1643), further destabilizes efforts to decode the catastrophe, thereby foregrounding instead the reactions of the hearers and interpreters.[84] At several removes from the site, the Messenger cannot offer definitive testimony of this last great stroke of temple-work, an iconoclastic and dissembling performance that literally strikes "with amaze[ment] ... all who behold" (SA 1635) and that invites comparison with the cunning, intrepid Jael, who, in Dalila's words, "Smote *Sisera* sleeping through the Temples nail'd" (SA 990).

Generating more questions than answers,[85] the Danites describe Samson as suicidal (SA 1574–5, 1580), as vengeful (SA 1581, 1650, 1702), as "tangl'd in the fold / Of dire necessity" (SA 1655–56), and as divinely directed (SA 1709–10). With no Judge to consult and only a "mangl'd body" of Truth (CPW 2:549) left in Samson's wake, fully authoritative readings of the tragic hero's catastrophe prove impossible. The Chorus and Manoa declare Samson's victory and impose closure on the final act, which, however, is again disturbed by unspent passions.[86] "Even the most believing readers with the most traditional approach to Samson's heroism and regeneration" will not finally experience catharsis, resulting in "a strikingly open-eyed vision."[87] As for the poem's biblical source text, the Book of Judges not only remains silent on Samson's liberation of the Israelites (Judges 16:30–1) but also continues in the next chapter (17) with the story of Micah, in which we learn that "In those dayes there was no king in Israel, but every man did that which was right in his owne eyes."[88]

Samson Agonistes develops its meaning through the accommodation of its different perspectives and its built-in reception history that adds a new chapter to the divorce tracts and that extends the poem beyond the fifth act – a compelling illustration of the expansiveness of Milton's vision. The dramatic poem ultimately encourages explorations of the creative dynamics and "brotherly dissimilitudes" engendered by the ways poetry enlarges the "horizon of expectation."[89] Reviving William Empson's critique of orthodox Christian readings of the poem and his robust portrayal of Delilah/Dalila in support of the argument that "Milton gives his strongest arguments to Samson's opponent," Victoria Kahn draws attention to the unexpected similarities *Samson Agonistes* develops between its two tragic characters. She points out further that Milton is disinclined to permit "similarities [to] erase differences"; rather, he invites the reader's discrimination.[90] This chapter on Milton's last literary and specifically poetic articulation of nationhood has sought to show that the process of relating Samson and Dalila complicates the "*diagonial* contraries" between

Hebrew and Philistine, not, as it turns out, because Philistine nationalism has been found legitimate but because Israelite chosenness remains at
issue. The contest between Samson and the Philistines results in the end
in a representation of nationhood at variance with itself, as the reining in,
un-mixing, or eradication of foreign elements leaves the restoration of the
nation's separate status still in question.[91]

Epilogue

Evidence supplied by the corpus of his prose works reveals that Milton was "too mercurial for the cultural constraints of mere Englishness," Thomas N. Corns cogently argues.[1] Blair Worden likewise observes that Milton was an internationalist who fully recognized that the concepts of nationhood he advanced, the republic of letters in which he was immersed, the principles of Humanism to which he subscribed, and the Reformed religion he championed spilled across intellectual and national boundaries. "He was, after all," Worden observes, "the most cosmopolitan of figures, a man of commanding international connections and outlook," who used his pen in the fight to restore liberty not only for the English but for peoples across the nations.[2] At the same time, however, Milton's nationalism is prominently displayed in his works. Redirecting the focus of Humanists and internationalists like Thomas More and Desiderius Erasmus,[3] Milton channelled his involvement in a Continental republic of letters into the writing of a Protestant national identity, God having revealed himself "first to his English-men" (CPW 2:553). Indeed Milton's "love of and concern for 'my country' are ubiquitously expressed" and the "honourable achievements of his country" are his own.[4]

Milton was keenly interested in the development of an English literary tradition, which he would be instrumental in establishing in honour of God and country. The idea of "'English literature' itself cannot be separated from the writing of the nation,"[5] as Worden implied and as Andrew Hadfield rightly observed, but the reverse also holds, and arguably no English author was as convinced of the importance of writing the nation into being as Milton. From *Lycidas* and *Reason of Church-Government* through to *Samson Agonistes*, Milton was imagining, producing, and transmitting a canon of English literature. Although nationalism is, as John Guillory argued, a chief impetus for canon making through the creation of an imaginary cultural unity,[6] Milton's understanding of the nation as a construct or imagined community advanced his appreciation of the ways that a body of work "doctrinal and exemplary to a Nation" (CPW 1:815) could support the conception and celebration of nationhood. The corpus of writings he produced was the composite achievement of the poet and polemicist, who named himself Miltoni Angli after the nation with which his identity was entangled.

Although Milton may have registered an awareness that England constituted "scarce … a third part of the Brittish name" (CPW 2:231), he forcefully asserted the dominance of the English in the empire. Still, the shifting directions and competing articulations of the nation affect Milton's investment in his cause and result, as the first four chapters showed, in inconsistent positions on issues ranging from elect nationalism to Presbyterianism, the role of magistrates, the expansionary aspirations of the English, the revolution and the Cromwellian regime, and the constitution of the *sanior pars* that ultimately represents Milton's England. As this book has also sought to demonstrate, the investment is specifically tied to practices, policies, and positions on tolerance, which Milton formulates and refines over the course of his career, altering them in conjunction with personal and often with politico-historical circumstances, including in the aftermath of the civil war, the rise of an increasingly dictatorial government. The later tracts, notably those on disestablishment, no longer entertain the possibility of a state supporting policies consistent with toleration and with the constitution of what Milton called the "true" nation.

The literary evidence presented here also reveals that the category of nationhood becomes simultaneously narrower and more universal. The redefinition of the relationship between Israel and England sheds light on this paradox and connects my Chapter 4 reading of the Hebrew prototypes invoked by early modern philosophers and political and religious thinkers with the book's final chapters. Milton's progressive embrace of a minority position that rendered Christianity and elect nationhood discontinuous with a Jewish past prepares the way for the major poems' meditations on the troubled Israel-England parallel. The Hebraic tradition lends itself to the writing of foundational Christian narratives, which is precisely what Michael's typological story in the final prophetic book of *Paradise Lost* becomes. At the same time, the national epic is less concerned with the founding of an elect nation than with the mapping of a global vision both imperialist and tolerationist. The double messages and ambiguities of chosen nationhood, internationalism, and universalism likewise animate the chapter on the divorce tracts and *Samson Agonistes*, works that test the limits of tolerance for foreignness and wrestle with the question of mixed marriages. In light of the striking portrayal of the Philistine Dalila in *Samson Agonistes*, Milton's orientalist tendencies – whereby he codes the ethnic or racial other (the Irish, the Turks, the Jews, the Amerindians, and even Dalila herself [SA 710–24]) as inferior, barbaric, and justly dominated – give way to more subtle readings that unsettle the poem's seeming antithetical nature and its representation of national election.

Milton, Toleration, and Nationhood has analysed Milton's participation in the conception of a protean English identity, inflected by the definitions of, as well as the controversies over, early modern tolerationism. By showing that Milton's writings serve as a significant medium for exploring ideas of the nation, toleration, and the conjunctions between the two, this study supports the re-examination by literary critics and historians of key assumptions about early modern literature, culture, and politics, as well as contemporary approaches to these topics. While maintaining that nationhood is a phenomenon emerging in Milton's time, I have acknowledged a distinction between early modern nationalist sentiment and contemporary definitions of (Western) nationalism that foreground political policy over all other considerations.[7] In contrast to the modernist theories of the nation founded on assumptions about the decline of dynasties and religion, I have argued, also in accordance with Andrew Escobedo's observation, that early national consciousness evolved *alongside* other consciousnesses, notably that of religion in its various cultural, philosophical, political, and also international manifestations and practices.[8] In the case of England, national identity was manifested as much in religious commitments and conflicts as in civic and political ties, which were frequently expressions and extensions of religious convictions.

In conjunction with current critical movements, *Milton, Toleration, and Nationhood* participates in challenging notions of literature as an isolated, ahistorical category, offering instead a model for studying the relationship of literature and nationhood, and specifically in terms of early discourses on toleration. The investigations of discourses of and debates on toleration in this book on the mimetically constructed nation represent a methodological departure from established Milton scholarship in which the subject has largely been a subcategory. At the same time, this study suggested that Milton was not headed to the kind of political liberalism and philosophical thought supported by natural religion and science. Milton's philosophy thus differs from that of John Locke, whose theories of toleration would pave the way for the abandonment of the divine faculty of reason and conscience for empiricism and human understanding. In the final decades of the seventeenth century, the distance between religion and (secular) politics widened and altered conceptions of toleration. As well, justifications for the constraint of conscience and dissent would be couched in the rhetoric of reason of state, pragmatism, public and national order, and economic benefit.[9]

This project has attempted to complicate historiographical approaches contributing to the Whig tradition that was supported by liberal and Marxist-informed analyses. The revisionist interrogation thereof exposed continuities underlying English politics while deemphasizing the shaping role of culture and literature and the function of religion in the writing of the nation's cultural and political history. In line with the post-revisionist movement in historiography and literary criticism, this book has resisted historical continuums and presentist predilections to make Milton a nationalist or tolerationist of our time.[10] My focus instead has been on the interactions between early modern cultural, religious, and political representation and the literary means by which nation and toleration became subjects of contestation and negotiation. Locating Milton's works in relation to the literary and historical contexts in which they were generated ultimately shows how receptive and disruptive his oeuvre was to the multiple articulations of toleration and nationhood in his day.

Notes

1 Introduction

1 Roger Williams, "Epistle Dedicatory," *The Hireling Ministry None of Christs, or A Discourse touching the Propagating the Gospel* (London, 1652), pp. 13, 19. See also Joan S. Bennett, "Catholicism," in Stephen B. Dobranski (ed.), *Milton in Context* (Cambridge: Cambridge University Press, 2010), pp. 248–57.

2 Christopher Hodgkins, *Reforming Empire: Protestant Colonialism and Conscience in British Literature* (Columbia: University of Missouri Press, 2002), p. 3.

3 Benedict Anderson, *Imagined Communities: Reflections on the Origin and Spread of Nationalism* (1983, rev. edn, London and New York: Verso, 1991); Tom Nairn, *The Break-up of Britain* (London: Verso, 1981), p. 348; Nairn, *Faces of Nationalism: Janus Revisited* (London & New York: Verso, 1997); Nairn, "Religion and Nationalism: Symposium in Honour of Professor Adrian Hastings," *Nations and Nationalism* 9, 1 (2003), 5–28. See Homi K. Bhabha's reworking of Nairn's concept of the nation as a "modern Janus" in "Introduction: Narrating the Nation," in Homi K. Bhabha (ed.), *Nation and Narration* (New York: Routledge, 1990), pp. 2–3. Literary studies on the early nation include Richard Helgerson, *Forms of Nationhood: The Elizabethan Writing of England* (Chicago: University of Chicago Press, 1992); Claire McEachern, *The Poetics of English Nationhood, 1590–1612* (Cambridge: Cambridge University Press, 1996/2006); Adrian Hastings, *The Construction of Nationhood: Ethnicity, Religion and Nationalism* (Cambridge: Cambridge University Press, 1997; rpt 1999); David J. Baker, *Between Nations: Shakespeare, Spenser, Marvell, and the Question of Britain* (Stanford, CA: Stanford University Press, 1997); Jean E. Howard and Phyllis Rackin, *Engendering a Nation: A Feminist Account of Shakespeare's English Histories* (New York: Routledge, 1997); Andrew Hadfield's reflections on the value of literary evidence for the writing of the nation are especially illuminating (*Literature, Politics and National Identity: Reformation to Renaissance* [Cambridge: Cambridge University Press, 1994], pp. 1–22); Andrew Hadfield, "The English and Other People," in Thomas N. Corns (ed.), *A Companion to Milton* (Oxford: Blackwell, 2001), pp. 174–90; Willy Maley, *Nation, State and Empire in English Renaissance Literature: Shakespeare to Milton* (New York: Palgrave Macmillan, 2003); Andrew Escobedo, *Nationalism and Historical Loss in Renaissance England: Foxe, Dee, Spenser, Milton* (Ithaca,

NY: Cornell University Press, 2004); Patrick Schwyzer, *Literature, Nationalism, and Memory in Early Modern England and Wales* (Cambridge: Cambridge University Press, 2004); Paul Stevens, "Milton and National Identity," in Nicholas McDowell and Nigel Smith (eds.), *The Oxford Handbook of Milton* (Oxford: Oxford University Press, 2009), 242–62; David Loewenstein and Paul Stevens (eds.), *Early Modern Nationalism and Milton's England* (Toronto, ON: University of Toronto Press, 2008); Stevens, "Milton's Nationalism and the Rights of Memory," in E. J. Bellamy, Patrick Cheney, and Michael Schoenfeldt (eds.), *Imagining Death in Spenser and Milton* (London: Palgrave Macmillan, 2003), pp. 171–84; Raymond D. Tumbleson, *Catholicism in the English Protestant Imagination: Nationalism, Religion, and Literature, 1660–1745* (Cambridge: Cambridge University Press, 1998); Rachel Trubowitz, "Body Politics in *Paradise Lost*," *PMLA* 21, 2 (2006), 388–404.

4 Elie Kedourie, *Nationalism* (London: Hutchinson, 1960). Krishan Kumar, *The Making of English National Identity* (Cambridge: Cambridge University Press, 2003), p. 103; see also pp. 57, 117; Ernest Gellner, *Nations and Nationalism* (Ithaca, NY: Cornell University Press, 1983); E. J. Hobsbawm, *Nations and Nationalism since 1780: Programme, Myth, Reality* (Cambridge: Cambridge University Press, 1990, 2nd edn 1992, 1997); Colin Kidd, *British Identities before Nationalism: Ethnicity and Nationhood in the Atlantic World, 1600–1800* (Cambridge: Cambridge University Press, 1999); Anthony Giddens, *The Nation-State and Violence* (Berkeley: University of California Press, 1985), p. 120.

5 Anderson, *Imagined Communities*, p. 7.

6 Adrian Hastings, *Construction of Nationhood*, p. 5.

7 See, for example, Blair Worden, *Literature and Politics in Cromwellian England: John Milton, Andrew Marvell, Marchamont Nedham* (Oxford: Oxford University Press, 2007); David Loewenstein and John Marshall (eds.), *Heresy, Literature and Politics in Early Modern English Culture* (Cambridge: Cambridge University Press, 2006); David Armitage, *The Ideological Origins of the British Empire* (Cambridge: Cambridge University Press, 2000); David Norbrook, *Writing the English Republic: Poetry, Rhetoric, and Politics, 1627–1660* (Cambridge: Cambridge University Press, 1999); Nigel Smith, *Literature and Revolution in England, 1640–1660* (New Haven, CT: Yale University Press, 1994); Christopher Hill, *Milton and the English Revolution* (New York: Viking, 1978).

8 Paul Stevens, "Milton's Janus-faced Nationalism: Soliloquy, Subject, and the Modern Nation State," *Journal of English and Germanic Philology* 100, 2 (2001), 254. Until recently, Milton studies has been more attentive to the poet-polemicist's revolutionary politics and his contributions to radicalism, republicanism, imperialism, and liberalism. See N.H. Keeble's *The Literature of Nonconformity in Later Seventeenth-Century England* (Leicester: Leicester University Press, 1987); Nigel Smith's *Perfection Proclaimed: Language and Literature in English Radical Religion* (Oxford: Clarendon Press, 1989); Nicholas McDowell's *The English Radical Imagination: Culture, Religion, and Revolution, 1630–1660* (Oxford: Clarendon Press, 2003). Sharon Achinstein's *Literature and Dissent*

in Milton's England (Cambridge: Cambridge University Press, 2003) advances Loewenstein's *Representing Revolution in Milton and his Contemporaries: Religion, Politics and Polemics in Radical Puritanism* (Cambridge: Cambridge University Press, 2001) by examining the republican Milton's sympathy with the culture of radicalism through the Restoration period. Also concentrating on Milton's relationship to radical ideologies without directly addressing toleration are Michael Wilding, *Dragon's Teeth: Literature in the English Revolution* (Oxford: Clarendon Press, 1987) and Kristen Poole, *Radical Religion from Shakespeare to Milton: Figures of Nonconformity in Early Modern England* (Cambridge: Cambridge University Press, 2000). The scholarship on Milton's republicanism and liberalism includes Nicholas von Maltzahn's *Milton's "History of Britain": Republican Historiography in the English Revolution* (Oxford: Clarendon Press, 1991), the equally engaging and influential work of Z.S. Fink, J.G.A Pocock, Quentin Skinner, and Blair Worden, the contributions to David Armitage, Armand Himy, and Quentin Skinner (eds.), *Milton and Republicanism* (Cambridge: Cambridge University Press, 1995), which offer multiple definitions of republicanism and of Milton's understanding of it, and Janel Mueller, "Contextualizing Milton's Nascent Republicanism," in P.G. Stanwood (ed.), *Of Poetry and Politics: New Essays on Milton and His World* (Binghamton, NY: Medieval and Renaissance Texts and Studies, 1995), pp. 263–282, which posits an origin for Milton's republican sentiment by way of an analysis of the discourse of estates in *Of Reformation* (1641). Advancing Annabel Patterson's observation in *Reading Between the Lines* (Madison: University of Wisconsin Press, 1993) that seventeenth-century republican ideas are conveyed as much through literature as political tracts or formal political theory (p. 225), David Norbrook's *Writing the English Republic* locates Milton's works in the context of a political and literary republicanism. Graham Parry and Joad Raymond's edited collection *Milton and the Terms of Liberty* (Cambridge: D.S. Brewer, 2002) analyses Milton's writings in terms of a socio-political context, with attention to Milton's republicanism and neo-Roman theories of the liberties of states and citizens. On Milton's relationship to empire, see David Quint, *Epic and Empire: Politics and Generic Form from Virgil to Milton* (Princeton, NJ: Princeton University Press, 1993); David Armitage, "John Milton: Poet against Empire," in David Armitage, Armand Himy and Quentin Skinner (eds.), *Milton and Republicanism* (Cambridge: Cambridge University Press, 1995); J. Martin Evans, *Milton's Imperial Epic: Paradise Lost and the Discourse of Colonization* (Ithaca, NY: Cornell University Press, 1996); Paul Stevens, "*Paradise Lost* and the Colonial Imperative," *Milton Studies* 34 (1996), 3–21; and Balachandra Rajan and Elizabeth Sauer (eds.), *Milton and the Imperial Vision* (Pittsburgh, PA: Duquesne University Press, 1999).

9 On the imaginative act of nation formation, see Linda Colley, who adopts Anderson's definition of a nation as "an imagined political community" in reading Britain as "an invented nation" (*Britons: Forging the Nation, 1707–1837* [1992; New Haven, CT: Yale University Press, 2009], pp. 5–6). See also Anthony Smith, "The Nation: Imagined, Invented, Reconstructed?" *Millennium, Journal of*

International Studies 20, 3 (1991), 353–68. On nations as constructs, see Gellner, *Nations and Nationalism*, pp. 48–9, 53, and Hobsbawm, who supports Gellner's theory of the "element of artefact" in the making of nations" (*Nations and Nationalism since 1780*, p. 10). See also Tony Claydon and Ian McBride, "The Trials of the Chosen Peoples: Recent Interpretations of Protestantism and National Identity in Britain and Ireland," in Tony Claydon and Ian McBride (eds.), *Protestantism and National Identity: Britain and Ireland, c. 1650–c. 1850* (Cambridge: Cambridge University Press, 1998), p. 5.

10 Helgerson, *Forms of Nationhood*, p. 6.

11 See William Kolbrener, "Those Grand Whigs, Bentley and Fish," *Milton's Warring Angels: A Study of Critical Engagements* (Cambridge: Cambridge University Press, 1997), pp. 107–32.

12 Don M. Wolfe (gen. ed.), *Complete Prose Works of John Milton*, 8 vols. (New Haven, CT: Yale University Press, 1953–82).

13 A. S. P. Woodhouse (ed. and intro.), *Puritanism and Liberty: Being the Army Debates (1647–9) from the Clarke Manuscripts with Supplementary Documents*, Foreword by A. D. Lindsay (London: J.M. Dent and Sons, 1938, rpt. 1966).

14 Arthur E. Barker, *Milton and the Puritan Dilemma 1641–1660* (Toronto, ON: University of Toronto Press, 1942).

15 On the Historicist critics of Milton, see Woodhouse, "The Historical Criticism of Milton," *PMLA* 66 (1951), 1038n1.

16 Northrop Frye, *The Return of Eden* (Toronto, ON: University of Toronto Press, 1965), p. 115; Stavely, *The Politics of Milton's Prose Style* (New Haven, CT: Yale University Press, 1975), p. 1.

17 Michael Lieb and John T. Shawcross (eds.), *Achievements of the Left Hand: Essays on the Prose of John Milton* (Amherst: University of Massachusetts Press, 1974).

18 James Grantham Turner, "The Poetics of Engagement," in David Loewenstein and James Grantham Turner (eds.), *Politics, Poetics, and Hermeneutics in Milton's Prose* (Cambridge: Cambridge University Press, 1990), esp. pp. 259–62. See also Blair Worden's recent contributions to the debate over Milton's mediums (*God's Instruments: Political Conduct in the England of Oliver Cromwell* [Oxford: Oxford University Press, 2012], pp. 355–8).

19 Annabel Patterson, "Why Is There No Rights Talk in Milton's Poetry?" in Christophe Tournu and Neil Forsyth (eds.), *Milton, Rights and Liberties* (New York: Peter Lang, 2007), pp. 197–209.

20 CPW 1:816. Gordon Campbell and Thomas N. Corns, *John Milton: Life, Work, and Thought* (Oxford: Oxford University Press, 2008), p. 149.

21 Additionally, Milton regularly interpolates poems or poetic passages in his prose. See "Verses from the Prose Works," in Harris Francis Fletcher (comp. and ed.), *John Milton's Complete Poetical Works*, 4 vols. (Urbana: University of Illinois Press, 1943), vol. 1, pp. 376–80.

22 Thomae Thomasii, *Dictionarium Linguae Latinae et Anglicanae* (Canterbury, 1587), n.p.

23 On the discourse of the nation, see Homi K. Bhabha, "Introduction: Narrating the Nation," pp. 1–7.

24 "Nationhood," Oxford English Dictionary, 3rd ed. June 2003; online version December 2011. http://www.oed.com.proxy.library.brocku.ca/view/Entry/125299; accessed 11 January 2012.

25 Thomas Davis, "The West's Asleep," *The Spirit of the Nation: Ballads and Songs by the Writers of "The Nation"* (Dublin: James Duffy, 1845), p. 72, l, 10.

26 See Will Kymlicka, "Two Models of Pluralism and Tolerance," in David Heyd (ed.), *Toleration: An Elusive Virtue* (Princeton, NJ: Princeton University Press, 1996), pp. 81–105; Keith P. Luria, "Separated by Death? Burials, Cemeteries, and Confessional Boundaries in Seventeenth-Century France," *French Historical Studies* 24, 2 (2001), 185–222; Benjamin J. Kaplan, "Fictions of Privacy: House Chapels and the Spatial Accommodation of Religious Dissent in Early Modern Europe," *American Historical Review* 107 (2002), 1031–64; Walsham, "Church Papists," Chapter 4 of *Church Papists: Catholicism, Conformity and Confessional Polemic in Early Modern England* (Woodbridge, UK: The Boydell Press, 1993), pp. 73–99; Judith Pollmann, "The Bond of Christian Piety: The Individual Practice of Tolerance and Intolerance in the Dutch Republic," in R. Po-chia Hsia and Henk Van Nierop (eds.), *Calvinism and Religious Toleration in the Dutch Golden Age* (Cambridge: Cambridge University Press, 2002), pp. 53–71.

27 On the use of literary evidence in studying the early history of toleration in Milton's time, see Sharon Achinstein and Elizabeth Sauer, "Introduction," in Sharon Achinstein and Elizabeth Sauer (eds.), *Milton and Toleration* (Oxford: Oxford University Press, 2007), pp. 1–20.

28 Alexandra Walsham, *Charitable Hatred: Tolerance and Intolerance in England, 1500–1700* (Manchester: Manchester University Press, 2006), p. 234; Blair Worden, "Toleration and the Cromwellian Protectorate," in W. J. Sheils (ed.), *Persecution and Toleration*, Studies in Church History 21 (Oxford: Basil Blackwell, 1984), p. 209; N. H. Keeble, "Milton and Puritanism," in Thomas N. Corns (ed.), *Companion to Milton*, p. 126. Feisal G. Mohamed astutely characterizes "the limits on religious toleration inscribed within the principle of liberty of conscience" in "Donne, Milton, and the Two Traditions of Religious Liberty," in Michael Hattaway (ed.), *A New Companion to English Renaissance Literature and Culture*, 2 vols. (Oxford: Blackwell, 2010), vol. 1, p. 299.

29 J. C. Davis, "Religion and the Struggle for Liberty," *Historical Journal* 35, 3 (1992), 513, 515; Blair Worden, "Toleration and the Cromwellian Protectorate," pp. 209–10.

30 James Hay, Earl of Carlisle, *Collonel James Hays Speech to the Parlament upon the Debate Concerning Toleration...*([London], 1655), pp. 4, 5.

31 Oliver Cromwell, *The Writings and Speeches of Oliver Cromwell*, W.C. Abbott (ed.), 4 vols. (New York: Russell & Russell, 1970), vol. 1, p. 677.

32 Oliver Cromwell to the Consuls and Senators of Bremen" (1654), CPW 5.2:680.

33 Richard Perrinchief, *Samaritanism Revised and Enlarged: Or, a Treatise ... Demonstrating the Piety, Equity, and Necessity of Putting the Laws in Execution against Popish and Puritan Recusants* (London, 1669), p. 130.

34 Hugo Grotius, *De Juri Belli ac Pacis Libri Tres* (1625), Francis W. Kelsey (trans.) (New York: Oceana Publications, 1964), vol. 1, ch 1.XVII.2, p. 49.

35 Whiggish histories of toleration include W[ilbur] K. Jordan, *The Development of Religious Toleration in England*, 4 vols. (Cambridge, MA: Harvard University Press, 1932–40); more recently John Coffey, *Persecution and Toleration in Protestant England, 1558–1689* (New York: Longman, 2000); Cary J. Nederman and John Christian Laursen (eds.), *Beyond the Persecuting Society: Religious Toleration Before the Enlightenment* (Philadelphia: University of Pennsylvania Press, 1998); Ole Peter Grell and Roy Porter (eds.), *Toleration in Enlightenment Europe* (Cambridge: Cambridge University Press, 1999); Jonathan Israel, "Spinoza, Locke and the Enlightenment Battle for Toleration," in Ole Peter Grell and R. Porter (eds.), *Toleration in Enlightenment Europe* (Cambridge: Cambridge University Press, 2000), pp. 102–13; Perez Zagorin, *How the Idea of Religious Toleration came to the West* (Princeton, NJ: Princeton University Press, 2003). For a critique, see Nicholas Tyacke, "The 'Rise of Puritanism' and the Legalizing of Dissent, 1571–1719," in Ole Peter Grell, Jonathan I. Israel, and Nicholas Tyacke (eds.), *From Persecution to Toleration: The Glorious Revolution in England* (Oxford: Clarendon Press, 1991), p. 17. The portrait of Milton as a staunch defender of rights and liberties has been interrogated of late. See, for example, the essays in Achinstein and Sauer (eds.), *Milton and Toleration*, which resist the "progressive" analyses of Milton's positions on liberty.

36 J. W. McKenna, "How God became an Englishman," in D.J. Guth and J.W. McKenna (eds.), *Tudor Rule and Revolution: Essays for G. R. Elton from his American Friends* (Cambridge: Cambridge University Press, 1982), pp. 27, 42.

37 But even before then, God was claimed for England. See Patrick Collinson, "Biblical Rhetoric: The English Nation and National Sentiment in the Prophetic Mode," *This England: Essays on the English Nation and Commonwealth in the Sixteenth Century* (New York: Palgrave Macmillan, 2011), pp. 172–3. See also Patrick Collinson, *The Birthpangs of Protestant England: Religious and Cultural Change in the Sixteenth and Seventeenth Centuries* (London: Macmillan, 1988), p. 4; Christopher Hill, *The English Bible and the Seventeenth-Century Revolution* (London: Penguin, 1993), p. 266, and Richard Helgerson, *Forms of Nationhood*, p. 263. Cf. William Haller on God's English identity (*Foxe's Book of Martyrs and the Elect Nation* [London: Jonathan Cape, 1963], p. 245). N.B. Claydon and McBride, who usefully characterize elect status as aspirational rather than descriptive ("The Trials of the Chosen Peoples," pp. 26–9).

38 See Walter Ullmann, "'This Realm of England is an Empire,'" *Journal of Ecclesiastical History* 30, 2 (1979), 175–203, and L.B. Smith, "This Realm of England Is an Empire," *This Realm of England: 1399 to 1688*, 7th ed. (Lexington, MA: D.C. Heath and Co., 1992), pp. 112–30.

39 Sir Thomas Smith, *Certaigne Psalmes or Songues of David translated into Englishe Meter*, in *Literary and Linguistic Works*, Part 1, Bror Danielsson (ed.), *Stockholm Studies in English*, 12 (Stockholm: Almqvist and Wiksell, 1963), p. 33. See also Cathy Shrank, *Writing the Nation in Reformation England 1530–1580* (Oxford: Oxford University Press, 2004), p. 10.

40 Cathy Shrank distinguishes the English Reformation from the somewhat later movement of English Protestantism (*Writing the Nation in Reformation*

England, p. 9). David Loades, "Literature and National Identity," in David Loewenstein and Janel Mueller (eds.), *The Cambridge History of Early Modern English Literature* (Cambridge: Cambridge University Press, 2002), p. 213.

41 Hastings, *The Construction of Nationhood*, p. 60.

42 Milton, *Of Reformation*, CPW 1:604; Jesse Lander queries readings of Foxe's advancement of *elect* nationalism ("Foxe's *Books of Martyrs*: Printing and Popularizing the *Acts and Monuments*," in Claire McEachern and Debora Shuger [eds.], *Religion and Culture in Renaissance England* [Cambridge: Cambridge University Press, 1997], pp. 70–1).

43 Christopher Haigh, *English Reformations: Religion, Politics, and Society under the Tudors* (Oxford: Clarendon Press, 1993), p. 280; see also Eamon Duffy, *The Stripping of the Altars: Traditional Religion in England 1400–1580* (New Haven, CT: Yale University Press, 1992).

44 Linda Gregerson, *The Reformation of the Subject: Spenser, Milton, and the English Protestant Epic* (Cambridge: Cambridge University Press, 1995), p. 4.

45 McKenna, "How God became an Englishman," p. 43.

46 Liah Greenfeld, *Nationalism: Five Roads to Modernity* (Cambridge, MA: Harvard University Press, 1992), p. 71.

47 Walsham, *Charitable Hatred*, p. 234.

48 Christopher Hill, "The Protestant Nation," *The Collected Essays of Christopher Hill, Volume Two: Religion and Politics in Seventeenth Century England* (Brighton: Harvester Press, 1986), pp. 28–9. See also E. H. Kantorowicz, *The King's Two Bodies; A Study in Mediaeval Political Theory* (1957, rpt. Princeton, NJ: Princeton University Press, 1970).

49 Edward Chamberlayne, *Angliae Notitia, or The Present State of England* (London, 1669), pp. 28, 29. 1670 edn., p. 58.

50 Edward Chamberlayne, *Angliae Notitia, or The Present State of England* (London, 1670), pp. 56–7.

51 Edward Chamberlayne, *Angliae Notitia, or The Present State of England* (London, 1704), p. 61.

52 Collinson, "Biblical Rhetoric," *This England*, pp. 175, 174; see also *This England*, pp. 5, 193; Hill, *The English Bible*, p. 264.

53 Joad Raymond, "Complications of Interest: Milton, Scotland, Ireland, and National Identity in 1649," *The Review of English Studies* 55, 220 (2004), 335–6; See also Colin Kidd, *British Identities*, pp. 211–4.

54 McEachern, *Poetics of Nationhood*, p. 61; Claire McEachern, "Literature and National Identity," in *The Cambridge History of Early Modern English Literature*, p. 327. Haller, *Foxe's "Book of Martyrs" and the Elect Nation* (London: Jonathan Cape, 1963), p. 245; Katharine R. Firth, *The Apocalyptic Tradition in Reformation Britain, 1530–1645* (Oxford: Oxford University Press, 1979); Jesse Lander, "Foxe's *Books of Martyrs*: Printing and Popularizing the *Acts and Monuments*," pp. 69–92. On England's peculiar identity and the relationship between insularity and colonialism in Elizabethan England, see Jeffrey Knapp, *An Empire Nowhere: England, America, and Literature from "Utopia" to "The Tempest"* (Berkeley: University of California Press, 1992).

55 Armitage, *The Ideological Origins of the British Empire*, pp. 79, 96.
56 Anthony D. Smith, "Neo-Classicist and Romantic Elements in the Emergence of Nationalist Conceptions," in Anthony D. Smith (ed.), *Nationalist Movements* (London: Macmillan, 1976), pp. 74–87; Smith, *Antiquity of Nations* (Cambridge: Polity Press, 2004); Smith, "'Set in the silver sea': English National Identity and European Integration," *Nations and Nationalism* 12, 3 (2006), 445.
57 Anthony D. Smith, "Nation and Covenant: The Contribution of Ancient Israel to Modern Nationalism," *Proceedings of the British Academy* 151 (2007), 222.
58 Anthony D. Smith, *Chosen Peoples: Sacred Sources of National Identity* (Oxford: Oxford University Press, 2003, rpt 2008), pp. 58–60.
59 Greenfeld, *Nationalism*, pp. 76–7; H. Belloc, *Milton* (Philadelphia: Lippincott, 1935), p. 22.
60 See Greenfeld, *Nationalism*, p. 70. Elie Kedourie's 1960 *Nationalism* offers an early study of nationalism, which he roots in a secular doctrine. Smith supplies a religious lineage for Kedourie's secularized nationalism (Anthony D. Smith, "Nation and Covenant," 213–55).
61 Claydon and McBride, "The Trials of the Chosen Peoples," p. 6.
62 Helgerson, *Forms of Nationhood*, p. 252.
63 Thomas Edwards, "Epistle Dedicatory," *Reasons Against the Independant Government of Particular Congregations. . .* (London, 1641), sig. A2v.
64 Cf. Stephen R. Honeygosky, *Milton's House of God: The Invisible and Visible Church* (Columbia: University of Missouri Press, 1993), which discusses the interdependence of the invisible and visible church as characterizing Milton's ecclesiology.
65 Michael Neill, "Broken English and Broken Irish: Nation, Language, and the Optic of Power in Shakespeare's Histories," *Shakespeare Quarterly* 45, 1 (1994), 3.
66 Hadfield, *Literature, Politics and National Identity*, p. 11. Hadfield cautions scholars against attempting "to subsume Anglo-Irish relations under the umbrella of the British question" while insisting that Anglo-Irish history be "conceived alongside the history of Britain and Britishness" (*Shakespeare, Spenser and the Matter of Britain* [London: Palgrave Macmillan, 2004], p. 7). Joad Raymond warns against isolating Irish-English relations from the relations among the three kingdoms (Raymond, "Complications of Interest," 332). "It is in Ireland that we find arguably the most fraught relationship with Britishness," discovers Willy Maley. On Ireland as a site of contention for national identities, see Willy Maley, "The British Problem: Three Tracts on Ireland by Spenser, Bacon, and Milton," in Brendan Bradshaw and Peter Roberts (eds.), *British Consciousness and Identity: The Making of Britain, 1533–1707* (Cambridge: Cambridge University Press, 1998), pp. 161; 159–84.
67 Claire McEachern, "Literature and National Identity," p. 313.
68 Campbell and Corns, *John Milton: Life*, p. 216.

69 Peter Lake, "Presbyterianism, The Idea of a National Church and the Argument from Divine Right," in Peter Lake and Maria Dowling (eds.), *Protestantism and the National Church in Sixteenth-Century England* (New York: Methuen, 1987), pp. 193–222; Patrick Collinson, "The Cohabitation of the Faithful with the Unfaithful," in *From Persecution to Toleration*, pp. 51–75; Collinson, "Biblical Rhetoric: The English Nation and National Sentiment in the Prophetic Mode," *This England: Essays on the English Nation and Commonwealth*, p. 183.

70 J. W. Gough, *Fundamental Law in English Constitutional History* (Oxford: Clarendon Press, 1955), p. 1.

71 Loewenstein, *Representing Revolution in Milton and his Contemporaries*, p. 11.

72 On the radicals' pro-tolerationist positions and the articulation thereof, see Gary De Krey, "Rethinking the Restoration: Dissenting Cases for Conscience, 1667–1672," *Historical Journal* 38, 1 (1995), 53–83.

73 On Milton's strained relationship to the Philo-Semitic tradition of his time, see Jeffrey S. Shoulson, *Milton and the Rabbis: Hebraism, Hellenism, and Christianity* (New York: Columbia University Press, 2001), and Nicholas von Maltzahn, "Making Use of the Jews: Milton and Philo-Semitism," in Douglas A. Brooks (ed.), *Milton and the Jews* (Cambridge: Cambridge University Press, 2008), pp. 57–82.

74 Feisal G. Mohamed, "Donne, Milton, and the Two Traditions of Religious Liberty," in Michael Hattaway (ed.), *A New Companion to English Renaissance Literature and Culture*, 2 vols. (Oxford: Blackwell, 2010), vol. 1, p. 298; see also Mohamed, "Liberty Before and After Liberalism: Milton's Shifting Politics and the Current Crisis in Liberal Theory," *University of Toronto Quarterly* 77 (2008), 940–60.

75 See John Coffey, "Puritanism and Liberty Revisited: The Case for Toleration in the English Revolution," *The Historical Journal* 41, 4 (1998), 961–85.

76 Nathaniel Hardy, *The Arraignment of Licentious Liberties and Oppressing Tyrannie. In a Sermon Preached ... Febr. 24. 1646* (London, 1647), pp. 10, 14.

77 See especially Richard Helgerson, "The Voyages of a Nation," *Forms of Nationhood*, pp. 149–91, and Bruce McLeod's equally admirable *Geography of Empire in English Literature, 1580–1745* (Cambridge: Cambridge University Press, 1999).

78 Bruce McLeod, "The 'Lordly Eye': Milton and the Strategic Geography of Empire," in *Milton and the Imperial Vision*, p. 55.

79 Cawley discusses the literature that informed Milton's *Brief History of Moscovia* (*Milton and the Literature of Travel* [Princeton, NJ: Princeton University Press, 1951], p. 86).

80 Cawley, *Milton and the Literature of Travel*, p. 87.

81 Victoria Kahn, "Disappointed Nationalism: Milton in the Context of Seventeenth-Century Debates about the Nation-State," in *Early Modern Nationalism and Milton's England*, pp. 249–72.

82 Elizabeth Sauer, "Milton's 'Peculiar' Nation," in *Milton and the Jews*, pp. 35–56.

83 Shoulson, *Milton and the Rabbis*, p. 235.

84 David Goodblatt offers a critical survey of the extensive scholarship on ethnicity and nationhood in his study on Jewish nationalism in antiquity (*Elements of Ancient Jewish Nationalism* [Cambridge: Cambridge University Press, 2006]).

85 Stephen M. Fallon, *Milton's Peculiar Grace: Self-Representation and Authority* (Ithaca, NY: Cornell University Press, 2007), p. 251; David Norbrook, "The True Republican: Putting the Politics Back into Milton," *Times Literary Supplement* (2 February 1996), 5.

86 CPW 8:421; Walsham, *Charitable Hatred*, p. 5.

1 "Temple-worke": Milton's Literary Ecclesiology

1 Thomas Hill, *The Season for Englands Selfe-Reflection, and Advancing Temple-work: Discovered in a Sermon Preached to the two Houses of Parliament ... Aug. 13. 1644* (London, 1644), p. 3.

2 Joan S. Bennett, *Reviving Liberty: Radical Christian Humanism in Milton's Great Poems* (Cambridge, MA: Harvard University Press, 1989), p. 106.

3 Thomas Edwards, "Epistle Dedicatory," *Reasons Against the Independant Government of Particular Congregations: As also Against the Toleration of such Churches to be erected in this Kingdome* (London, 1641), sig. A2v.

4 Ken Simpson, *Spiritual Architecture and "Paradise Regained": Milton's Literary Ecclesiology* (Pittsburgh, PA: Duquesne University Press, 2007), p. 112. On the visible and invisible churches, see Peter Lake and Anthony Milton, who discuss the Laudians' rejection of a true "invisible" church of orthodox believers (Peter Lake, "The Laudian Style: Order, Uniformity and the Pursuit of the Beauty of Holiness in the 1630s," and Anthony Milton, "The Church of England, Rome, and the True Church: The Demise of a Jacobean Consensus," in Kenneth Fincham [ed.], *The Early Stuart Church, 1603–1642* [Stanford, CA: Stanford University Press, 1993], pp. 161–85, 187–210, esp. 200). Like Achsah Guibbory, I align Milton's expansive vision of the Church with a nation that allows for "dissimilarities, difference, variety of peoples, ideas and visions" (*Christian Identity, Jews, and Israel in Seventeenth-Century England* [Oxford: Oxford University Press, 2010], p. 119). For Milton's notion of the invisible church, see also CPW 6:498–501.

5 Milton, Commonplace Book, Ruth Mohl (ed. and trans), in vol. 1, *Complete Prose Works*, p. 420; Sir Thomas Smith, *De Republica Anglorum: The Maner of Gouernement or Policie of the Realme of England* (London, 1583), pp. 4–5.

6 Milton, *Christian Doctrine*, CPW 6:173, 506. Election becomes for him a condition of merit and conversion. See CPW 6:543. Milton cites Rom. 4:12, Gal. 5:3, and John 7.22–3.

7 CPW 6:507. George Gifford declared "We still esteemeth them (though not al) as the Lords chosen people" (*A Sermon Preached at Pauls Crosse the Thirtie Day of*

May. 1591 [London, 1591], [sig. C6v]). On the fraught identification of the early modern English Christians with ancient Israel, see Achsah Guibbory's *Christian Identity* (2010).

8 *An Answer to a Booke Entituled, An Humble Remonstrance. In which, The Originall of Liturgy, Episcopacy is discussed ... Written by SMECTYMNUUS* (London, 1641).

9 Joseph Hall, *A Humble Remonstrance to the High Court of Parliament* (London, 1641), p. 8.

10 Hall, *A Humble Remonstrance*, pp. 24, 23. In his *Defence of the Humble Remonstrance, Against the frivolous and false exceptions of Smectymnuus. Wherein The Right of Leiturgie and Episcopacie is clearly vindicated* (London, 1641), Hall refers to Titus, Bishop of Crete and Timothy, Bishop of Ephesus, and the "averred Episcopacy of *Timothy* and *Titus*" (pp. 96, 112).

11 Hall, *A Humble Remonstrance*, pp. 40, 43.

12 On the genre of the animadversion, see Joad Raymond, *Pamphlets and Pamphleteering in Early Modern Britain* (Cambridge: Cambridge University Press, 2003), pp. 202–75.

13 *An Answer to a Booke*, p. 82.

14 *An Answer to a Booke*, p. 84.

15 Joseph Hall, *A Short Answer to the Tedious Vindication of Smectymnuus. By the Author of Humble Remonstrance* (London, 1641).

16 CPW 1:650; Cf. Hall, *Defence of the Humble Remonstrance*, pp. 120–1.

17 William Walwyn, *The Compassionate Samaritane: Unbinding the Conscience* ([London,] 1644), p. 17.

18 Milton, "On the New Forcers of Conscience under the Long Parliament" (1646), in John Carey (ed.), *Milton, The Complete Shorter Poems*, l. 20. See also CPW 2:539.

19 Milton, *Paradise Lost*, 12.521, 525–6, 526–8.

20 See "A Postscript," Preface and Notes by Don M. Wolfe," CPW 1:961–5. (This chapter, "Temple-worke," otherwise cites the original edition of *An Answer to a Booke* [1641]). Robert Greville, Lord Brooke also discredits the "Grand Principle of Episcopall policie, *No Bishop, No King*" in *A Discourse Opening the Nature of that Episcopacie, which is Exercised in England* (London, 1641), pp. 48, 45–8.

21 The identification was largely substantiated by Gordon Campbell and Thomas N. Corns in *John Milton: Life, Work, and Thought* (Oxford: Oxford University Press, 2008), p. 139.

22 Milton, *Of Reformation*, CPW 1:529; *An Answer to a Booke*, p. 102 (misnumbered p. 92).

23 Nigel Smith, "Anti-Episcopal Tracts," in Nicholas McDowell and Nigel Smith (eds.), *The Oxford Handbook of Milton* (Oxford: Oxford University Press, 2009), p. 171.

24 Janel Mueller, "Embodying Glory: The Apocalyptic Strain in Milton's *Of Reformation*," in David Loewenstein and James Grantham Turner (eds.), *Politics, Poetics, and Hermeneutics in Milton's Prose* (Cambridge: Cambridge University Press, 1990), p. 34.

25 Milton, *Of Reformation*, CPW 1:549. Milton would repeat the point in the *Reason of Church-Government*: 1 Peter 5 "commits to the Presbyters only full authority both of feeding the flock, and Episcopating" (CPW 1:760).

26 *An Answer to a Booke*, p. 34.

27 Sir Thomas Aston, *A Remonstrance against Presbitery ... Together with a Short Survey of the Presbyterian Discipline ... its Principles destructive to the Laws and Liberties of the People* (n.p. 1641), Sect. 1.

28 Aston, *A Remonstrance against Presbitery*, Sect. 14. On the early seventeenth-century complaint about Presbyterians installing a pope in every parish, see CPW 1:570n180.

29 Aston, *A Remonstrance against Presbitery*, Sect. 17.

30 George Digby, *The Third Speech of the Lord George Digby, to the House of Commons, Concerning Bishops* (n.p., [Feb. 9] 1641), p. 17.

31 Brooke, *A Discourse Opening the Nature of that Episcopacie*, p. 47.

32 Brooke, *A Discourse Opening the Nature of that Episcopacie*, p. 72.

33 Milton, *Lycidas*, in *Milton, The Complete Shorter Poems*, ll. 108–31; 132.

34 Milton, *Lycidas*, ll. 119, 125.

35 See James Egan's study of *Areopagitica*, which analyses the stylistic relationships between the treatise and popular tolerationist tracts in "*Areopagitica* and the Tolerationist Rhetorics of the 1640s," *Milton Studies* 46 (2007), 165–90.

36 *Certain Briefe Treatises, Written by Diverse Learned Men, Concerning the Ancient and Moderne Government of the Church. Wherein ... the Primitive Institution of EPISCOPACIE is Maintained* (Oxford, 1641).

37 Andrewes, *A Summarie View of the Government*, in *Certain Treatises*, p. 7.

38 Andrewes, *A Summarie View of the Government*, in *Certain Treatises*, p. 25.

39 Andrewes, *A Summarie View of the Government*, in *Certain Treatises*, p. 32.

40 Bucer, Rainolds, and Ussher, *The Originall of Bishops and Metropolitans*, *Certain Treatises*, p. 46.

41 Campbell and Corns, *John Milton: Life*, p. 149.

42 [Hubert Languet], *Vindiciae contra Tyrannos: A Defence of Liberty against Tyrants. Or, Of the lawfull power of the Prince over the people, and of the people over the Prince* (London, 1648), pp. 44–5. Milton mentions the tract in *Defensio Secunda* (1654), CPW 4:659.

43 *The Manner of the Impeachment of the 12 Bishops, accused of High Treason* (London, rpt Edinburgh, 1641), p. 2.

44 Edwards, *Reasons Against the Independant Government*, p. 20. For a trenchant analysis of the tract in the context of the controversy over church government, see Ann Hughes, *Gangraena and the Struggle for the English Revolution* (Oxford: Oxford University Press, 2004), pp. 34–41.

45 Edwards, *Reasons Against the Independant Government*, p. 23.

46 Brooke, *A Discourse Opening the Nature of that Episcopacie*, p. 108.

47 Campbell and Corns consider the juxtaposition of toleration and intolerance in *Areopagitica*. Although already disappointed by the Presbyterian response to his tracts, Milton still believed "he was in dialogue with moderate, rational, scholarly men like Calamy and Marshall" (*John Milton: Life*, p. 173). Corns

makes the same point in "Milton, Roger Williams, and Limits of Toleration," in Sharon Achinstein and Elizabeth Sauer (eds.), *Milton and Toleration* (Oxford: Oxford University Press, 2007), p. 83. Cf. Nicholas von Maltzahn, who, in a comparison of Milton with Andrew Marvell, finds that the former was consistently hostile to Presbyterians from as early as 1641 ("Milton, Marvell and Toleration," *Milton and Toleration*, pp. 86–104).

48 Katherine Chidley, *Justification of the Independant Churches of Christ. Being an Answer to Mr. Edwards his Booke, which hee hath written against the Government of Christs Church, and Toleration of Christs Publike Worship* (London, 1641), sig. *2, pp. 22–3. See Marcus Nevitt's astute analysis of Chidley in the context of 1640s religious controversy in "'Justification Cannot Be Self-Justification': Katherine Chidley and the Discourses of Religious Toleration," in *Women and the Pamphlet Culture of Revolutionary England, 1640–1660* (Aldershot: Ashgate, 2006), pp. 21–48.

49 Chidley, *Justification of the Independant Churches*, p. 21.

50 Chidley, *Justification of the Independant Churches*, p. 29.

51 John Lanseter, *Lanseters Lance for Edwards'es Gangrene: or, A ripping up, and laying open some rotten … matter in Mr. Thomas Edwards his Gangren* (London, 1646), sig. A2r.

52 Lanseter, *Lanseters Lance*, sig. A2v.

53 Thomas Edwards, *The Third Part of Gangraena. Or, A New and Higher Discovery of the Errors, Heresies, Blasphemies, and Insolent Proceedings of the Sectaries of these Times* (London, 1646), pp. 170–71.

54 The "visible church" is defined as "all those who expressed outward belief by obedient participation in the worship organised by the Church" (John Fielding, "Arminianism in the Localities: Peterborough Diocese, 1603–1642," in Kenneth Fincham [ed.], *The Early Stuart Church, 1603–1642* [Stanford, CA: Stanford University Press, 1993], p. 95).

55 Thomas Hill, *The Season for Englands Selfe-Reflection, and Advancing Temple-work* (London, 1644), "Epistle Dedicatory," sig. A3. For political and religious uses of temple-work in sermons, see Achsah Guibbory, "Israel and the 'Fast Sermons' during the English Revolution," in David Loewenstein and Paul Stevens (eds.), *Early Modern Nationalism and Milton's England* (Toronto, ON: University of Toronto Press, 2008), pp. 115–38.

56 Hill, *The Season for Englands Selfe-Reflection*, p. 34.

57 [John Taylor], *Religions Enemies. With a Brief and Ingenious Relation, as by Anabaptists, Brownists, Papists, Familists, Atheists and Foolists, sawcily presuming to tosse Religion in a Blanquet* (London, 1641), p. 6.

58 Thomas Goodwin, Philip Nye, et al., *An Apologeticall Narration, Humbly Submitted to the Honourable Houses of Parliament* (London, 1644), pp. 23, 24.

59 *An Apologeticall Narration*, p. 22.

60 *An Anatomy of Independency, or A Brief Commentary, and Moderate Discourse upon The Apologeticall Narration … laying naked the dangers of their Positions* (London, 1644), p. 13.

61 Thomas Edwards, *Antapologia: Or, A Full Answer to the Apologeticall Narration of Mr Goodwin, Mr Nye, Mr Sympson, Mr Burroughs, Mr Bridge, Members of*

the Assembly of Divines. Wherein is handled many of the Controversies of these Times (London, [13 July] 1644), pp. 282–5.

62 Herbert Palmer, *The Necessity and Encouragement, of Utmost Venturing for the Churches Help ... a Sermon, Preached to the Honorable House of Commons, on the day of the Monethly solemn Fast, 28. June, 1643* (London, 1643), pp. 9, 20.

63 Palmer, *The Necessity and Encouragement*, pp. 20, 26.

64 Henry Burton, *A Vindication of Churches, Commonly Called Independent: Or A Briefe Answer to two Books; the one, intituled, Twelve considerable serious Questions, touching Church-Government: The other, Independency examined, unmasked, refuted, &c. Both lately published by William Prinne* (London, 1644), p. 31.

65 Burton, *A Vindication of Churches*, p. 40.

66 Burton, *A Vindication of Churches*, pp. 40–41.

67 Herbert Palmer, *The Glasse of Gods Providence Towards His Faithfull Ones. Held forth in a Sermon preached ... against the ungodly Toleration pleaded for under pretence of Liberty of Conscience* (London, [Nov.] 1644), p. 57. The widespread disapproval of Milton's position on divorce is also evidenced in the works of Ephraim Pagitt, Nathaniel Hardy, William Prynne, Daniel Featley, Thomas Edwards, and Robert Baillie, among others. In his twinned Trinity Manuscript Sonnets XI and XII (1647, 1646; printed 1673), Milton would cast the (largely Presbyterian) deriders of his tolerationist tracts as foolish calumniators.

68 John Ward, *God Judging Among the Gods. Opened in a Sermon before the Honourable House of Commons* (London, 1645), p. 31.

69 CPW 2:491. The House of Lords passed the Bishops' Exclusion Bill on 5 February 1642 and the king accepted it, allegedly at the behest of his wife, on 13 February 1642 (Samuel R. Gardiner, *History of England from the Accession of James I to the Outbreak of the Civil War, 1603–1642*, 10 vols. [London: Longmans, Green, and Co., 1884], vol. 10, pp. 163, 165–6). Presbyterianism would be established by law on 28 January 1645.

70 Andrew Escobedo, "The Invisible Nation: Church, State, and Schism in Milton's England," in *Early Modern Nationalism and Milton's England*, p. 192.

71 Escobedo, "The Invisible Nation," pp. 194, 192; see also pp. 195–6.

72 Even after he formalizes his theory of disestablishment, he would be compelled to acknowledge a function for magistrates as civil authorities, specifically in the exorcising of a politicized popery and idolatry. See Chapter 4 of this book.

73 Brooke, *A Discourse Opening the Nature of that Episcopacie*, p. 95.

74 Arthur E. Barker, *Milton and the Puritan Dilemma 1641–1660* (Toronto, ON: University of Toronto Press, 1942), p. 80.

75 Sirluck notes the limited authority enjoyed by the Court in the fourth century BCE, authority Isocrates sought to restore (CPW 2:486n1).

76 David Loewenstein and John Morrill, "Literature and Religion," in David Loewenstein and Janel Mueller (eds.), *The Cambridge History of Early Modern English Literature* (Cambridge: Cambridge University Press, 2002), p. 685. See also Loewenstein's "Toleration and the Specter of Heresy in Milton's England," in *Milton and Toleration*, p. 65.

77 Robert Baillie/Baylie, *Satan the Leader in Chief to All Who Resist the Reparation of Sion. As it was cleared in a Sermon … Febr. 28. 1643* (London, 1644), pp. 36, 37.

78 Baillie, *Satan the Leader*, pp. 4–5, sig. A4v.

79 Baillie, *Satan the Leader*, sig. A2v; see also pp. 34–35.

80 Robert Baillie, *Anabaptism, the true fountaine of Independency, Brownisme, Antinomy, Familisme, and the most of the other errours, which for the time doe trouble the Church of England, unsealed* (London, 1647), sig. *2v, p. 100.

81 Stephen Marshall, *A Sacred Panegyrick, or a Sermon of Thanks-giving* (London, 1644), p. 26. On Marshall and the hammering out of the doctrine and discipline of church government in the Westminster Assembly, see Sharon Achinstein, "'A Law in this Matter to Himself': Contextualizing Milton's Divorce Tracts," in Nicholas McDowell and Nigel Smith (eds.), *The Oxford Handbook of Milton* (Oxford: Oxford University Press, 2009), pp. 177–8.

82 Thomas Fuller, *A Pisgah-sight of Palestine and The Confines Thereof, with the History of the Old and New Testament Acted Thereon* (London, 1650), bk 3.2, p. 361.

83 Burton, *A Vindication of Churches*, pp. 1–2.

84 Thomas Hill, *The Good Old Way, Gods Way To Soule-Refreshing Rest: Discovered in a Sermon Preached … Apr. 24. 1644* (London, 1644), sig. A4r.

85 Hill, *The Good Old Way*, p. 39.

86 Hill, *The Good Old Way*, p. 40

87 Hill, *The Good Old Way*, p. 41.

88 On this point, see Simpson's *Spiritual Architecture and "Paradise Regained."*

89 Thomas Cartwright, *An Answere Unto a Letter of Master Harrisons* (c. 1573) in *An Answere to Master Cartwright His Letter For Joyning with the English Churches: whereunto the true copie of his sayded letter is annexed* (London, [1585]), pp. 90, 91, 89.

90 George Gifford, *A Sermon preached at Pauls Crosse the thirtie day of May. 1591* (London, 1591), sig. [B5v–B6r].

91 Matt. 13:24–30; CPW 2:564; Hans R. Guggisberg, "The Defence of Religious Toleration and Religions Liberty in Early Modern Europe: Arguments, Pressures, and some Consequences," *History of European Ideas* 4 (1983), 38.

92 Loewenstein, "Toleration and the Specter of Heresy in Milton's England," in *Milton and Toleration*, p. 69. In *Of Reformation*, Milton had asked: "What more binding then Conscience? what more free then *indifferency?*" (CPW 1:585).

93 CPW 2:554. Cf. Thomas Hill's concluding appeal in *Good Old Way*, p. 52.

94 Cf. Col. 3:12–3.

95 Roger Williams, *The Bloudy Tenent, of Persecution, for Cause of Conscience, Discussed in a Conference betweene Truth and Peace* (London, 1644), p. 18.

96 Williams, *Bloudy Tenent*, sig. a2v; p. 183. See Thomas Corns's instructive comparisons between Milton's limited and Williams's broad toleration in "Milton, Roger Williams, and Limits of Toleration," *Milton and Toleration*, pp. 72–85.

97 CPW 1:797. See also "The Digression in Milton's History of England" (ca. 1647–8), a variation on Milton's *Character of the Long Parliament and Assembly*

of Divines in 1641 (1681), in which Milton remarks that "civilitie, prudence, love of the public" are not native to the British but must be cultivated through "the knowledge of Antient and illustrious deeds" (CPW 5.1:451).

2 Reduction: Civilizing Conquests in Ireland

1 Sir James Perrott, *The Chronicle of Ireland 1584–1608*, Herbert Wood (ed.) (Dublin: Stationary Office, 1933), p. 4.

2 On the British problem, see J. G. A. Pocock, "British History: A Plea for a New Subject" (1973), *Journal of Modern History* 47 (1975), 601–28, rpt. *The Discovery of Islands: Essays in British History* (Cambridge: Cambridge University Press, 2005), pp. 24–43. Pocock argues for "an Age of the Three Kingdoms" that encompasses the whole early modern era. See also Willy Maley's comprehensive bibliographic note in *Nation, State and Empire in English Renaissance Literature: Shakespeare to Milton* (New York: Palgrave Macmillan, 2003), pp. 150–1n8; David J. Baker, *Between Nations: Shakespeare, Spenser, Marvell, and the Question of Britain* (Stanford, CA: Stanford University Press, 1997); David J. Baker and W. Maley, "Introduction: An Uncertain Union," in David J. Baker and Willy Maley (eds.), *British Identities and English Renaissance Literature* (Cambridge: Cambridge University Press, 2002), pp. 1–8; Andrew Hadfield, *Shakespeare, Spenser and the Matter of Britain* (London: Palgrave Macmillan, 2004), pp. 1–11. See especially Kerrigan's magisterial *Archipelagic English: Literature, History, and Politics 1603–1707* (Oxford: Oxford University Press, 2008). On the New British History (or the British problem) as an expression of "historical imperialism," see Patrick Collinson, *This England: Essays on the English Nation and Commonwealth in the Sixteenth Century* (New York: Palgrave Macmillan, 2011), p. 2. Cf. Milton's "relentless Anglicizing" as shrewdly and admirably discussed in Paul Stevens's "Archipelagic Criticism and Its Limits: Milton, Geoffrey of Monmouth, and the Matter of England," *The European Legacy* 17, 2 (2012), 151–164.

3 David Cairns and Shaun Richards, *Writing Ireland: Colonialism, Nationalism, and Culture* (Manchester, UK: Manchester University Press, 1988), p. 3. Monmouth's *Historia Regnum Britanniae* (ca. 1136) served as a significant source for Spenser and for Milton in the first book of his *History of Britain*. See also Stevens above.

4 Tony Claydon and Ian McBride, "The Trials of the Chosen Peoples: Recent Interpretations of Protestantism and National Identity in Britain and Ireland," in Tony Claydon and Ian McBride (eds.), *Protestantism and National Identity: Britain and Ireland, c. 1650–c. 1850* (Cambridge: Cambridge University Press, 1998), p. 22.

5 Michael Neill, "Broken English and Broken Irish: Nation, Language, and the Optic of Power in Shakespeare's Histories," *Shakespeare Quarterly* 45, 1 (1994), 3.

6 David Hempton, *Religion and Political Culture in Britain and Ireland* (Cambridge: Cambridge University Press, 1996), p. 145; Raymond D. Tumbleson, *Catholicism in the English Protestant Imagination: Nationalism,*

Religion, and Literature, 1660–1745 (Cambridge: Cambridge University Press, 1998), p. 11; see also Peter Lake, "Anti-popery: the Structure of a Prejudice," in Richard Cust and Ann Hughes (eds.), *Conflict in Early Stuart England: Studies in Religion and Politics, 1603–1642* (London: Longman, 1989), pp. 72–106, and Andrew Hadfield, "Milton and Catholicism," in Sharon Achinstein and Elizabeth Sauer (eds.), *Milton and Toleration* (Oxford: Oxford University Press, 2007), pp. 186–99.

7 Alexandra Walsham, *Charitable Hatred: Tolerance and Intolerance in England, 1500–1700* (Manchester, UK: Manchester University Press, 2006), p. 5. See also John Coffey, *Persecution and Toleration in Protestant England, 1558–1689* (New York: Longman, 2000), p. 146.

8 Thomas N. Corns, "Milton and the Characteristics of a Free Commonwealth," *Milton and Republicanism*, p. 32.

9 Oxford English Dictionary, "Reduction," I.2.a. "An Act for the English order, habite and language," Anno 28. H.8. fo. 128. Cap. XV., *The Statutes of Ireland, Beginning the Third Yere of K. Edward the Second, and Continuing untill . . . King James* (Dublin, 1621), p. 129.

10 Sir Thomas Smith to Sir William Fitzwilliam, 8 November 1572 (Oxford, Carte MSS, vol. 57, no. 236), qtd in Nicholas Canny, "The Ideology of English Colonization from Ireland to America," *William and Mary Quarterly* 30, 4 (1973), 588–9. "Secretary Sir Thomas Smith to the Lord Deputy" (8 Nov. 1572), in Hans Claude Hamilton (ed.), *Calendar of the State Papers relating to Ireland, of the Reigns of Henry VIII, Edward VI, Mary, and Elizabeth. 1509–1573*, 11 vols. (London: Longman, 1860), vol. 1, p. 488.

11 Edmund Spenser, *A vewe of the present state of Ireland* in W. L. Renwick (ed.), *"A View of the Present State of Ireland" by Edmund Spenser* (London: Scholaritis Press, 1934), p. 13.

12 Spenser, *A View of the State of Ireland, Written Dialogue-wise betweene Eudoxus and Irenaeus, By Edmund Spenser Esq. in the yeare 1596*, in James Ware (ed.), *The Historie of Ireland, Collected by Three Learned Authors viz. Meredith Hanmer . . ., Edmund Campion . . . and Edmund Spenser* (Dublin, 1633), sig. 3v. STC 25067a.

13 Milton, *A Masque Presented at Ludlow Castle*, in *Milton, Complete Shorter Poems*, l. 60. Philip Schwyzer, "Purity and Danger on the West Bank of the Severn: The Cultural Geography of *A Masque Presented at Ludlow Castle*," *Representations* 60 (1997), 35.

14 Ruth Mohl (ed.), Milton's Commonplace Book, CPW 1:465. Such entries indicate Milton read the 1633 edition of Spenser's *View*; see also CPW 1:496.

15 Spenser, *A View of the State of Ireland*, p. 1. The original text read "salvage nacion." See Spenser, *A vewe of the present state of Ireland*, p. 3.

16 Spenser, *A View of the State of Ireland*, p. 1.

17 Spenser, *A View of the State of Ireland*, pp. 8–9.

18 Willy Maley, "Forms of Discrimination in Spenser's *A View of the State of Ireland* (1596; 1633): From Dialogue to Silence," in *Nation, State and Empire in English Renaissance Literature*, p. 72.

19 *A Treatice of Ireland; by John Dymmok*, ed. Rev. Richard Butler (Dublin: For the Irish Archaeological Society, University of Dublin Press, 1842), p. 6. B. M. Harl. MSS. 1291, fo. 41v

20 Spenser, *A View of the State of Ireland*, p. 34. Later he chastises the Old English, the first colonizers of Ireland, for their incivility, which renders them "wilde and meere *Irish*" (p. 105).

21 Fynes Moryson, *The Itinerary of Fynes Moryson*, vol. 4. (Glasgow, Scotland: James MacLehose and Sons, 1908), p. 236.

22 Nicholas Canny, *The Upstart Earl: A Study of the Social and Mental World of Richard Boyle First Earl of Cork 1566–1643* (Cambridge: Cambridge University Press, 1982), p. 130.

23 Francis Bacon, "Considerations Touching the Queen's Service in Ireland," vol. 10 in James Spedding, Robert Leslie Ellis, and Douglas Denon Heath (eds.), *The Works of Francis Bacon*, 15 vols. (London: Longman, 1868–92), p. 47.

24 Bacon, "Considerations Touching the Queen's Service," in *Works of Francis Bacon*, vol. 10, pp. 47–8, 49, 51, 50.

25 Bacon, "Certain Considerations Touching the Plantation in Ireland," in *Works of Francis Bacon*, vol. 11, pp. 116–26.

26 Sir John Davies, "A Letter to the Earl of Salisbury, in 1610; Giving an Account of the Plantation in Ulster," in Sir John Davies, *Historical Tracts by John Davies* (London, 1786), p. 289.

27 Sir John Davies, *A Discoverie of the True Causes why Ireland was never entirely Subdued, nor brought under Obedience of the Crowne of England, untill the Beginning of his Majesties happie Raigne* (London, 1612), p. 281.

28 Davies, *Discoverie of the True Causes*, p. 282.

29 Anthony Pagden, *Lords of All the World: Ideologies of Empire in Spain, Britain and France, c. 1500–1800* (New Haven, CT: Yale University Press, 1995), p. 12.

30 Davies, *Discoverie of the True Causes*, pp. 6–8. Cf. Patrick Kelly, "Conquest Versus Consent as the Basis of the English Title to Ireland in William Molyneux's *Case of Ireland ... Stated* (1698)," in Ciaran Brady and Jane Ohlmeyer (eds.), *British Interventions in Early Modern Ireland* (Cambridge: Cambridge University Press, 2005), pp. 334–56.

31 Robert Greville, Lord Brooke, *A Discourse Opening the Nature of that Episcopacie, which is Exercised in England* (London, 1641), p. 48.

32 CPW 1:798. Alan Ford, *The Protestant Reformation in Ireland, 1590–1641* (Portland, OR: Four Courts Press, 1997), p. 220.

33 CPW 1:800, 800n41. See also Davies, *A Discoverie of the True Causes*, 8–9; and *A Geographicall Description of the Kingdome of Ireland ... As also Declaring the Right and Titles of the Kings of England unto that Kingdom* (London, 1642), Part II, p. 30.

34 Roger Williams, *Hirelings Ministry None of Christs, or A Discourse touching the Propagating the Gospel* (London, 1652), p. 25: [Note: No sword to be used against the most horrid *Blasphemies* & *Heresies*, but the two edged sword of the *Word*, the sword of the *Spirit* of *God*.]

35 Daniel Harcourt, *The Levites Lamentation* (1643), p. 3; rpt as *The Clergies Lamentation: Deploring the sad Condition of the Kingdome of Ireland, by reason*

of the unparallel'd cruelties and murders exercised by the inhumane Popish Rebells upon many thousand Protestants in the Province of Ulster (London, 1644).

36 Walsham, *Charitable Hatred*, p. 46.

37 Harcourt, *The Levites Lamentation*, p. 23.

38 CPW 3:482. Arguably such distinctions come into play when Samson spares the "vulgar" while bringing down the house on the Philistines in *Samson Agonistes*, l. 1659.

39 Michael Lieb, *Milton and the Culture of Violence* (Ithaca, NY: Cornell University Press, 1994), pp. 139n9; see also Lieb, *Poetics of the Holy: A Reading of "Paradise Lost"* (Chapel Hill: University of North Carolina Press, 1981), pp. 246–312.

40 Oliver Cromwell, *The Writings and Speeches of Oliver Cromwell*, W. C. Abbott (ed.), 4 vols. (New York: Russell & Russell, 1970), vol. 2, p. 224.

41 *The Character of the Long Parliament and Assembly of Divines in 1641* (London, 1681) was composed c. 1647–8.

42 CPW 5.1:127. On the frequent allusions to Rome and its "civilizing mission" in the discourse on Ireland, see Canny, "The Ideology of English Colonization from Ireland to America," *William and Mary Quarterly* 30 (1973), 575–98.

43 Thomas N. Corns, "Milton and the Limitations of Englishness," in David Loewenstein and Paul Stevens (eds.), *Early Modern Nationalism and Milton's England* (Toronto, ON: University of Toronto Press, 2008), p. 211. I cite Corns's examples from Milton's *History*. See also Gordon Campbell and Thomas N. Corns, *John Milton: Life, Work, and Thought* (Oxford: Oxford University Press, 2008), p. 356.

44 See, for example, CPW 5.1:132–45. Nicholas von Maltzahn ascribes Milton's disparagement of non–English Britons to the challenges of uniting Britain in the 1640s (*Milton's "History of Britain": Republican Historiography in the English Revolution* [Oxford: Oxford University Press, 1991], p. 33).

45 The first translation of William Camden's *Britannia* (1586) was *Britain, or A Chorographicall Description of . . . England, Scotland, and Ireland*, Philémon Holland (trans.), (London, 1610), p. 63.

46 A motley crew of Ulster Presbyterians, Catholics, and royalists was then assembled under Ormond. See Pádraig Lenihan, *Consolidating Conquest: Ireland 1603–1727* (Harlow: Pearson Longman, 2008), p. 117.

47 PRO, Order Book of the Council of State, (28 March 1649), #1, in Mary Anne Everett Green (ed.), *Calendar of State Papers, Domestic, 1649–1650* (London: Longman & Co., 1875), p. 57. David Masson, *The Life of John Milton*, 6 vols. (London, 1859–94), vol. 4, pp. 87, 98. See also J. Milton French (ed.), *The Life Records of John Milton*, 5 vols. (New York: Gordian Press, 1966), vol. 2, p. 240.

48 Thomas N. Corns, "Milton's *Observations upon the Articles of Peace*: Ireland under English Eyes," in David Loewenstein and James Grantham Turner (eds.), *Politics, Poetics, and Hermeneutics in Milton's Prose* (Cambridge: Cambridge University Press, 1990), p. 125.

49 Christopher Hill, "Seventeenth-century English Radicals and Ireland," in Patrick J. Corish (ed.), *Radicals Rebels and Establishments: Historical Studies* 15 (Appletree Press: Belfast, 1985), p. 35.

50 David Loewenstein, *Representing Revolution in Milton and his Contemporaries: Religion, Politics, and Polemics in Radical Puritanism* (Cambridge: Cambridge University Press, 2001), p. 200.

51 Willy Maley, "Milton and 'the complication of interests' in Early Modern Ireland," in Balachandra Rajan and Elizabeth Sauer (eds.), *Milton and the Imperial Vision* (Pittsburgh, PA: Duquesne University Press, 1999), p. 342n6. Maley insists that Hill's "even" should read "especially" (Maley, "How Milton and Some Contemporaries Read Spenser's *View*," in Brendan Bradshaw, Andrew Hadfield, and Willy Maley [eds.], *Representing Ireland: Literature and the Origins of Conflict, 1534–1660* [Cambridge: Cambridge University Press, 1993], p. 202).

52 Milton, *Observations upon the Articles of Peace with the Irish Rebels*, in Merritt Y. Hughes (ed.), CPW 3:301.

53 On the implications thereof, see Joad Raymond, "Complications of Interest: Milton, Scotland, Ireland, and National Identity in 1649," *Review of English Studies* 55 (2005), 315–45. Willy Maley pointed out earlier that *Observations* is not about Ireland but Scotland (Maley, "Milton and 'the complication of interests'" [p. 164]). John Kerrigan affirms that *Observations* is "best understood in an Anglo-Scottish context" (*Archipelagic English*, p. 231). Raymond interprets the comparative minimal attention that Milton devotes to the Articles as an uncomfortable reticence on Milton's part about the politics of the English colonial situation in Ireland (Raymond, "Complications of Interest," 321). Mary C. Fenton, by contrast, determines that even after 1649, Milton's writings under Cromwell do not express "any significant ambivalence" on the subject of Cromwell's involvement in the campaign (Fenton, *Milton's Places of Hope: Spiritual and Political Connections of Hope with Land* [Aldershot: Ashgate, 2006], p. 90).

54 "An Act declaring the effect of Poynings act," Anno 28. H.8. fo. 164. Cap. XX, *The Statutes of Ireland, Beginning the Third Yere of K. Edward the Second, and Continuing untill … King James* (Dublin, 1621), pp. 164–66; Davies, "Sir John Davies's Speech to the Lord-Deputy of Ireland … 1613," in Sir John Davies, *Historical Tracts by John Davies* (Dublin, 1787), pp. 287–313.

55 CPW 3:478. The greatest threat to the republic in 1649 came from the Irish rather than the Scots, Cromwell concluded, just before accepting his command in Ireland and a year and a half before his invasion of Scotland: "I had rather bee overrun with a Cavalerish interest [than] of a Scotch interest; I had rather bee overrun with a Scotch interest then an Irish interest" (Whitehall, 23 March 1649, in Sir William Clarke, *The Clarke Papers. Selections from the Papers of William Clarke, Secretary to the Council of the Army, 1647–1649, and to General Monck and the Commanders of the Army in Scotland, 1651–1660,* C. H. Firth [ed.], 4 vols. [Camden Society, 1894], vol. 2, p. 205). See also Ian Gentles, "The Conquest of Ireland," *The New Model Army in England, Ireland and Scotland, 1645–1653* (Oxford: Blackwell, 1992), p. 351.

56 CPW 3:309, 311.

57 CPW 3:314, 315. Milton found precedents for the resistance to absolutism and for support of the doctrine of elective monarchy in François Hotman's

Franco-Gallia: Or An Account of the Ancient Free State of France (Geneva, 1573) and, as mentioned in Chapter 1, in [Hubert Languet], *Vindiciae contra Tyrannos: A Defence of Liberty against Tyrants ... A Treatise written in Latin and French by Junius Brutus, and translated ... into English* (London, 1648) (see Merritt Y. Hughes [ed.], CPW 3:177).

58 Phil Kilroy, *Protestant Dissent and Controversy in Ireland 1660–1714* (Cork, Ireland: Cork University Press, 1994), p. 16.

59 *A Solemn League and Covenant, for Reformation, and Defence of Religion, the Honour and Happinesse of the King, and the Peace and Safety of the three Kingdoms of England, Scotland, and Ireland* (London, 1643).

60 Anthony D. Smith, "Nation and Covenant: The Contribution of Ancient Israel to Modern Nationalism," *Proceedings of the British Academy* 151 (2007), 242.

61 CPW 3:307n19. Presbyterian Herbert Palmer refers to the *Solemn League and Covenant* in terms of the covenant between God and his people in *The Glasse of Gods Providence Towards His Faithfull Ones. Held forth in a Sermon preached ... applied specially to a more carefull observation of our late Covenant, and particularly against the ungodly Toleration pleaded for under pretence of Liberty of Conscience* (London, 1644), p. 57.

62 *A Necessary Representation*, CPW 3:297. See also Herbert Palmer, who discusses the violation of the terms of the covenant in *The Glasse of Gods Providence* (pp. 50, 54).

63 *A Necessary Examination of a Dangerous Design and Practice against the Interest and Soveraignty of the Nation and Common-wealth of England, by the Presbytery at Belfast ... in their ... Treasonable Libel ... A Necessary Presentation of the Present and Eminent Danger ...* (London, 1649), p. 9.

64 *A Necessary Examination of a Dangerous Design*, p. 20.

65 Kilroy, *Protestant Dissent and Controversy*, p. 17.

66 See Articles 3 and 6, *A Solemn League and Covenant*, 5, 6.

67 Council of State, Day's Proceedings (26 March 1649), #32, *Calendar of State Papers, Domestic, 1649–1650*, vol. 1, p. 52.

68 Nicholas McDowell, "Milton's Regicide Tracts and the Uses of Shakespeare," in Nicholas McDowell and Nigel Smith (eds.), *The Oxford Handbook of Milton* (Oxford: Oxford University Press, 2009), p. 263. Joad Raymond, "Complications of Interest," 317.

69 See Gentles, *The New Model Army*, pp. 330–1. The pro-Parliamentary tract, *A great and bloudy fight neer Droghedah in Ireland* (London, 1649), p. 6, includes an account of the Levellers' plea "For a dissolution of this present Parl. And for electing a free Representative" (Norah Carlin, "The Levellers and the Conquest of Ireland in 1649," *The Historical Journal* 30 [1987], 274).

70 *Mercurius Pragmaticus*, no. 52 (24 Apr.–1 May 1649), 24 Apr., sig. Qqq2v–Qqq3r, esp. 30 Apr., sig. Qqq4v.

71 *The English Souldiers Standard, to Repaire to; for Wisdom and Understanding in these dolefull back-sliding Times* (n.p., 1649), p. 9. While arguing that the anonymous tract, copies of which the Council of State ordered to be seized, was in various ways pro-Leveller, Norah Carlin questions the attribution of *English*

Souldiers Standard to William Walwyn ("The Levellers and the Conquest," 277). The Levellers themselves are ridiculed on p. 11 of the tract.

72 *Tyranipocrit, Discovered with his wiles, wherewith he vanquisheth* (Rotterdam, 1649), p. 35.

73 Cromwell, *The Writings and Speeches of Oliver Cromwell*, vol. 2, p. 199. *A Declaration of the Lord Lieutenant* was printed 21 March 1650.

74 Cromwell, *The Writings and Speeches of Oliver Cromwell*, vol. 2, pp. 197–8.

75 Thomas May, *The History of the Parliament of England*, 3 books (London, 1647), bk 2, ch. 1, pp. 4–5, 5.

76 Sir John Temple, *The Irish Rebellion: or the History of the Beginning and First Progress of the General Rebellion Raised Within the Kingdom of Ireland, Upon the Three and Twentieth Day of October, 1641* (London, 1646).

77 May, *The History of the Parliament of England*, bk 2, ch. 1, p. 4.

78 Cromwell, *The Writings and Speeches of Oliver Cromwell*, vol. 2, p. 205.

79 Joad Raymond, "The Daily Muse, or Seventeenth-Century Poets Read the News," *The Seventeenth Century* 10 (1995), 189–218.

80 Andrew Marvell, "An Horatian Ode," in Elizabeth Story Donno (ed.), *The Complete Poems* (Harmondsworth: Penguin, 1972; rpt. 1985), ll. 73–4.

81 Cromwell, *The Writings and Speeches of Oliver Cromwell*, vol. 2, p. 287.

82 Qtd. in Gentles, *The New Model Army*, p. 383.

83 "An Act for the Setling of Ireland," in C. H. Firth and R. S. Rait (eds.), *Acts and Ordinances of the Interregnum, 1642–1660*, 3 vols. (London: Wyman & Sons, 1911), vol. 2, p. 598.

84 Christopher Hill, *God's Englishman: Oliver Cromwell and the English Revolution* (London: Weidenfeld and Nicolson, 1970), p. 122.

85 John Morrill, "The Rule of Saints and Soldiers: The Wars of Religion in Britain and Ireland 1638–1660," in Jenny Wormald (ed.), *The Seventeenth Century* (Oxford: Oxford University Press, 2008), p. 112.

86 Roger Williams, Preface, "To all such *Honourable* and *Pious* hands, whom the present *Debate* touching the propagating of CHRIST'S Gospel concernes," *Hirelings Ministry None of Christs*, sig. A3v, A4r.

87 Williams, *Hirelings Ministry None of Christs*, pp. 12–13.

88 James Harrington, *The Commonwealth of Oceana*, in J. G. A. Pocock (ed.), *The Political Works of James Harrington* (Cambridge: Cambridge University Press, 1977), p. 159.

89 1 June 1652, *A Perfect Diurnall of Some Passages and Proceedings of . . . the Armies in England, Ireland, & Scotland*, 130 (31 May – 7 June 1652), 1927, 1928. These pages are misnumbered, having been used for the previous pages.

90 John P. Prendergast, *The Cromwellian Settlement of Ireland* (New York: P. M. Haverty, 1868), pp. 87, 110, 244.

91 14 August 1656, *The Calendar of State Papers Colonial, America, and West Indies, Volume 1, 1574–1660*, W. Noël Sainsbury (ed.) (London: Longman, 1860), p. 447.

92 Antonia Fraser, *Cromwell, The Lord Protector* (New York: Knopf, 1974), pp. 522, 534. See also Charles P. Korr, *Cromwell and the New Model Foreign Policy: England's Policy Toward France, 1649–1658* (Berkeley: University of California Press, 1975), pp. 115, 144, 145.

93 "*H. Cromwell*, major general of the forces in *Ireland*, to secretary *Thurloe*" (18 September 1655), in Thomas Birch (ed.), *A Collection of the State Papers of John Thurloe*, 7 vols. (London, 1742), vol. 4, p. 40.

94 On the debate between Gookin and Lawrence, see Sarah Butler, "Settlement, Transplantation and Expulsion: A Comparative Study of the Placement of Peoples," in Brady and Ohlmeyer (eds.), *British Interventions*, pp. 280–98; see also Patricia Coughlan's "Counter-Currents in Colonial Discourse: The Political Thought of Vincent and Daniel Gookin," in Jane H. Ohlmeyer (ed.), *Political Thought in Seventeenth-Century Ireland: Kingdom or Colony* (Cambridge: Cambridge University Press, 2000), pp. 56–82.

95 Vincent Gookin, *The Great Case of Transplantation in Ireland Discussed* (London, 1655), p. 29.

96 T. C. Barnard, "Planters and Policies in Cromwellian Ireland," *Past and Present* 61, 1 (1973), 43.

97 Gookin, *The Great Case of Transplantation*, pp. 25–6.

98 Richard Lawrence, *The Interest of Ireland in its Trade and Wealth Stated* (Dublin, 1682), part 2, p. 84.

99 Richard Lawrence, *The Interest of England in the Irish Transplantation* (London, 1655), p. 16; the judgement is repeated on pp. 25, 26. On the significance of "planting," also see Mary C. Fenton, "Milton's View of Ireland: Reform, Reduction, and Nationalist Polity," *Milton Studies* 44 (2005), 207, and Fenton, "Milton's Hope: Domestic Land Ownership and The Paradise Within," *SEL: Studies in English Literature 1500–1900* 43, 1 (2003), 151–80.

100 Lawrence, *The Interest of Ireland*, p. 16. James Butler, Duke of Ormond, who became Lord Lieutenant in Dublin, arranged for the publication of Lawrence's 1682 *Interest of Ireland* (T. C. Barnard, "Interests in Ireland: the 'fanatic zeal and irregular ambition' of Richard Lawrence," in *British Interventions*, p. 301).

101 Vincent Gookin, *The Author and Case of Transplanting the Irish into Connaught Vindicated from the unjust Aspersions of Col. Richard Laurence* (London, 1655), p. 41.

102 Gookin, *The Great Case of Transplantation*, p. 20. On the implications of this point about language, see Robert C. Simington, *The Transplantation to Connacht 1654–58* (Shannon: Irish University Press, 1970), pp. xxv–xxvi.

103 Gerard Boate, *Ireland's Naturall History ... Published by Samuel Hartlib, Esq For the Common Good of Ireland, and more especially, for the benefit of the Adventurers and Planters therein* (London, 1657), p. 8. Thomas May makes the same point about the English Pale and the English inhabitants who "declared themselves for the Rebels" (*The History*, bk 2, ch. 1, p. 11).

104 "The humble petition of the Officers within the precincts of *Dublin, Caterlough, Wexford*, and *Kilkenny*," [John Hall (ed.)], *Mercurius Politicus*, no. 251 (29 March–5 April 1655), 5237.

105 Lawrence, *Interest of England*, p. 15.

106 Gookin, *Author and Case of Transplanting*, p. 40.

107 Gookin, *Author and Case of Transplanting*, p. 40.

108 *The Weekly Post*, no. 283 (31 July 31–7 August 1655), 1908. Fleetwood retained his post as Lord Deputy of Ireland for two years after returning to England.

109 Gookin, *The Great Case of Transplantation*, p. 29.
110 T. C. Barnard, "Crises of Identity among Irish Protestants, 1641–1685," *Past and Present* 127 (May 1990), 72.
111 John W. Blake, "Transportation from Ireland to America, 1653–60," *Irish Historical Studies* 3 (1942–3), 275.
112 Nicholas Canny, *Making Ireland British, 1580–1650* (Oxford: Oxford University Press, 2001), p. 571; in the 1650s, 34,000 Irish soldiers enlisted in continental armies (Gentles, *The New Model Army*, p. 381).
113 "From Nieuport the Dutch Ambassador in England" (4 June 1655), in *A Collection of the State Papers of John Thurloe*, vol. 3, p. 477.
114 T. C. Barnard, "Crises of Identity," 72–3.
115 "A letter from several officers in *Ireland* to the protector" (1655), in *A Collection of the State Papers of John Thurloe*, vol. 3, p. 467.
116 "*Fleetwood*, lord deputy of *Ireland*, to secretary *Thurloe*" (23 May 1655), in *A Collection of the State Papers of John Thurloe*, vol. 3, p. 468.
117 Milton, "Sonnet XV. On the late Massacre in Piedmont," in *Milton, Complete Shorter Poems*, ll. 1–2.
118 *The Weekly Post*, no. 231 (12–19 June 1655), 1842.
119 Stouppe, *A Collection of the Several Papers…Concerning the Bloody and Barbarous Massacres…of many thousands of Reformed, or Protestants dwelling in the Vallies of Piedmont* (London, 1655), title page; Dedication, sig. A3; pp. 23, 27, 37; "An Abstract of a Letter writen from the Vale of *Perouse* the *17 of April 1655*," *A Collection of the Several Papers*, p. 27. "A Narrative of the bloody Persecution of the Protestants in Savoy," *The Weekly Post*, n. 231 (12–19 June, 1655), 1842, 1843.
120 Stouppe, *Collection of the Several Papers*, p. 3; Cromwell, vol. 3, p. 707. Cf. Paris, 12 June 1655, *A Collection of the State Papers of John Thurloe*, vol. 3, p. 502.
121 Stouppe, *Collection of the Several Papers*, p. 40.
122 Stouppe, *Collection of the Several Papers*, p. 41.
123 "Extracts of several letters from mr. *Leger*, pastoral and divinity reader at Geneva" (22 May 1655), in *A Collection of the State Papers of John Thurloe*, vol. 3, p. 459.
124 Stouppe, *Collection of the Several Papers*, p. 43.
125 See Stephen Marshall, *Meroz Cursed, or A Sermon Preached to the Honourable House of Commons, At their late Solemn Fast, Febr. 23. 1641* (London, 1642), p. 22.

3 Natural Law: Milton's Post-revolutionary Defences of England

1 *Observations upon the Articles of Peace*, CPW 3:312. *A Defence of the People of England*, William J. Grace (Preface and Notes), Donald Mackenzie (trans.), CPW 4:323, 430–1.
2 John Milton, "To the Lord General Cromwell," in *Milton, Complete Shorter Poems*, ll. 1; 9b–10a; 13b–14a; 11b.

3 See, for example, Blair Worden, "Milton's *Second Defence*," *Literature and Politics in Cromwellian England: John Milton, Andrew Marvell, Marchamont Nedham* (Oxford: Oxford University Press, 2007), pp. 262–88; Worden, "Marchamont Nedham and the Beginnings of English Republicanism, 1649–1656," in David Wootton (ed.), *Republicanism, Liberty, and Commercial Society, 1649–1776* (Stanford, CA: Stanford University Press, 1994), pp. 45–81; Martin Dzelzainis, "Milton's Classical Republicanism," in David Armitage, Armand Himy, and Quentin Skinner (eds.), *Milton and Republicanism* (Cambridge: Cambridge University Press, 1995), pp. 3–24; Thomas N. Corns, "Milton and the Characteristics of a Free Commonwealth," in *Milton and Republicanism*, pp. 25–42; and David Norbrook, *Writing the English Republic: Poetry, Rhetoric and Politics, 1627–1660* (Cambridge: Cambridge University Press, 1999), pp. 209–11 (*Defensio Prima*) and pp. 331–7 (*Defensio Secunda*).

4 David Loewenstein, "Milton's Prose and the Revolution," in N. H. Keeble (ed.), *Writing of the English Revolution* (Cambridge: Cambridge University Press, 2001), p. 99. Loewenstein's description is also applicable to the 1651 *Defensio*.

5 N. H. Keeble, "Introduction," in N. H. Keeble (ed.), *Writing of the English Revolution*, p. 8n26. See also N. H. Keeble, "Restoration or Revolution?" *The Restoration: England in the 1660s* (Oxford: Blackwell, 2002), pp. 46–57; Michael Wilding, *Dragons Teeth: Literature in the English Revolution* (Oxford: Clarendon Press, 1987), p. 91; Cf. Christopher Hill, "The Word 'Revolution' in Seventeenth-Century England," in Richard Lawrence Ollard and Pamela Tudor-Craig (eds.), *For Veronica Wedgwood: These Studies in Seventeenth-Century History* (London: Collins, 1986), pp. 134–51; and David Loewenstein, *Representing Revolution in Milton and his Contemporaries: Religion, Politics, and Polemics in Radical Puritanism* (Cambridge: Cambridge University Press, 2002), p. 9.

6 John Adamson, *The Noble Revolt: The Overthrow of Charles I* (London: Weidenfeld and Nicolson, 2007, 2009); David Cressy, *England on the Edge: Crisis and Revolution, 1640–1642* (Oxford: Oxford University Press, 2006).

7 On these historiographical questions, see N. H. Keeble, "Introduction," *Writing the English Revolution*, p. 6; John Morrill, "The Causes and Course of the British Civil Wars," *Writing the English Revolution*, pp. 13–31; and Annabel Patterson, "The Very Name of the Game," in Thomas Healy and Jonathan Sawday (eds.), *Literature and the English Civil War* (Cambridge: Cambridge University Press, 1990), pp. 21–37.

8 On post-revisionism, see, for example, Kevin Sharpe, *Remapping Early Modern England: The Culture of Seventeenth-Century Politics* (Cambridge: Cambridge University Press, 2000), esp. pp. 3–27.

9 [Marchamont Nedham], *A True State of the Case of the Commonwealth* (London, 1654), p. 5.

10 Christopher Hill, *Milton and the English Revolution* (New York: Viking Press, 1978), p. 167.

11 Gordon Campbell and Thomas N. Corns, *John Milton: Life, Work and Thought* (Oxford: Oxford University Press, 2008), pp. 229–30. Dugard was also the printer of the Racovian Catechism, for which he was tried in 1652 (2 April 1652, *Journal of the House of Commons*, vol. 7: 1651–1660 [1802], pp. 113–4.

URL: http://www.british-history.ac.uk/report.aspx?compid=23976&strquery =dugard Date accessed: 23 January 2013.)

12 *Joannis Miltoni Anglo Pro Populo Anglicano Defensio*, Clinton W. Keyes (ed.), Samuel Lee Wolff (trans.), vol. 7 (1932), in F. A. Patterson (gen. ed.), *The Works of John Milton*, 18 vols. (New York: Columbia University Press, 1931–8), pp. 356, 357. The phrase also appears earlier in the remark that the state maintains relations with "its sound and uncontaminated part alone" (*si sanæ et integræ tantum partis*), vol. 7, pp. 28–9.

13 CPW 4:507. In his Commonplace Book, Milton documents the major branches of law outlined in Justinian's *Institutes*, book 1: "De jure naturali, gentium et civili": natural, international, and civil law (*Works of John Milton*, vol. 18, p. 166). Lynne Greenberg argues that "this framework is foundational to Milton's later thinking" ("Law," in Stephen B. Dobranski [ed.], *Milton in Context* [Cambridge: Cambridge University Press, 2010], p. 330).

14 Cyriack Skinner, Milton's pupil, friend, and amanuensis, defines constitution as the "distinguishing Principles of Government" that would advance civil liberties ("The Life of Mr. John Milton by John Phillips," in Helen Darbishire [ed.], *The Early Lives of Milton* [London: Constable, 1932, reissued 1965], p. 26). On the attribution of "The Life of Mr. John Milton by John Phillips" to Cyriack Skinner, see vol. 2 of *The New Cambridge Bibliography of English Literature: 1660–1800*, George Watson (ed.) (Cambridge: Cambridge University Press, 1974), p. 481, and Gordon Campbell, "The Life Records," in Thomas N. Corns (ed.), *Companion to Milton* p. 484.

15 John Lilburne, *Londons Liberty in Chains Discovered. And, Published by Lieutenant Colonell John Lilburn, prisoner in the Tower of London* (London: October 1646), p. 41.

16 James Hay, Earl of Carlisle, *Collonel James Hays Speech to the Parlament upon the Debate Concerning Toleration...* ([London], 1655), p. 6.

17 Michael P. Zuckert, *Natural Rights and New Republicanism* (Princeton, NJ: Princeton University Press, 1994), p. 126.

18 Joan S. Bennett, *Reviving Liberty: Radical Christian Humanism in Milton's Great Poems* (Cambridge, MA: Harvard University Press, 1989), p. 47.

19 CPW 1:571. Cf. *Eikonoklastes*, CPW 3:458.

20 Barbara Lewalski, *Life of John Milton: A Critical Biography* (Oxford: Blackwell, 2000), p. 255; John Kerrigan, *Archipelagic English: Literature, History, and Politics, 1603–1707* (Oxford: Oxford University Press, 2008), p. 54.

21 See Quentin Skinner, *Liberty Before Liberalism* (Cambridge: Cambridge University Press, 1998, 2008).

22 *A Second Defence of the English People*, Donald A. Roberts (Preface and Notes), Helen North (trans.), CPW 4:654, 653–4.

23 Cedric C. Brown, "Great Senates and Godly Education: Politics and Cultural Renewal in Some Pre- and Post-revolutionary Texts of Milton," *Milton and Republicanism*, p. 44.

24 Keith W. Stavely, *The Politics of Milton's Prose Style* (New Haven, CT: Yale University Press, 1975), pp. 112–3.

25 See Prasanta Chakravarty, *Like Parchment in the Fire: Literature and Radicalism in the English Civil War* (New York: Routledge, 2006).

26 Gerrard Winstanley, *The Law of Freedom in a Platform: or, True Magistracy Restored* (London, 1652), p. 58.

27 John Goodwin, *Right and Might well Met, or A Briefe and Unpartiall Enquiry into the ... Proceedings of the Army* (London, 1649), p. 15.

28 Salmasius, *Defensio Regia pro Carolo I* (1649), Kathryn A. McEuen (trans.), CPW 4.2:1020.

29 Don M. Wolfe, Introduction, "*Defensio Regia* of Salmasius," CPW 4:107.

30 Sir Robert Filmer, "Observations on Mr. Milton *Against Salmasius*," in Peter Laslett (ed.), *Patriarcha and Other Political Works of Sir Robert Filmer* (Oxford: Blackwell, 1949), p. 251.

31 Bruce Boehrer, "Elementary Structures of Kingship: Milton, Regicide, and the Family," *Milton Studies* 23 (1987), 108.

32 See Johann P. Sommerville, "Literature and National Identity," in David Loewenstein and Janel Mueller (eds.), *The Cambridge History of Early Modern English Literature* (Cambridge: Cambridge University Press, 2002), p. 469. See also J. P. Sommerville, *Royalists and Patriots: Politics and Ideology in England 1603–1640* (London: Longman, 1999).

33 James I, King of England, *The True Lawe of Free Monarchies: Or the Reciprock and Mutuall Dutie Betwixt a Free King and His Naturall Subjects* (London, 1603), sig. B2v, D3r.

34 Thomas Hobbes, *Behemoth; or an Epitome of the Civil Wars of England, From 1640 to 1660* (London, 1679), 151. Hobbes, *Leviathan*, C. B. Macpherson (ed.) (Harmondsworth, UK: Penguin Books, 1968), p. 267.

35 David Owen, *Anti-Paraeus, or A Treatise in the Defence of the Royall Rights of Kings* (York, 1642), pp. 54, 57.

36 Cf. Milton in 1649 (*Tenure*, CPW 3:254).

37 John Canne, *The Golden Rule, Or, Justice Advanced* (London, 1649), p. 22.

38 Claire McEachern, *The Poetics of English Nationhood, 1590–1612* (Cambridge: Cambridge University Press, 1996/2006), p. 10.

39 Milton, *Tenure of Kings*, CPW 3:210. The contest over Romans 13:1–2 is described in CPW 3:58–64, which compares instructively with the debate over Romans 13:7 (CPW 4:376–7). Cf. Lancelot Andrewes's 1601 court sermon "Of the giving *Caesar* his due," a defence of subsidies based on Romans 13:7 and natural law.

40 William J. Grace, "Preface to *A Defence*," CPW 4:294.

41 CPW 4:480; 492. See also p. 501. See also Janelle Greenberg, *The Radical Face of the Ancient Constitution* (Cambridge: Cambridge University Press, 2001), pp. 236–42.

42 Winstanley, *Law of Freedom*, p. 65.

43 "The Act Erecting a High Court of Justice for the King's Trial" (6 January 1649), Samuel Rawson Gardiner (ed.), *The Constitutional Documents of the Puritan Revolution 1625–1660*, 3rd ed. (Oxford: Clarendon Press, 1889; rpt 1962), p. 357.

44 See J. G. A. Pocock, *The Ancient Constitution and the Feudal Law* (Cambridge, 1957; New York: Norton, 1967), pp. 30–55. See also Maurice Ashley, *Magna Carta in the Seventeenth Century* (Charlottesville: University Press of Virginia, 1965).

45 Lilburne, *Londons Liberty in Chains*, p. 40.

46 William Walwyn, *Englands lamentable slaverie* (London, 1645), p. 5.

47 *A Remonstrance of Many Thousand Citizens, and other Free-born People of England ... Occasioned through the Illegal and Barbarous Imprisonment of ... John Lilburne* ([London], 1646), p. 15. See also John Warr's objections to the elitism and abuses of the legal system since the time of the Conquest (*The Corruption and Deficiency of the Lawes of England* [London, 1649], pp. 9–10).

48 Iain M. MacKenzie, *God's Order and Natural Law: The Works of the Laudian Divines* (Aldershot and Burlington, VT: Ashgate, 2002), p. 62.

49 Skinner, "The Life of Mr. John Milton by John Phillips," p. 26. As noted above, Darbishire had attributed the work to Phillips.

50 Arthur P. Monahan, *Consent, Coercion and Limit: The Medieval Origins of Parliamentary Democracy* (Kingston, ON and Montreal, QB: McGill-Queen's University Press, 1987), p. 140.

51 Martin Dzelzainis, "Introduction," *John Milton, Political Writings*, Martin Dzelzainis (ed.); Claire Gruzelier (trans.) (Cambridge: Cambridge University Press, 1991), p. xxiv.

52 John Goodwin, *Right and Might well Met, or A briefe and unpartiall enquiry into the ... procedings of the Army* (London, 1649), p. 14.

53 *Mercurius Politicus*, no. 21 (Oct. 24–31, 1650), 342–43; 341–42; *Mercurius Politicus*, no. 78 (29 Nov.-4 Dec. 1651), 1237. Even dissenters wavered between inclusive and limited concepts of the people; see Brian Manning, *The English People and the English Revolution* (London: Heinemann, 1976; 2nd ed. London, 1991), e.g., p. 279.

54 A. S. P. Woodhouse, (ed. and intro.), *Puritanism and Liberty: Being the Army Debates [1647–9]*, Foreword by A. D. Lindsay (London: J. M. Dent and Sons, 1938, rpt. 1966), p. 93.

55 CPW 4:457. See also CPW 4:648.

56 See also CPW 4:317 and 422n2 4:317.

57 See Christopher Hill, "Liberty and Equality: Who are the People"? *Liberty Against the Law: Some Seventeenth-Century Controversies* (London: Penguin Press, 1996), pp. 242–51; Zuckert, *Natural Rights*, pp. 81–2. See also Hill, *Milton and the English Revolution* (New York: Viking Press, 1978), pp. 168–70. Hill surveys Daniel Taylor's, Oliver Cromwell's, Colonel John Jones's, and Thomas Scott's definitions of "the people". On Winstanley's qualifications of the "people," see Hill, *The World Turned Upside Down: Radical Ideas during the English Revolution* (New York: Viking Press, 1972), p. 135.

58 Armand Himy discusses the balancing of the democratic and elitist principles that define Milton's view of state politics ("*Paradise Lost* as a Republican 'tractatus theologico-politicus,'" *Milton and Republicanism*, pp. 118–34).

59 Filmer, "Observations on Mr. Milton *Against Salmasius*," pp. 252, 256.

60 John Lilburne, *As You Were or The Lord General Cromwel and the Grand Officers of the Armie their Remembrancer* ([Amsterdam], 1652), p. 16. The quoted section from the *Defensio* appears in CPW 4:535–6. See also Loewenstein, *Representing Revolution*, p. 39.

61 Lilburne, *As You Were*, pp. 16, 17.

62 Paul A. Rahe, *Against Throne and Altar: Machiavelli and Political Theory under the English Republic* (Cambridge: Cambridge University Press, 2008), p. 234.

63 Worden, *Literature and Politics in Cromwellian England*, p. 268. In the meantime, Newcomb also printed an enlarged edition of *Eikonoklastes* in 1650 and would print the 1658 *Defensio Prima* and *The Readie and Easie Way* in 1660, among other Milton imprints.

64 Worden, *Literature and Politics*, pp. 271, 288. Worden noted earlier that the continuity between the two *Defences* extends to the common "revolutionary purpose" they both hailed ("John Milton and Oliver Cromwell," in Ian Gentles, John Morrill, and Blair Worden [eds.], *Soldiers, Writers and Statesmen of the English Revolution* [Cambridge: Cambridge University Press, 1998], p. 257). David Norbrook also stated that Milton's discussion of the Protectorate in *Defensio Secunda* appears in a work originating in the republic (*Writing the English Republic*, p. 331).

65 Cf. Laura Lunger Knoppers's reading of the tract in "Late Political Prose," in Thomas N. Corns (ed.), *Companion to Milton*, pp. 309–25.

66 David Norbrook, *Writing the English Republic*, p. 437.

67 Milton, "To Mr Cyriack Skinner Upon His Blindness," in *Milton, Complete Shorter Poems*, ll. 12, 11.

68 Milton to Henry Oldenburg (6 July 1654), J. Milton French, *The Life Records*, 5 vols. (London: Rutgers University Press, 1949–58), vol. 3, p. 410.

69 Lewalski, *Life of John Milton*, p. 307.

70 Stephen M. Fallon, *Milton's Peculiar Grace: Self-Representation and Authority* (Ithaca, NY: Cornell University Press, 2007), p. 171.

71 CPW 4:596. Corns, "Milton and the Characteristics of a Free Commonwealth" in *Milton and Republicanism*, p. 27.

72 Payne Fisher and other poets cast Cromwell in the role assigned to Augustus, although Milton was, like Nedham, among those who did not (Norbrook, *Writing the English Republic*, pp. 328–9).

73 Worden, *Literature and Politics in Cromwellian England*, p. 291.

74 [John Hall], *A Letter Written to a Gentleman in the Country, touching the Dissolution of the Late Parliament* (London, 1653), pp. 1; 15–16. The title page of the British Library copy attributes the *Letter* to John Milton.

75 [Nedham], *A True State*, p. 5. Henry Stubbe, *Essay in Defence of the Good Old Cause, or A Discourse concerning the Rise and Extent of the power of the Civil Magistrate in reference to Spiritual Affairs... and A Vindication of The Honorable Sir Henry Vane from the false aspersions of Mr. Baxter* (London, 1659), Preface, sig. 4r–4v, sig. 5r.

76 [Nedham], *A True State*, pp. 22–3.

77 On the rhetorical relationship between compliment and criticism, see Kevin Sharpe, *Criticism and Compliment: The Politics of Literature in the England of Charles I* (Cambridge: Cambridge University Press, 1987).

78 CPW 4:676, 677.

79 The scholarly debate over the encomiastic or critical nature of the portrait of Cromwell in *Defensio Secunda* was ignited by Austin Woolrych's "Milton and Cromwell: A Short but Scandalous Night of Interruption?" in Michael Lieb and John Shawcross (eds.), *Achievements of the Left Hand: Essays on the Prose of John Milton* (Amherst: University of Massachusetts Press, 1974), pp. 185–218. For an analysis of the panegyric as (covertly) ironic, see Blair Worden, "Milton and Marchamont Nedham," *Milton and Republicanism*, pp. 175–8; as balanced, see Norbrook, *Writing the English Republic*, pp. 331–7, and Laura Knoppers, *Constructing Cromwell: Ceremony, Portrait, and Print, 1645–1661* (Cambridge: Cambridge University Press, 2000), pp. 93–5; as laudatory, see Robert Thomas Fallon, who resists the reading of the panegyric as critical of its subject ("*A Second Defence*: Milton's Critique of Cromwell?" *Milton Studies* 39 [2000], 167–83), and Warren Chernaik, who argues that Milton's panegyric is unambiguously celebratory in its commendation of the "guardian" of liberty in a republican government ("Victory's Crest: Milton, the English Nation, and Cromwell," in David Loewenstein and Paul Stevens [eds.], *Early Modern Nationalism and Milton's England* [Toronto, ON: University of Toronto Press, 2008], pp. 93–4). On Milton's reading of Cromwell in light of Raleigh's *Cabinet Council* and the 1658 *Defensio*, see Martin Dzelzainis, "Milton and the Protectorate in 1658," in *Milton and Republicanism*, pp. 181–205, and Paul Stevens, who resists Dzelzainis's theory of an ironic repudiation of Cromwell's single rule ("Milton "Renunciation" of Cromwell: The Problem of Raleigh's *Cabinet Council*," *Modern Philology* 98 [2001], 363–92).

80 *Joannis Miltoni Anglo Pro Populo Anglicano Defensio Secunda*, in Eugene J. Strittmatter (ed.), George Burnett, rev. Moses Hadas (trans.), vol. 8 of *The Works of John Milton*, pp. 238–9.

81 Compare the directives Michael issues to Adam to build the paradise within (PL 12.381–5).

82 Hugo Grotius, *De Jure Belli ac Pacis Libri Tres* (1625), Francis W. Kelsey (trans.) (New York: Oceana Publications, 1964), vol. 2, 2.18.2, p. 440; also quoted in a different translation in [Nedham], *Mercurius Politicus* no. 21 (24–31 Oct. 1650), 342.

83 George Bishop, *Mene Tekel, or The Council of Officers of the Army, Against The Declarations, &c. of the Army. Wherein is flatly proved … that the Sixth Article of the late Address of the said Council … changeth the Cause of Liberty of Conscience, from the Good Old One, to a Bad New One…* (London, 1659), p. 4.

84 Bishop, *Mene Tekel*, p. 6.

85 My argument departs from Dzelzainis's and Worden's positions on Milton's original (1654) and reasserted (1658) condemnation of Cromwell and the Protectorate (Dzelzainis, "Milton and the Protectorate in 1658," in *Milton and Republicanism*, p. 205; Worden, "John Milton and Oliver Cromwell," in *Soldiers, Writers and Statesmen*, p. 263).

86 David Loewenstein, "Milton and the Poetics of Defense," in David Loewenstein and James Grantham Turner (eds.), *Politics, Poetics, and Hermeneutics in Milton's Prose* (Cambridge: Cambridge University Press, 1990), pp. 187–8.

87 *A Proclamation for Calling In, and Suppressing of Two Books Written by John Milton, the One Intituled, Johannis Miltoni Angli Pro Populo Anglicano Defensio . . . and the Other in Answer to a Book Intituled, The Pourtraicture of His Sacred Majesty in His Solitude and Sufferings . . .* (London, 1660). See *Mercurius Publicus*, no. 37 (6–13 Sept. 1660), 578, and *The Parliamentary Intelligencer*, no. 37 (3–10 Sept. 1660), 589.

88 John Milton, *A Defence of the People of England by John Milton . . . in answer to Salmasius's defence of the King*, Joseph Washington (trans.) ([London,] 1692).

89 Gilbert Burnet, Martin Joseph Routh, and Thomas Burnet, *History of His Own Time*, 6 vols. (Oxford: Clarendon Press, 1823), vol. 5, p. 107; Locke, *A Letter Concerning Toleration*, M. Montuori (ed.) (The Hague: Martinus Nijhoff, 1963), p. 95.

90 See BL 8122.a.47. Cf. BL 8005.c.24.

4 Disestablishment: Divorce of Church and State

1 Milton, Commonplace Book, James Holly Hanford (ed.), Nelson Glenn McCrea (trans.), in vol. 18, *The Works of John Milton*, gen. ed. Frank Allen Patterson, 18 vols. (New York: Columbia University Press, 1931–8), p. 164. Cf. Commonplace Book, Ruth Mohl (ed. and trans), CPW 1:421.

2 Victoria Silver develops the links among epistemology, legal theory, theology, and equity in "Milton's Equitable Grounds of Toleration," in Sharon Achinstein and Elizabeth Sauer (eds.), *Milton and Toleration* (Oxford: Oxford University Press, 2007), pp. 144–70; Susanne Woods studies the form and stylistic features of the tracts as they influence author–text–reader interactions, the destabilization of cultural identity, and definitions of liberty ("Elective Poetics and Milton's Prose: *A Treatise of Civil Power* and *Considerations Touching the Likeliest Means to Remove Hirelings Out of the Church*," in David Loewenstein and James Grantham Turner [eds.], *Politics, Poetics, and Hermeneutics in Milton's Prose* [Cambridge: Cambridge University Press, 1990], pp. 193–211). Cf. Harry Smallenburg's stylistic analysis in "Government of the Spirit," in Michael Lieb and John T. Shawcross (eds.), *Achievements of the Left Hand: Essays on the Prose of John Milton* (Amherst: University of Massachusetts Press, 1974), pp. 219–37. See also Barbara K. Lewalski, "Milton: Political Beliefs and Polemical Methods, 1659–60," *PMLA* 74 (1959), 191–202. See note 63 below for the recent critical tradition on *Of True Religion*.

3 John Milton, *Considerations Touching the Likeliest Means to Remove Hirelings Out of the Church* (August 1659), in CPW vol. 7 (1980), Robert W. Ayers (ed.) and William B. Hunter, Jr. (Preface and Notes), p. 275.

4 *Englands Settlement, Upon the Two Solid Foundations of the Peoples Civil and Religious Liberties. Collected out of Divers Petitions, Declarations, and Remonstrances; Wherein is Discovered the General Genius of the Nation* (London,

12 Sept. 1659), p. 24. *Humble Petition of thousands of well-affected Gentlemen, Freeholders … of the County of Kent, and City of Canterbury* (London, 4 June 1659).

5 Austin Woolrych, "Introduction," in CPW 7:73.

6 See Sharon Achinstein, *Literature and Dissent in Milton's England* (Cambridge: Cambridge University Press, 2003), pp. 129–30; Michael P. Zuckert, *Natural Rights and New Republicanism* (Princeton, NJ: Princeton University Press, 1994), p. 79; and Robert Thomas Fallon, who maintains that liberty of conscience was for Milton the condition for political freedom (*Milton in Government* [University Park: The Pennsylvania State University Press, 1993], pp. 179, 188, 212).

7 Milton, *Lycidas*, in *Milton, Complete Shorter Poems*, l. 114.

8 CPW 3:310–1. See the discussion thereof in Chapter 2, "Reduction."

9 Balachandra Rajan, "Warfaring and Wayfaring: Milton and the Globlization of Tolerance," in Elizabeth Sauer (ed.), *Milton and the Climates of Reading: Essays by Balachandra Rajan* (Toronto, ON: University of Toronto Press, 2006), p. 143.

10 N. H. Keeble, "'Nothing nobler then a free Commonwealth': Milton's Later Vernacular Republican Tracts," in Nicholas McDowell and Nigel Smith (eds.), *The Oxford Handbook of Milton* (Oxford: Oxford University Press, 2009), pp. 305–24.

11 See Adrian Hastings, *The Construction of Nationhood: Ethnicity, Religion and Nationalism* (Cambridge: Cambridge University Press, 1997), p. 3, and Claire McEachern, *The Poetics of English Nationhood, 1590–1612* (Cambridge: Cambridge University Press, 1996/2006), p. 12.

12 Alexandra Walsham, *Charitable Hatred: Tolerance and Intolerance in England, 1500–1700* (Manchester: Manchester University Press, 2006), p. 234. See also John Coffey, *Persecution and Toleration in Protestant England, 1558–1689* (Harlow: Longmans, 2000).

13 Milton, *A Treatise of Civil Power in Ecclesiastical Causes* (16 February 1659), CPW 7:251. *The humble Advice of the Assembly of Divines… sitting at Westminster, Concerning a Confession of Faith* (London, 1647), ch. 20 (pp. 35–6), ch. 23 (pp. 41–2).

14 Blair Worden, "Toleration and the Cromwellian Protectorate," in W. J. Sheils (ed.), *Persecution and Toleration, Studies in Church History* (Oxford: Basil Blackwell, 1984), p. 209. On the rise of the Erastian state and the ideal of a national Church, see Walsham, *Charitable Hatred*, pp. 49–92.

15 *The Humble Petition and Advice* (London, 1657), p. 14; Austin Woolrych, "Milton and Cromwell, 'A Short But Scandalous Night of Interruption'?" *Achievements of the Left Hand*, p. 200.

16 Thomas Case, *Spirituall Whoredom Discovered in a Sermon Preach'd Before the Honourable House of Commons* (London, 1647), p. 34.

17 Roger Williams, *Hireling Ministry None of Christs, or A Discourse touching the Propagating the Gospel* (London, 1652), p. 18.

18 Samuel Fisher, *Christianismus Redivivus, Christndom Both un-christ'ned and new-christ'ned* (London, 1655), p. 537.

19 Stephen Marshall, *The Power of the Civil Magistrate in Matters of Religion, Vindicated* (London: G. Firmin, 1657), pp. 3, 21, 21.

20 Robert South, *Ecclesiasticall Policy the Best Policy: Or, Religion The Best Reason of State*, in *Interest Deposed, and Truth Restored ... in Two Sermons* (Oxford, 1660), p. 11.

21 Thomas Collier, *The Decision & Clearing of the great Point now in Controversie about ... the Civill Magistrate* (London, 1659), p. 16. Mark R. Bell, *Apocalypse How: Baptist Movements during the English Revolution* (Macon, GA: Mercer University Press, 2000), pp. 140–1.

22 John Coffey, "Puritanism and Liberty Revisited: The Case for Toleration in the English Revolution," *The Historical Journal* 41, 4 (1998), 973.

23 Ernest Barker, *Oliver Cromwell and the English People* (Cambridge: Cambridge University Press, 1937), pp. 167–8.

24 *Certaine briefe Observations and Antiquaeries* (1644), pp. 7–8; Henry Robinson [and Henry Burton], *An Answer to Mr. William Prynn's Twelve Questions concerning Church Government* (London, 1644), p. 7. John Coffey rules out John Goodwin as the author of *Certaine briefe Observations*, suggesting instead Robinson or John Price (Coffey, *John Goodwin and the Puritan Revolution: Religion and Intellectual Change in Seventeenth-Century England* [Woodbridge, U.K.: Boydell Press, 2006], p. 301). Burton's *A Vindication of Churches* (1644), discussed in Chapter 1 of this book, also responds to Prynne's defence of a national church.

25 Williams, *Hirelings Ministry*, p. 3; cf. *The Bloudy Tenent, of Persecution, for cause of Conscience* (London, 1644), sig. a2v, p. 183; Milton, *The Likeliest Means*, CPW 7:288.

26 Coffey, "Puritanism and Liberty Revisited," 972.

27 CPW 7:256. See Joan S. Bennett, *Reviving Liberty: Radical Christian Humanism in Milton's Great Poems* (Cambridge, MA: Harvard University Press, 1989), p. 129.

28 *Humble Petition and Advice*, p. 2.

29 "An Act of the better observation of the Lord's Day" was passed on 26 June 1657 (C. H. Firth and R. S. Rait [eds.], *Acts and Ordinances of the Interregnum 1642–1660*, 3 vols. [London: H. M. Stationery Off., 1911], vol. 2, p. 1167).

30 Marshall, *Power of the Civil Magistrate*, pp. 6–7.

31 Marshall, *Power of the Civil Magistrate*, pp. 10, 19.

32 E.g., *The Humble Petition of Many Inhabitants ... of London* (London: Printed for Thomas Brewster and Livewell Chapman, 12 May 1659) and the afore-mentioned *Humble Petition of thousands ... of the County of Kent, and City of Canterbury* (1659), both cited in *Englands Settlement* (1659), p. 24.

33 "Moses Wall to Milton," CPW 7:511.

34 John Hale, "England as Israel in Milton's Writings," *Early Modern Literary Studies* 2.2 (1996), 3.46.1, 7.

35 Christopher Hill's contention that Milton always "assumed that God had a special interest in the English people" requires qualification (Hill, *Milton and the English Revolution* [New York: Viking, 1977], p. 282).

36 William Prynne, *A Gospel Plea ... for ... the Ancient Settled Maintenance and Tithes of the Ministers of the Gospel* (London, Sept. 1653), p. 4.

37 Prynne, "To the Reader," *Gospel Plea*, sig. b1r.
38 John Canne, *A Second Voyce from the Temple to the Higher Powers* (London, 1653), p. 12. Canne's prequel appeared in June. See also ch. 3, p. 82 above.
39 Canne, *A Second Voyce*, p. 15.
40 Prynne, *A Gospel Plea*, sig. b3.
41 William Prynne, *A true and perfect Narrative of What was done* (1659), 50, qtd in J. Milton French (ed.), *The Life Records of John Milton*, 5 vols. (New York: Gordian Press, 1966), vol. 4, p. 266.
42 Woolrych, "Milton and Cromwell," p. 200.
43 *Englands Settlement, Upon the Two Solid Foundations*, pp. 2, 3. Representative of anti-tithe petitions, the broadside *The Humble Representation and desires of divers Freeholders and others … within the County of Bedford* (London, 16 June 1659) refers to "the *Good old Cause* of justice and freedom."
44 *Englands Settlement, Upon the Two Solid Foundations*, pp. 5, 6.
45 *Englands Settlement, Upon the Two Solid Foundations*, pp. 8, 9, 11.
46 Collier, *Decision & Clearing*, p. 7.
47 *Englands Settlement, Upon the Two Solid Foundations*, pp. 16, 25. H. S. defends "a just and innocent *Toleration*" in *The Common-wealth of Israel, or A Brief Account of Mr. Prynne's Anatomy of the Good Old Cause* (London, 1659), p. 2. Several days beforehand, on 13 May 1659, Prynne published *The Re-publicans and Others Spurious Good Old Cause, Briefly and Truly Anatomized*.
48 Henry Stubbe, *Essay in Defence of the Good Old Cause, or A Discourse concerning the Rise and Extent of the power of the Civil Magistrate in reference to Spiritual Affairs* (London, 1659), Preface, sig. *4v; pp. 4, 9, 10, 17, etc. Stubbe's constitutional document, "Miscellaneous Positions concerning Government," in *A Letter to an Officer of the Army* used the same refrain. The tract also distinguished between "the nation" and the "people" while reserving the latter term for those who promoted the cause of liberty (Stubbe, *A Letter to an Officer of the Army Concerning a Select Senate mentioned by them in their Proposals to the late Parliament … Whereunto are added sundry Positions about Government, and an Essay towards a secure Settlement* [London, 26 October 1659], p. 62, Article XVI). "To be part of the *people* it is not *necessary* that one *actually* have *land* in such or such a Countrey" (p. 52, Art. XVIII), though a citizen would need to have defended the Good Old Cause, as the members of the army did. Stubbe proposed that the parliament be "chosen by the *whole Nation*, and not the *people* onely" (p. 62, Art. XVI). See also James R. Jacob, *Henry Stubbe, Radical Protestantism and the Early Enlightenment* (Cambridge: Cambridge University Press, 1983), pp. 28–9.
49 Stubbe, *Essay in Defence*, p. 133.
50 See John Marshall, *John Locke: Resistance, Religion and Responsibility* (Cambridge: Cambridge University Press, 1994), pp. 6–7.
51 Stubbe, *Essay in Defence*, pp. 55–9
52 Stubbe, *Essay in Defence*, p. 32. George Bishop identified "the *Good Old Cause*" as "(chiefly) *Liberty of Conscience*" (*Mene Tekel, or The Council of Officers of the Army, Against The Declarations, &c. of the Army* [London, 1659], p. 4). See Chapter 3, "Natural Law," for the full citation.

53 *Englands Settlement, Upon the Two solid foundations*, pp. 25; 16, 17.

54 *Englands Settlement Mistaken, or, A Short Survey of a Pamphlet called England's Settlement* (London, 1660), p. 9.

55 See Woolrych, "Introduction," in CPW 7:55, 7:94. Harrington's 1659 *Aphorisms Political* probably offers a corrective to *Considerations* (Aphorisms 35, 37, 38 [CPW 7:521]). *The Censure of the Rota* (London, 1660) reviled Milton as a Church robber (pp. 8–9).

56 James Harrington, *A Discourse upon this Saying: "The Spirit of the Nation is not yet to be trusted with Liberty…,"* in J. G. A Pocock (ed.), *The Political Works of James Harrington* (Cambridge: Cambridge University Press, 1977), p. 742.

57 Andrew Browning (ed.), *English Historical Documents 1660–1714* (London: Eyre and Spottiswoode, 1953), p. 378.

58 Roger L'Estrange, *Toleration discuss'd* (London, 1663), p. 86; Thomas Tomkins, *The Inconveniences of Toleration* (London, 1667), p. 6.

59 Samuel Pepys, *The Diary of Samuel Pepys*, Robert Latham and William Matthews (eds.), 11 vols. (Berkeley: University of California Press, 1970–83), vol. 9 (1688–9), p. 60.

60 N. H. Keeble, *The Restoration: England in the 1660s* (Oxford: Blackwell, 2002), p. 124.

61 Gordon Schochet, "Samuel Parker, Religious Diversity, and the Ideology of Persecution," in Roger D. Lund (ed.), *The Margins of Orthodoxy: Heterodox Writing and the Cultural Response, 1660–1750* (Cambridge: Cambridge University Press, 1995), pp. 132–4.

62 Gary S. De Krey, "Rethinking the Restoration: Dissenting Cases for Conscience, 1667–72," *The Historical Journal* 38 (1995), 57–60.

63 The scholarship on *Of True Religion* has concentrated more on the language and stance of Milton's anti-popery than on his positions on visions of disestablishment, toleration, and nationhood. See, for example, Reuben Márquez, Jr. Sánchez, "'The Worst of Superstitions': Milton's *Of True Religion* and the Issue of Religious Tolerance," *Prose Studies* 9 (1986), 21–38, to which Martin Dzelzainis partly responds in "Milton's *Of True Religion* and the Earl of Castlemaine," *The Seventeenth Century* 7, 1 (1992), 53–69; Raymond D. Tumbleson, "*Of True Religion* and False Politics: Milton and the Uses of Anti-Catholicism," *Prose Studies* 15 (1992), 253–70, rpt with changes in *Catholicism in the English Protestant Imagination: Nationalism, Religion, and Literature, 1660–1745* (Cambridge: Cambridge University Press, 1998); John Shawcross, "'Connivers and the Worst of Superstitions': Milton on Popery and Toleration," *Literature & History* 7, 2 (Autumn 1998), 51–69; Hong Won Suh, "Belial, Popery, and True Religion: Milton's *Of True Religion* and Antipapist Sentiment," in Kristin A. Pruitt and Charles W. Durham (eds.), *Living Texts: Interpreting Milton* (Selinsgrove, PA: Susquehanna University Press, 2000), pp. 283–99; Katsuhiro Engetsu, "The Publication of the King's Privacy: *Paradise Regained* and *Of True Religion* in Restoration England," in Graham Parry and Joad Raymond (eds.), *Milton and the Terms of Liberty* (Cambridge: D. S. Brewer, 2002), 163–74. Cf. my "Milton's *Of True Religion*, Protestant Nationhood, and the Negotiation of Liberty," *Milton Quarterly* 40, 1 (2006), 1–19.

64 *His Majesties Declaration to All His Loving Subjects, March 15th 1671/2* (London, 1671/2), pp. 6, 4. Robert McWard, *The English Ballance, Weighing the Reasons of Englands present Conjunction with France, against the Dutch. With some Observes upon his Majesties Declaration, of Liberty to Tender Consciences* (n.p., 1672), p. 42.

65 "An Act for preventing Dangers which may happen from Popish Recusants" (1673), in J. P. Kenyon (ed.), *The Stuart Constitution: Documents and Commentary*, 2nd edn. (Cambridge: Cambridge University Press, 1986), p. 385.

66 "Epistle," *The Christian Doctrine*, CPW 6:121, 123.

67 Janel Mueller, "Milton on Heresy," in Stephen B. Dobranski and John P. Rumrich (eds.), *Milton and Heresy* (Cambridge: Cambridge University Press, 1998), p. 36.

68 *His Majesties Declaration* (1672), p. 7.

69 On Milton's conciliatory gestures, see my "Milton's *Of True Religion*, Protestant Nationhood," 9–12.

70 Christopher Hill, "The Protestant Nation," *The Collected Essays of Christopher Hill*, Volume II: *Religion and Politics in Seventeenth Century England* (Brighton: Harvester Press, 1986), p. 28.

5 Geography: Spatial Poetics

1 Richard Hakluyt, "A preface to the Reader as touching the principall Voyages and discourses in this first part," *The Principal Navigations, Voyages, Traffiques and Discoveries of the English Nation, made by Sea or overland … within the compass of these 1600 yeres* (London, 1599), n.p.

2 Leo Africanus, title page, *A Geographical Historie of Africa, Written in Arabicke and Italian by John Leo a More...* (1526), John Pory (trans.) (London, 1600).

3 Allan H. Gilbert, *A Geographical Dictionary of Milton* (New Haven, CT: 1919; New York: Russell & Russell, 1968), p. viii.

4 Milton, "The Authour's Preface," in George B. Parks (ed.), *A Brief History of Moscovia: and Of other less-known Countries lying eastward of Russia as far as Cathay. Gathered from the Writings of several Eye-witnesses* (London, 1682), CPW 8:474.

5 Christopher GoGwilt, *The Fiction of Geopolitics* (Stanford, CA: Stanford University Press, 2000), p. 2. On geography as a political discourse, see J. B. Harley, "Maps, Knowledge, and Power," in Denis Cosgrove and Stephen Daniels (eds.), *The Iconography of Landscape: Essays on the Symbolic Representation, Design and Use of Past Environments* (Cambridge: Cambridge University Press, 1988), pp. 277–312; Ann Blair, *The Theater of Nature: Jean Bodin and Renaissance Science* (Princeton, NJ: Princeton University Press, 1997), pp. 174–5.

6 Michel Foucault, "Questions on Geography," in Colin Gordon (ed.), *Power / Knowledge: Selected Interviews and Other Writings, 1972–1977* (New York: Pantheon Books, 1980), p. 68.

7 Lesley B. Cormack, *Charting an Empire: Geography at the English Universities, 1580–1620* (Chicago: University of Chicago Press, 1997), p. 11.

8 J. B. Harley and David Woodward (eds.), *Cartography in Prehistoric, Ancient, and Medieval Europe and the Mediterranean*, vol. 1 of *The History of Cartography* (Chicago: University of Chicago Press, 1987), p. 9; John L. Allen, "Lands of Myth, Waters of Wonder: The Place of the Imagination in the History of Geographical Exploration," in David Lowenthal and Martyn J. Bowden (eds.), *Geographies of the Mind: Essays in Historical Geosophy in Honor of John Kirtland Wright* (New York: Oxford University Press, 1976), pp. 41–62.

9 Foucault, "Questions on Geography, p. 73. On the contribution of maps to the remaking of national subjects, see Richard Helgerson, *Forms of Nationhood: The Elizabethan Writing of England* (Chicago: University of Chicago Press, 1992), chs. 3, 4.

10 Michel de Certeau, *The Practice of Everyday Life*, Stephen Rendell (trans.) (Berkeley: University of California Press, 1984), pp. 117–8.

11 For studies on Milton and geography, see Allan H. Gilbert, *A Geographical Dictionary of Milton*; George Wesley, *Milton's Literary Milieu* (Chapel Hill: University of North Carolina Press, 1939/New York: Russell & Russell, 1964); and Robert R. Cawley, who underscores the significance of the vision in impressing Adam with the consequences of disobedience (*Milton and the Literature of Travel* [Princeton, NJ: Princeton University Press, 1951], pp. 9–10, 22).

12 Foucault, "Questions on Geography," pp. 70–1.

13 John Dee, *The Mathematicall Preface* (1570), in Captain Thomas Rudd, *Euclides Elements of Geometry: The first VI Books* (London, 1651), sig. E4v. See also the early modern definition of geography in Nathanael Carpenter, *Geography Delineated Forth in Two Bookes. Containing the Sphaericall and Topicall Parts Thereof* (Oxford, 1625), p. 1.

14 Dee, *Mathematicall Preface*, sig. G2v.

15 Edward Phillips, "Cosmography," in *The New World of Words: or, A Universal English Dictionary*, 7th ed. (London, 1720), sig. Y1v;, originally published in folio in 1658.

16 John M. Headley, "Geography and Empire in the Late Renaissance: Botero's Assignment, Western Universalism, and the Civilizing Process," *Renaissance Quarterly* 53, 4 (Winter, 2000), 1119–55.

17 William B. Sherman, *John Dee: The Politics of Reading and Writing in the English Renaissance* (Amherst: University of Massachusetts Press, 1995), pp. 128–200; Lesley B. Cormack, "Britannia rules the waves?: Images of Empire in Elizabethan England," in Andrew Gordon and Bernhard Klein (eds.), *Literature, Mapping, and the Politics of Space in Early Modern Britain* (Cambridge: Cambridge University Press, 2001), pp. 45–68.

18 Abraham Ortelius, "*Theatrum Orbis Terrarum: Theatre of the Whole World: Set Forth by ... Abraham Ortelius* (London, 1606), n.p. Translated by W. B. (i.e., William Bedwell?), whose initials appear on the third leaf recto, *Theatrum* was Milton's favourite atlas, according to Whiting (*Milton's Literary Milieu*, pp. 97, 122).

19 Ann Blair, *The Theater of Nature: Jean Bodin and Renaissance Science* (Princeton, NJ: Princeton University Press, 1997), pp. 153–79. Cosmography represented the world theatre at large (e.g., Gerardus Mercator's *Atlas, sive Cosmographicae Meditationes de fabrica mundi et fabricati figura*).

20 Ortelius, "Abraham Ortelius ... to the courteous Reader" (1570), *Theatrum Orbis Terrarum*, n.p.

21 On the *Lusiads* as a poem about nationhood, see Richard Helgerson, *Forms of Nationhood*, pp. 155–76, 189–90. For a brilliant postcolonial critique, see Balachandra Rajan, "Milton and Camões: Reinventing the Old Man," "Post-Imperial Camões": Special Issue of *Portuguese Literary and Cultural Studies* 9 (Fall 2002), 177–87, rpt. in Elizabeth Sauer (ed.), *Milton and the Climates of Reading: Essays by Balachandra Rajan* (Toronto, ON: University of Toronto Press, 2006), pp. 123–34.

22 R. A. Skelton, "Bibliographical Note," *The Theatre of the Whole World*, R. A. Skelton, (ed.) (Amsterdam: Theatrum Orbis Terrarum, 1968), xvii.

23 Richard Hakluyt, "A preface," *The Principal Navigations, Voyages, Traffiques and Discoveries of the English Nation, made by Sea or overland*, n.p.

24 Cormack, "Britannia rules the waves?" pp. 52–3.

25 Leo Africanus, "Dedication "To ... Sir Robert Cecil," *A Geographical Historie of Africa*, n.p.

26 See Elizabeth Sauer, "Toleration and Translation: The Case of Las Casas, Phillips, and Milton," *Philological Quarterly* 86, 1 & 2 (2006), 271–91.

27 Samuel Purchas, "Epistle Dedicatorie," *Hakluytus Posthumus or Purchas his Pilgrimes; Contayning a History of the World, in Sea Voyages and Lande Travells, by Englishmen and Others*, 4 vols. (London: William Stansby, 1625), vol. 1, n.p.

28 Loren E. Pennington, "*Hakluytus Posthumus*: Samuel Purchas and the Promotion of English Overseas Expansion," *The Emporia State Research Studies* 14, 3 (1966), 11.

29 Cormack, *Charting an Empire*, p. 140.

30 See Christopher Ivic, "Mapping British Identities: Speed's *Theatre of the Empire of Great Britaine*," in David J. Baker and Willy Maley (eds.), *British Identities and English Renaissance Literature* (Cambridge: Cambridge University Press, 2002), pp. 135, 153 n3. On Milton's engagement with Speed, see William Riley Parker, *Milton: A Biography*, 2 vols. (Oxford: Clarendon Press, 1968), vol. 2, p. 802.

31 Cormack, *Charting an Empire*, pp. 18–9.

32 CPW 5.1:239–40. See also CPW 5.1:337, 342.

33 *Gerardi Mercatoris Atlas. sive Cosmographicae meditationes de fabrica Mundi et fabricati figura ...* (Amsterdam: C. Nicolaius and J. Hondius, 1595); Henry Hexham, *Atlas: or, A Geographicke description ...* (Amsterdam: Henricus Hondius, 1607).

34 *Atlas Novus, sive theatrum orbis terrarium* (Amsterdam: Joannes Janssonius, ca. 1656).

35 On Blaeu, see Cornelius Koeman, *Joan Blaeu and His Grand Atlas* (Amsterdam: Theatrum Orbis Terrarum, 1970).

36 Milton's Private Correspondence [Letter 30], "To … Peter Heimbach" (8 November 1656), in CPW 7:494–5. Milton likely inquired about a six-volume set of *Novus Atlas*. See also Johannes Keuning, "The *Novus Atlas* of Johannes Janssonius," *Imago Mundi: A Review of Early Cartography* 8 (1951/1967), 71–98. Amy Lee Turner argues that Milton consulted a 1650 single volume called *Atlas Maritimus* (Turner, "Milton and Jansson's Sea Atlas," *Milton Quarterly* [1970], 36–9). Turner states that Milton used Jansson's maps, but the Jansson/Jansonius source in *Moscovia* is taken from Purchas (CPW 8:538n46).

37 Johannes Keuning, "The History of an Atlas: Mercator-Hondius," *Imago Mundi: A Review of Early Cartography* 4 (1947), 38.

38 Headley, "Geography and Empire in the Late Renaissance," 1125.

39 Peter Heylyn, *Cosmographie: In Four Bookes. Containing the Chorographie and Historie of the whole World* (London, 1652), 4.1.48.

40 See Hartlib's diary, *Ephemerides,* in the Sheffield University Library; printed in G. H. Turnbull, *Hartlib, Dury and Comenius* (London: Hodder and Stoughton, 1947), pp. 40–1. See Robert R. Cawley, *Milton's Literary Craftsmanship* (Princeton, NJ: Princeton University Press, 1941) and "Geography and Milton," in William B. Hunter (gen. ed.), *A Milton Encyclopedia*, 9 vols. (Lewisburg, PA: Bucknell University Press, 1978–83), vol. 3, pp. 122–5. Milton, *A Brief History of Moscovia: and Of other less-known Countries*, in CPW, vol. 8, pp. 471–538.

41 Lewes Roberts, *The Treasure of Traffike or a Discourse of Forraigne Trade. Wherein is shewed the benefit and commoditie arising to a Common-Wealth or Kingdome, by the skilfull Merchant* (London, 1641), pp. 92–3. A similar pride in English nationalism is exhibited in *The History of Britain*, written about the same time as *A Brief History*.

42 On "para-colonial," see John Michael Archer, *Old Worlds: Egypt, Southwest Asia, India, and Russia in Early Modern English Writing* (Stanford, CA: Stanford University Press, 2001), pp. 1–22, and the references to *Paradise Lost* as a para-colonial epic (p. 99).

43 Milton, "Authour's Preface," *Brief History of Moscovia*, CPW 8:475. The material on Russia is taken from the first volume of Richard Hakluyt's *Principal Navigations* (3 vols., 1598–1600, see 1:466–70 on Russia) and the third volume of Samuel Purchas's *Hakluytus Posthumus, or Purchas His Pilgrimes* (London, 1625), which Milton owned and consulted. See Milton's affixed list of sources, CPW 8:537–8. See also Robert Markley, "'The destin'd Walls / Of *Cambalu*': Milton, China, and the Ambiguities of the East," in *Milton and the Imperial Vision*, pp. 191–213 (rpt. Markley, *The Far East and the English Imagination, 1600–1730* [Cambridge: Cambridge University Press, 2006], pp. 70–103).

44 Cawley, *Milton and the Literature of Travel*, p. 44.

45 Milton, "Authour's Preface," *Brief History of Moscovia*, CPW 8:475; PL 11:387–8.

46 Leo Africanus, title page, *A Geographical Historie of Africa*.

47 Fowler (ed.), Milton, *Paradise Lost*, 535n1117. Cf. Karen Edwards, who states that the tree-shelter and the cincture "do not point to the difference between natives and Europeans but to their common ancestry" (*Milton and the Natural World: Science and Poetry in "Paradise Lost"* [Cambridge: Cambridge University Press, 1999], p. 153). See also Mary Nyquist, "Contemporary Ancestors of

de Bry, Hobbes, and Milton," in Paul Stevens and Patricia Simmons (eds.), "Milton in America," *The University of Toronto Quarterly* 77, 3 (2008), 837–75.

48 On this passage, see also Balachandra Rajan, "Banyan Trees and Fig Leaves: Some Thoughts on Milton's India," *Milton and the Climates of Reading*, pp. 81–4.

49 Deut. 34. Michael Lieb refers to "Milton's fondness for high-place revelations" and cites Greenhill's *An Exposition of the Prophet Ezekiel* (1650) in *Poetics of the Holy: A Reading of "Paradise Lost"* (Chapel Hill: University of North Carolina Press, 1981), pp. 147, 167.

50 Thomas Fuller, *A Pisgah-sight of Palestine and The Confines Thereof, with the History of the Old and New Testament Acted Thereon* (London, 1650), bk 2.1.21, p. 64; "Ezekiel his Visionary Land of Canaan," bk 5.1.1, p. 189.

51 John Lightfoot, *Horae Hebricae et Talmudicae* (Cambridge, 1658), qtd. in Jeffrey S. Shoulson, *Milton and the Rabbis: Hebraism, Hellenism, and Christianity* (New York: Columbia University Press, 2001), p. 19.

52 Jordanes, *The Gothic History of Jordanes: In English Version*, Charles Christopher Mierow (intro., ed.) (1915; Cambridge: Speculum Historiale; New York: Barnes & Noble, Inc., 1966), 7.55, p. 65. Cf. Strabo, *The Geography of Strabo: With an English Translation by Horace Leonard Jones*, 8 vols. (Cambridge, MA: Harvard University Press, 1961), vol. 5, 11.12.4, p. 299.

53 Cicero, *Cicero in Twenty-eight Volumes*, in Clinton Walker Keyes (trans.), *De Re Publica, De Legibus*, 16 vols. (Loeb Classical Library; Cambridge, MA: Harvard University Press, 1988), vol. 16, 6.16, pp. 269, 268. The work made its way into the medieval and early modern eras in the form of Macrobius's *Commentarii in Somnium Scipionis*. The English version appeared as *Foure Severall Treatises of M. Tullius Cicero conteyninge his most learned and eloquente discourses of frendshippe: oldage: paradoxes: and Scipio his dreame. All turned out of Latine into English, by Thomas Newton* (London, 1577).

54 Cicero, *Republic* 6.16, pp. 269, 268. For the reference to Cicero's Scipio, I am indebted to Denis Cosgrove, "Globalism and Tolerance in Early Modern Geography," *Annals of the Association of American Geographers*, 93, 4 (2003), 852–70. See also Frank Lestringant, *Mapping the Renaissance World: The Geographical Imagination in the Age of Discovery*, David Fausett (trans.), Stephen Greenblatt (Foreword) (Berkeley: University of California Press, 1994), p. 20.

55 Cicero, *Republic*, 6.24, p. 278.

56 On pietas, see Colin Burrow's study of the subject in *Epic Romance: Homer to Milton* (Oxford: Clarendon Press, 1993), pp. 38–51.

57 Joseph Addison, *Criticisms on Milton*, Henry Morley (Intro.) (London: Cassell & Co., 1905 edn, p. 176). In annotating the scene in their edition of *Paradise Lost*, William Kerrigan, John Rumrich, and Stephen M. Fallon cite Addison's remarks on "the vision of descendants given to Aeneas in the last book of the *Aeneid*" (William Kerrigan, John Rumrich, Stephen M. Fallon (eds.), *The Complete Poetry and Essential Prose of John Milton* [New York: The Modern Library, 2007], p. 595n356–8). In fact, Addison mentions that vision is

presented to "Virgil's hero, in the last of these poems," namely, *The Aeneid* (and not in the last book of *The Aeneid*) (Addison, *Criticisms on Milton*, p. 176).

58 Cawley, *Milton and the Literature of Travel*, pp. 9–10, 22.

59 Bruce McLeod, *The Geography of Empire in English Literature, 1580–1745* (Cambridge: Cambridge University Press, 1999), pp. 139–40.

60 Particularly learned examinations of the catalogues' place names in the epics include Robert Markley's "'The destin'd Walls / Of *Cambalu*,'" in *Milton and the Imperial Vision*, pp. 191–213, and John Michael Archer's "Milton and the Fall of Asia," in *Old Worlds: Egypt, Southwest Asia, India*, pp. 63–99. These analyses focus on the geographical significance of Middle and Far Eastern place names.

61 McLeod does not take *Paradise Regained* into his purview in *The Geography of Empire*, p. 140. See Jason P. Rosenblatt's correction of Robert R. Cawley's reading of the "growing conscience" that Milton acquired as a result of his post as Secretary for Foreign Tongues and his education in foreign policy (Rosenblatt, "Eden, Israel, England: Milton's Spiritual Geography," in John McVeagh (ed.), *All Before Them: Attitudes to Abroad in English Literature 1660–1780* [London: Ashfield, 1990], p. 50).

62 Peter Toohey, "Roman Epic," in Catherine Bates (ed.), *The Cambridge Companion to the Epic* (Cambridge: Cambridge University Press, 2010), pp. 37–8.

63 Vergil, *The Aeneid*, Sarah Ruden (trans.) (New Haven, CT: Yale University Press, 2008), 3.158–67.

64 In Milton's day, China and Cathay (of which Cambula was the capital) were identical (Markley, *The Far East and the English Imagination*, p. 70).

65 Most critical and historical studies of empire assign imperialism to the West and to the Atlantic world, for example, David Armitage, *The Ideological Origins of the British Empire* (Cambridge: Cambridge University Press, 2000); Michael Hardt and Antonio Negri, *Empire* (Cambridge, MA: Harvard University Press, 2000); Balachandra Rajan and Elizabeth Sauer (eds.), *Milton and the Imperial Vision* (Pittsburgh: Duquesne University Press, 1999); Anthony Pagden, *Lords of all the World: Ideologies of Empire in Spain, Britain and France c.1500–c.1800* (New Haven, CT: Yale University Press, 1998); J. Martin Evans, *Milton's Imperial Epic: "Paradise Lost" and the Discourse of Colonization* (Ithaca, NY: Cornell University Press, 1996); David Quint, *Epic and Empire: Politics and Generic Form from Virgil to Milton* (Princeton, NJ: Princeton University Press, 1993); Michael W. Doyle, *Empires* (Ithaca, NY: Cornell University Press, 1986). The catalogue of empires in book 11 of Milton's *Paradise Lost* puts Eastern empires on display.

66 George Sandys, *A Relation of a Journey begun An. Dom. 1610. Foure Bookes. Containing a Description of the Turkish Empire, of Egypt, etc.*, 2nd ed. (London, 1615).

67 Heylyn, "Epistle to the Reader," *Cosmographie*, sig. A4r.

68 Following on Milton editor A. W. Verity (see *Paradise Lost* [Cambridge: Cambridge University Press, 1910], 2:383, 440), Cawley's thesis is based on the

authoritative nature of Heylyn for Milton. George B. Parks, editor of CPW vol. 8, states that Milton consulted Heylyn's *Cosmographie*, which he must have had in his possession while dictating *Paradise Lost* (CPW 8:470), but Parks relies on Cawley for his information (CPW 8:457). Archer insists that *Cosmographie* influenced Milton greatly, especially in the account of Nimrod in *Paradise Lost*, book 12 (*Old Worlds: Egypt, Southwest Asia, India*, pp. 77–85). Cf. Markley, *The Far East and the English Imagination*, p. 96.

69 Letter 20, *The Works of John Milton*, 12:83. Cawley presumes that the blind Milton would have desired a less expensive atlas, like that of Heylyn's *Cosmographie*, which would be less likely to grieve him "'over [his] deprivation,'" that is, his blindness (*Milton and the Literature of Travel*, p. 21).

70 "Abraham Ortelius … to the courteous Reader" (1570), *Theatrum Orbis Terrarum*, n.p. STC 18855; Folger Library, shelf no. ac203117.

71 Foucault, "Questions on Geography," p. 75.

72 The analysis in this and the two previous sentences is indebted to Alastair Fowler's erudite reading of PL 11.388–95; 11.405; n387–8, 396–407.

73 Heylyn, *Cosmographie*, 4.2.170–1; Hakluyt, *Principal Navigations*, 3:636.

74 Geryon is a monster of fraud in Dante's *Inferno* 17.99 and a personification of Spanish oppression in Spenser's *Faerie Queene* 5.10.8.

75 Sandys, "To the Prince," *A Relation of a Journey*, n.p.

76 Heylyn, "To the Reader," *Cosmographie*, sig. [A6r]. Purchas, Raleigh, Peter Heylyn, Ortelius, and others foreground spatial strategies in Milton's own geopolitical readings. The *Cosmographie* especially informs the long geographic passage in PL 11.383–411, argues Cawley ("Geography and Milton," in *A Milton Encyclopedia*, vol. 3, p. 124; *Milton and the Literature of Travel*, pp. 12–23). Cf. Whiting, *Milton's Literary Milieu*, p. 120.

77 Claire McEachern, *The Poetics of English Nationhood, 1590–1612* (Cambridge: Cambridge University Press, 1996/2006), p. 31.

78 Guillaume de Salluste Du Bartas, *Du Bartas His Devine Weekes and Workes Translated: And Dedicated to the Kings most excellent Majestie by Josuah Sylvester* (London, 1611), pp. 315–34.

79 Barbara Lewalski, *Milton's Brief Epic: The Genre, Meaning, and Art of "Paradise Regained"* (Providence, RI: Brown University Press, 1966), p. 334.

80 PR 3.236–321; see Whiting, *Milton's Literary Milieu*, pp. 123–4.

81 Stephen Greenblatt, *Marvelous Possessions: The Wonder of the New World* (Chicago: University of Chicago Press, 1991), pp. 20–1.

82 J. B. Harley and David Woodward, (eds.), *Cartography in Prehistoric, Ancient, and Medieval Europe and the Mediterranean*, p. 7. Milton used the 1605 atlas of Ptolemy's *Geographia*, edited by Jodocus Hondius, for *Paradise Regained* 3.269–321 and 4.25–80.

83 By the Restoration era, the English, Milton lamented, sought to build "another *Rome* in the west" (CPW 7:423). See Blair Worden, "Milton's Republicanism and the Tyranny of Heaven," in Gisela Bock, Quentin Skinner, and Maurizio Viroli (eds.), *Machiavelli and Republicanism* (Cambridge: Cambridge University Press, 1990), pp. 225–46; and Andrew Barnaby, "'Another Rome in

the West?': Milton and the Imperial Republic, 1654–1670," *Milton Studies* 30 (1993), 67–84.

84 Walter MacKellar (ed.), *Paradise Regained*, vol. 4, *A Variorum Commentary on the Poems of John Milton* (London: Routledge and K. Paul, 1975), p. 188n74–5. MacKellar also points out that the Britons (of France), the Scythians, and Sarmatians were not absorbed into the Roman Empire at the time (pp. 187n70–9, 189n78).

85 Cf. Benedict Anderson, *Imagined Communities: Reflections on the Origin and Spread of Nationalism* (London: Verso, 1991), p. 93.

86 Rajan, "The Imperial Temptation," in *Milton and the Imperial Vision*, p. 299.

87 Vergil, *The Aeneid*, 1.276–9.

88 On Milton's use of the anti-imperial tradition, see Quint, *Epic and Empire*, p. 326.

89 See, for example, Sir Edward Dyer, "My Mind to Me a Kingdom Is," in William Byrd, *Psalmes, sonets, & and songs of sadnes and pietie, made into musicke of five parts* (London, 1588).

90 R. J. Mayhew, *Enlightenment Geography: The Political Languages of British Geography, 1650–1850* (New York: St. Martin's Press, 2000).

91 John A. Marino, "On the Shores of Bohemia: Recovering Geography," in John A. Marino (ed.), *Early Modern History and the Social Sciences: Testing the Limits of Braudel's Mediterranean, Sixteenth Century Essays and Studies*, vol. 61 (Kirksville, MO: Truman State University Press, 2002), p. 31.

92 See Lewalski, *Milton's Brief Epic*, pp. 290–3.

93 Milton, "Ad Patrem," in *Milton, Complete Shorter Poems*, l. 40, pp. 156, 159. See John Carey, "Milton's 'Ad Patrem,' 35–37," *The Review of English Studies* 15, 58 (1964), 180–4.

6 Exogamy: "Entercourse" with Philistines

1 A. D. Smith, *Chosen Peoples: Sacred Sources of National Identity* (Oxford: Oxford University Press, 2003, rpt 2008), p. 63.

2 Milton, "Ad Patrem," in *Milton, Complete Shorter Poems*, l. 85.

3 George Sandys, *Travels*, 7th ed. (London, 1673), p. 116; qtd in Allan H. Gilbert, *A Geographical Dictionary of Milton* (1919) (New York: Russell & Russell, 1968), p. 225.

4 Eid A. Dahiyat, "The Portrait of the Philistines in John Milton's *Samson Agonistes*," *Studia Anglica Posnaniensia* 14 (1982), 298. The poem's power, contends Dahiyat, is in its "being the least Christian of all Milton's major works" (p. 294).

5 See Dayton Haskin's prescient *Milton's Burden of Interpretation* (Philadelphia: University of Pennsylvania Press, 1994), esp. pp. 147–82. Dennis Kezar reviews the debate in Milton studies between regenerationist and sceptical/revisionist readers of *Samson Agonistes* in "Samson's Death by Theater and Milton's Art of Dying," *English Literary History* 66 (Summer 1999), 328–9 n.11, rpt. in *Guilty Creatures: Renaissance Poetry and the Ethics of Authorship* (Oxford: Oxford University Press, 2001), pp. 139–71. See also Barbara Kiefer Lewalski,

"Milton's Samson and the 'New Acquist of True [Political] Experience," *Milton Studies* 24 (1988), 233–34, and Stanley Fish, "Spectacle and Evidence in *Samson Agonistes*," *Critical Inquiry* 15, 3 (1989), 557 n.2.

6 Annabel Patterson, "Milton, Marriage and Divorce," in Thomas N. Corns (ed.), *A Companion to Milton* (Oxford: Blackwell, 2001), p. 279. See John G. Halkett's similar observation in "Marriage and Divorce," in William B. Hunter (gen. ed.), *A Milton Encyclopedia*, 9 vols. (Lewisburg, PA: Bucknell University Press, 1978–83), vol. 5, p. 75.

7 On Selden, see CPW 2:232; on Grotius, CPW 2:715, 4:615.

8 Samuel Pufendorf, *De Jure Naturae et Gentium. Libri Octo* (London, 1672), 6.1.24.

9 Milton, *The Reason of Church-Government*, CPW 1:823, 858; John T. Shawcross, *John Milton: The Self and the World* (Lexington: University of Kentucky Press, 1993), p. 256.

10 Harold Bloom, *The Visionary Company: A Reading of English Romantic Poetry* (1961), rev. ed. (Ithaca, NY: Cornell University Press, 1971), xix.

11 See also Sharon Achinstein, "'A Law in this Matter to Himself': Contextualizing Milton's Divorce Tracts," in Nicholas McDowell and Nigel Smith (eds.), *The Oxford Handbook of Milton* (Oxford: Oxford University Press, 2009), p. 180.

12 *Tetrachordon*, Arnold Williams (ed.), in Ernest Sirluck (ed.), vol. 2, *Complete Prose Works of John Milton*, p. 632; Lowell W. Coolidge (ed.), *The Doctrine and Discipline of Divorce*, CPW 2:347.

13 The 1644 edition included Milton's initials on the title page.

14 CPW 2:717. John Halkett, *Milton and the Idea of Matrimony: A Study in the Divorce Tracts and "Paradise Lost"* (New Haven, CT: Yale University Press, 1970), p. 12.

15 Canons XCIX–CIII; CV–CVIII, *Constitutions and Canons Ecclesiasticall* (London, 1604), Q3–Rv; Rv–R2v. On canon law, see R. H. Helmholz's *The Oxford History of the Laws of England* (New York: Oxford University Press, 2004) and Helmholz's *Roman Canon Law in Reformation England* (Cambridge: Cambridge University Press, 2004).

16 Jason P. Rosenblatt, *Torah and Law in "Paradise Lost"* (Princeton, NJ: Princeton University Press, 1994), p. 103. Although the frequency of the occurrence of "charity" in the divorce tracts has been recognized, the identification of charity with "divine universal law" has not, according to John Halkett, *Milton and the Idea of Matrimony*, p. 53.

17 Herbert Palmer, *Scripture and Reason Pleaded for Defensive Armes* (London, 1643), pp. 35–6.

18 Jason P. Rosenblatt, "John Selden's *De Jure Naturali … Juxta Disciplinam Ebraeorum* and Religious Toleration," in Allison P. Coudert and Jeffrey S. Shoulson (eds.), *Hebraica Veritas: Christian Hebraists and the Study of Judaism in Early Modern Europe* (Philadelphia: University of Pennsylvania Press, 2004), p. 105; CPW 2:350.

19 CPW 2:239. See also 2:329 and 2:335.

20 Hugo Grotius, *De Jure Belli ac Pacis. Libri Tres* (1625), Francis W. Kelsey (trans.) (New York: Oceana Publications, 1964), vol. 2, 5.IX.3 (pp. 236–7). Although citations of Grotius in the divorce tracts are all from his annotations

on the New Testament (CPW 2:329, 2:335, 2:344; 2:434; 2:715), connections between Grotian natural law and the divorce tracts as well as *Samson Agonistes* can be implied.

21 Grotius, *De Jure Belli*, vol. 1, 1.XVII.4, p. 49; see also CPW 2:264.

22 William Perkins, *A Godly and Learned Exposition of Christs Sermon in the Mount*, in *The Works of that Famous and Worthy minister of Christ in the Universitie of Cambridge, M. William Perkins. The third and last Volume* (London, 1631), p. 69. Perkins's sermon is on Matthew 5–7.

23 William Perkins, *Christian Oeconomie Or, A Short Survey of the Right Manner of Erecting and Ordering a Familie, According to Scriptures* (London, 1609), p. 103.

24 Gordon Campbell and Thomas N. Corns, *John Milton: Life, Work, and Thought* (Oxford: Oxford University Press, 2008), p. 164.

25 Thomas Edwards, *The First and Second Part of Gangraena: or A Catalogue and Discovery of Many of the Errours, Heresies, Blasphemies, and Pernicious Practices of the Sectaries of This Time*, 3rd ed. (London, 1646), p. 9.

26 William Prynne, *Twelve Considerable Serious Questions Touching Church Government* (London, 1644), title page; p. 7.

27 Herbert Palmer, *The Glasse of Gods Providence Towards His Faithfull Ones. Held forth in a Sermon ... against the ungodly Toleration pleaded for under pretence of Liberty of Conscience* (London, 1644), title page; 57. See also Robert Baillie's remark on Milton as a licentious divorcer in *Dissuasive from the Errours of the Time: Wherein the Tenets of the Principal Sects ... Are examined by the Touch-Stone of the Holy Scriptures* (London, 1645), p. 116.

28 "August 1653: An Act touching Marriages and the Registring thereof; and also touching Births and Burials," in C. H. Firth, R. S. Rait (eds.), *Acts and Ordinances of the Interregnum, 1642–1660*, 3 vols. (London: H. M. Stationery Off., 1911), vol. 2, pp. 715–18. CPW 7:299.

29 This synopsis of the changes in marriage legislation is partly indebted to Shigeo Suzuki's overview thereof ("Marriage and Divorce," in Stephen B. Dobranksi [ed.], *Milton in Context* [Cambridge: Cambridge University Press, 2010], pp. 384–5).

30 Alexander Ross, *Pansebeia: or, A View of all Religions in the World ... Together with a Discovery of all known Heresies* (London, 1653), pp. 400, 399.

31 Daniel Harcourt, *The Levites Lamentation* (1643), p. 5; rpt as *The Clergies Lamentation* (London, 1644). On the "Irish Philistims," see also Harcourt, *A New Remonstrance from Ireland, Containing an Exact Declaration of the Cruelties ... by the Bloudthirsty, Popish Rebells*" (London, 1643), p. 4.

32 Harcourt, *The Levites Lamentation*, p. 22, misnumbered p. 23.

33 "The humble petition of the Officers within the precincts of *Dublin, Caterlough, Wexford*, and *Kilkenny*," in [John Hall (ed.)], *Mercurius Politicus*, no. 251 (29 March–5 April 1655), 5237.

34 John Carey (ed.), *Samson Agonistes* in *Milton, Complete Shorter Poems*, p. 369 n312, n319.

35 See CPW 2:264. The tribes are the Hittites, Girgashites, Amorites, Canaanites, Perizzites, Hivites, and Jebusites.

36 Allan H. Gilbert, *A Geographical Dictionary of Milton* (1919; New York: Russell & Russell, 1968), p. 73.

37 Thomas Taylor, *The Progresse of Saints to Full Holinesse* (London, 1630), pp. 161–2.

38 Rachel Trubowitz, *Nation and Nurture in Seventeenth-Century English Literature* (Oxford: Oxford University Press, 2012), p. 193.

39 SA 312, 318–21, 322–4. Merritt Y. Hughes reads this passage as a comment on Dalila rather than the woman of Timna, in which case "unchaste" would be figurative or refer to her eventual choice of national loyalty over marriage fidelity (*Samson Agonistes*, in Merritt Y. Hughes [ed.], *John Milton: Complete Poems and Major Prose* [New York: Macmillan, 1957], p. 559 n321).

40 Josephus, *Jewish Antiquities*, H. St. J. Thackeray and Ralph Marcus (trans.), 9 vols. (Cambridge, MA: Harvard University Press, 1958), vol. 5, V.8.11, p. 139; Philo, *The Biblical Antiquities of Philo*, M. R. James (trans.) (London: Society for Promoting Christian Knowledge, 1917), XLIII.5.

41 Christopher Hill, *Milton and the English Revolution* (New York: Viking, 1977), pp. 429–30.

42 Thomas Fuller, "Ezekiel his Visionary Land of Canaan," *A Pisgah-sight of Palestine and The Confines Thereof, with the History of the Old and New Testament Acted Thereon* (London, 1650), bk 5.5.7, p. 198.

43 Tommaso de Vio Gaetani Cajetan, *Opera omnia quotquot in sacrae Scripturae expositionem reperiuntur*, 5 vols. (Lyons, 1639), vol. 2, p. 62.

44 F. Michael Krouse, *Milton's Samson and the Christian Tradition* (Princeton, NJ: Princeton University Press, 1949; rpt Archon Books, 1963), p. 76.

45 Joannis Seldeni, *De Jure Naturali & Gentium, Juxta Disciplinam Ebraeorum* (London, 1640), pp. 624, 625. See Jason P. Rosenblatt, *Renaissance England's Chief Rabbi: John Selden* (Oxford: Oxford University Press, 2006), p. 103. David Kimchi had also maintained that Samson's wives were proselytes (George F. Moore, *A Critical and Exegetical Commentary on Judges* [1895] [New York: Charles Scribner's Sons, 1918], p. 318).

46 See, for example, the cast of characters and SA 227, 724, 725, 885, 1193.

47 CPW 8:431. Grotius, *De Jure Belli ac Pacis. Libri Tres*, vol. 1, 1.XVI.1–8, pp. 45–8. See also Nicholas von Maltzahn, "Making Use of the Jews: Milton and Philo-Semitism," in Douglas A. Brooks (ed.), *Milton and the Jews* (Cambridge: Cambridge University Press, 2008), p. 69.

48 *SA* 890. According to Grotius, "the law of nature ... is also frequently called the law of nations" (*De Jure Belli*, vol. 1, 1.XIV.1, p. 44).

49 Grotius, *De Jure Belli*, vol. 2, 5.VIII.1, p. 234.

50 Grotius, *De Jure Belli*, vol. 2, 5.IX.3, p. 236; for Milton on Noachide laws, see CPW 3:586.

51 Cf. Stanley Fish, *How Milton Works* (Cambridge, MA: Harvard University Press, 2001), pp. 401, 427, 470. Fish reiterates this position in "'There Is Nothing He Cannot Ask': Milton, Liberalism, and Terrorism," in Michael Lieb and Albert C. Labriola (eds.), *Milton in the Age of Fish* (Pittsburgh, PA: Duquesne University Press, 2006), p. 254. The question of will and the exercise thereof is not wholly clear in Samson's case either, one might add. See William

Kerrigan, "The Irrational Coherence of *Samson Agonistes*," *Milton Studies* 22 (1986), 217–32.

52 Janel Mueller, "Just Measures: Versification in *Samson Agonistes*," *Milton Studies* 33 (1996), 72. Notably Mueller's meticulous prosodic analysis demonstrates the "damning connotations of the prosody with respect to Dalila" (p. 70). It is true that Dalila approaches Samson with "doubting feet" (SA 732).

53 SA 222–6, 231–3, 422–3. Some material in this paragraph and in several that follow is taken from Elizabeth Sauer, "Discontents with the Drama of Regeneration," in Peter C. Herman and Elizabeth Sauer (eds.), *The New Milton Criticism* (Cambridge: Cambridge University Press, 2012), pp. 124–9, with permission from Cambridge University Press.

54 Hope Parisi, "Discourse and Danger: Women's Heroism in the Bible and Dalila's Self-Defense," in Charles W. Durham and Kristin Pruitt McColgan (eds.), *Spokesperson Milton: Voices in Contemporary Criticism* (London: Associated University Presses, 1994), p. 264.

55 The remarks on the phrase are indebted to Mueller's "Just Measures," 73.

56 Mieke Bal, *Death and Dissymmetry: The Politics of Coherence in the Book of Judges* (Chicago: University of Chicago Press, 1988), p. 217.

57 Katherine Chidley, *The Justification of the Independant Churches of Christ* (London, 1641), sig. *2.

58 Norman T. Burns, "'Then Stood up Phineas': Milton's Antinomianism and Samson's," *Milton Studies* 33 (1996), 34. Dalila's heroic aspirations are corrupt, Hill concludes, while recognizing that "Milton gave Dalila the best arguments he possibly could" (*Milton and the English Revolution*, pp. 444, 443).

59 John Shawcross, *The Uncertain World of "Samson Agonistes"* (Cambridge: D.S. Brewer, 2001), pp. 70, 80, 138–45, 141. "Renovation" is Shawcross's preferred term for regeneration.

60 Kahn, "Disappointed Nationalism," in *Early Modern Nationalism and Milton's England*, p. 264.

61 The national god of the Philistines is among the fallen named in the epic catalogue of book 1 of *Paradise Lost*, 376–505.

62 Gordon Teskey, *Delirious Milton: The Fate of the Poet in Modernity* (Cambridge, MA: Harvard University Press, 2006), p. 192.

63 See Linda Gregerson on the nation's "collective aptitude for retentive imitation" ("Colonials Write the Nation: Spenser, Milton, and England on the Margins," in Balachandra Rajan and Elizabeth Sauer [eds.], *Milton and the Imperial Vision* [Pittsburgh, PA: Duquesne University Press, 1999], p. 188).

64 Jacqueline DiSalvo, "Make War Not Love: On *Samson Agonistes* and *The Caucasian Chalk Circle*," *Milton Studies* 24 (1988), 225.

65 Dahiyat, "The Portrait of the Philistines," 298. SA 1180.

66 CPW 1:385. Tasso's *Jerusalem Delivered* (1581) was first titled "Il Goffredo" (1580) (CPW 1:385 n2). On holy violence, see Alexandra Walsham, *Charitable Hatred: Tolerance and Intolerance in England, 1500–1700* (Manchester, UK: Manchester University Press, 2006), p. 46.

67 The reference is to the Egyptians, justly deceived by the Israelites, Milton decides (*The Christian Doctrine*, CPW 6:763–4).

68 *Testamenti Veteris Biblia Sacra, sive, Libri Canonici Priscae Iudaeorum Ecclesiae à Deo Traditi, Latini recèns ex Hebraeo Facti, Brevibúsque Scholiis Illustrati ab Immanuele Tremellio & Francisco Junio*, 2nd ed. (London, 1593), sig. Cc2v. Milton, *Christian Doctrine*, CPW 6:764.

69 CPW 2:335. Harris Fletcher argues that Milton read Buxtorf's *Biblia Hebraica Rabbinorum*, which contained commentaries of Rashi, Ibn Ezra, Levi ben Gerson, and David Kimchi (Fletcher, *Milton's Rabbinical Readings* [Urbana: University of Illinois Press, 1930], p. 38), although Rosenblatt in *Torah and Law in "Paradise Lost"* argues that Selden is Milton's primary source of Jewish learning (p. 85).

70 Divorce has not restored peace, James Grantham Turner rightly recognizes (*One Flesh: Paradisal Marriage and Sexual Relations* [Oxford: Clarendon, 1987], p. 228).

71 See Krouse, *Milton's Samson and the Christian Tradition*; Wittreich, *Interpreting "Samson Agonistes"*; R. W. Serjeantson, "*Samson Agonistes* and 'Single Rebellion,'" in *The Oxford Handbook of Milton*, pp. 613–31.

72 On Samson's sainthood in the early modern era, see Krouse, *Milton's Samson and the Christian Tradition*, p. 74, and Derek Wood, *Exiled from Light: Divine Law, Morality, and Violence in Milton's "Samson Agonistes"* (Toronto, ON: University of Toronto Press, 2001), p. 85; Thomas Taylor, *The Works of That Faithful Servant of Jesus Christ* (London, 1653), pp. 378–9.

73 Thomas Hayne, *The General View of the Holy Scriptures*, 2nd ed. (London, 1640), p. 216.

74 John P. Rumrich, "Samson and the Excluded Middle," in Mark R. Kelley and Joseph Wittreich (eds.), *Altering Eyes: New Perspectives on "Samson Agonistes"* (Newark: University of Delaware Press, 2002), pp. 325, 321.

75 Thomas Luxon, *Single Imperfection: Milton, Marriage and Friendship* (Pittsburgh, PA: Duquesne University Press, 2005), p. 164.

76 Burns, "'Then Stood up Phineas,'" 41; emphasis added.

77 Burns, "'Then Stood up Phineas,'" 42. See also Samuel S. Stollman, "Milton's Understanding of the 'Hebraic' in *Samson Agonistes*," *Studies in Philology*, 69, 3 (July 1972), 334–47; and Achsah Guibbory's *Christian Identity, Jews, and Israel in Seventeenth-Century England* (Oxford: Oxford University Press, 2010), pp. 284, 286.

78 Catherine Gimelli Martin, "The Phoenix and the Crocodile: Milton's Natural Law Debate with Hobbes Retried in the Tragic Forum of *Samson Agonistes*," in Claude J. Summers and Ted-Larry Pebworth (eds.), *The English Civil Wars in the Literary Imagination* (Columbia: University of Missouri Press, 1999), pp. 245, 269.

79 Yet whereas Edwards views antinomianism as the offspring of a monstrous toleration, Milton sees it as the result of "the restraint of some lawfull liberty" (CPW 2:278). On Edwards, see *The First and Second Part of Gangraena*, pp. 2–3.

80 Joan S. Bennett's brilliant regenerationist reading claims Samson "as a model for the regenerate Christian" while centring on an analysis of Samson's antinomianism as an expression of Milton's Christian Humanism and Christian

liberty (*Reviving Liberty: Radical Christian Humanism in Milton's Great Poems* [Cambridge, MA: Harvard University Press, 1989], pp. 120, 119–60). Offering a skeptical reading of the poem, Jane Melbourne, although attracted to *Reviving Liberty*, rejects Bennett's antinomian interpretation on the basis that Milton overwhelmingly writes about the consequences of disobedience ("The Bible and *Samson Agonistes*," *Studies in English Literature* 36 [1996], 127 n22; 122–3). Douglas Bush earlier announced, "no specifically Christian doctrines are admitted, no clear statement of the working of grace, not even in Samson's immortality …; no flights of angels sing him to his rest" (*John Milton: A Sketch of his Life and Writings* [London: Macmillan, 1964], p. 200). Rosenblatt's critique of the antinomian interpretations is a particularly valuable contribution to the scholarship on *Samson Agonistes* (*Renaissance England's Chief Rabbi*). Rosenblatt argues for the legitimacy of an interpretation of the poem's conclusion from the perspective of natural law and Mosaic Law, and the divorce tracts and the earlier sections of *Samson Agonistes* support such a reading (p. 106).

81 Grotius, *De Jure Belli*, vol. 2, 20.VIII.3, p. 473.

82 Josephus had edited out the prayer in his account of the event in the Philistine banqueting hall (*Jewish Antiquities*, vol. 5, 5.8.12, p. 141).

83 Hayne, *The General View*, p. 216. Cf. Catherine Gimelli Martin, who states that Milton deletes the prayer to justify true religion (*Milton Among the Puritans: The Case for Historical Revisionism* [Farnham: Ashgate, 2010], p. 288).

84 George F. Butler, "Donne's *Biathanatos* and *Samson Agonistes*," *Milton Studies* 34 (1997), 212.

85 Stanley Fish, "Spectacle and Evidence in *Samson Agonistes*," *Critical Inquiry* 15 (1989), 569. Cf. Rosenblatt, *Renaissance England's Chief Rabbi*, p. 110. Reprinted in *How Milton Works*, 432–73, Fish's reading of Milton's poem undermines much of the argument of Fish's book (Michael Lieb, "Returning the Gorgon Medusa's Gaze: Terror and Annihilation in Milton," in Albert C. Labriola and Michael Lieb [eds.], *Milton in the Age of Fish* [Pittsburgh, PA: Duquesne University Press, 2006], pp. 229–42).

86 See Wittreich, *Interpreting "Samson Agonistes*," 121. Parisi, "Discourse and Danger," p. 265.

87 Louis Schwartz, "The Nightmare of History: *Samson Agonistes*," in Angelica Duran (ed.), *A Concise Companion to Milton* (Oxford: Blackwell, 2006), p. 202.

88 Judges 17:6, 21:25. Robert T. Fallon, *Divided Empire: Milton's Political Imagery* (University Park: Pennsylvania State University, 1995), p. 171 n14.

89 *Areopagitica*, CPW 2:555. Wittreich, *Interpreting "Samson Agonistes*," p. 24.

90 Kahn, "Disappointed Nationalism," pp. 264, 265. Empson, "A Defense of Delilah," *Sewanee Review* 68 (1960), 240–55, reprinted in *Milton's God* (London: Chatto & Windus, 1961), pp. 211–28.

91 It is Dalila, Victoria Kahn states, who "represents Milton's understanding that there is no rational basis for preferring England to any other nation" ("Disappointed Nationalism," p. 266).

Epilogue

1 Thomas N. Corns, "Milton and the Limitations of Englishness," in David Loewenstein and Paul Stevens (eds.), *Early Modern Nationalism and Milton's England* (Toronto, ON: University of Toronto Press, 2008), p. 215.

2 CPW 8:15. Blair Worden, *Literature and Politics in Cromwellian England: John Milton, Andrew Marvell, Marchamont Nedham* (Oxford: Oxford University Press, 2007), p. 391.

3 Cathy Shrank, *Writing the Nation in Reformation England, 1530–1580* (Oxford: Oxford University Press, 2004), p. 3.

4 Worden, *Literature and Politics in Cromwellian England*, p. 391. CPW 8:7.

5 Andrew Hadfield, *Literature, Politics and National Identity: Reformation to Renaissance* (Cambridge: Cambridge University Press, 1994), p. 18.

6 Guillory, *Cultural Capital: The Problem of Literary Canon Formation* (Chicago: University of Chicago Press, 1993).

7 On the differences between early modern nationalist feeling and modern nationalism, see also Anna Suranyi, *The Genius of the English Nation: Travel Writing and National Identity in Early Modern England* (Newark: University of Delaware Press, 2008), p. 48.

8 Andrew Escobedo, "No Early-Modern Nations? Revising Modern Theories of Nationhood," in Elizabeth Sauer and Julia M. Wright (eds.), *Reading the Nation in English Literature: A Critical Reader* (New York: Routledge, 2010), p. 206.

9 Alexandra Walsham, *Charitable Hatred: Tolerance and Intolerance in England, 1500–1700* (Manchester: Manchester University Press, 2006), p. 49; John Marshall, *John Locke, Toleration and Early Enlightenment Culture* (Cambridge: Cambridge University Press, 2006); John Spurr, "England 1649–1750: Differences Contained?" in Steven N. Zwicker (ed.), *The Cambridge Companion to English Literature, 1650–1740* (Cambridge: Cambridge University Press, 1998), pp. 3–32; Mark Knights, "'Meer Religion' and the 'Church-state' of Restoration England: The Impact and Ideology of James II's Declarations of Indulgence," in Alan Houston and Steve Pincus (eds.), *A Nation Transformed: England after the Restoration* (Cambridge: Cambridge University Press, 2001), pp. 41–70.

10 "Making the future different from the past is Milton's creative territory," Gordon Teskey discerns ("Recent Studies in the English Renaissance Books Received," *SEL Studies in English Literature 1500–1900* 50, 1 [2010], 245).

Index

Lightning Source UK Ltd.
Milton Keynes UK
UKHW020812150619
344482UK00006B/56/P